Other Books and Series by Jeff Bowen

Applications for Enrollment of Chickasaw Newborn Act of 1905
Volumes I, II & III

Visit our website at **www.nativestudy.com** to learn more about these
and other books and series by Jeff Bowen

Applications for Enrollment of Chickasaw Newborn Act of 1905 Volume IV

Transcribed by
Jeff Bowen

NATIVE STUDY
Gallipolis, Ohio
USA

Other Books and Series by Jeff Bowen

1901-1907 Native American Census Seneca, Eastern Shawnee, Miami, Modoc, Ottawa, Peoria, Quapaw, and Wyandotte Indians (Under Seneca School, Indian Territory)

1932 Census of The Standing Rock Sioux Reservation with Births And Deaths 1924-1932

Census of The Blackfeet, Montana, 1897- 1901 Expanded Edition

Eastern Cherokee by Blood, 1906-1910, Volumes I thru XIII

Choctaw of Mississippi Indian Census 1929-1932 with Births and Deaths 1924-1931 Volume I
Choctaw of Mississippi Indian Census 1933, 1934 & 1937, Supplemental Rolls to 1934 & 1935 with Births and Deaths 1932-1938, and Marriages 1936-1938 Volume II

Eastern Cherokee Census Cherokee, North Carolina 1930-1939 Census 1930-1931 with Births And Deaths 1924-1931 Taken By Agent L. W. Page Volume I
Eastern Cherokee Census Cherokee, North Carolina 1930-1939 Census 1932-1933 with Births And Deaths 1930-1932 Taken By Agent R. L. Spalsbury Volume II
Eastern Cherokee Census Cherokee, North Carolina 1930-1939 Census 1934-1937 with Births and Deaths 1925-1938 and Marriages 1936 & 1938 Taken by Agents R. L. Spalsbury And Harold W. Foght Volume III

Seminole of Florida Indian Census, 1930-1940 with Birth and Death Records, 1930-1938

Texas Cherokees 1820-1839 A Document For Litigation 1921

Choctaw By Blood Enrollment Cards 1898-1914 Volumes I thru XVII

Starr Roll 1894 (Cherokee Payment Rolls) Districts: Canadian, Cooweescoowee, and Delaware Volume One
Starr Roll 1894 (Cherokee Payment Rolls) Districts: Flint, Going Snake, and Illinois Volume Two
Starr Roll 1894 (Cherokee Payment Rolls) Districts: Saline, Sequoyah, and Tahlequah; Including Orphan Roll Volume Three

Cherokee Intruder Cases Dockets of Hearings 1901-1909 Volumes I & II

Indian Wills, 1911-1921 Records of the Bureau of Indian Affairs Books One thru Seven;
 Native American Wills & Probate Records 1911-1921

Other Books and Series by Jeff Bowen

Turtle Mountain Reservation Chippewa Indians 1932 Census with Births & Deaths, 1924-1932

Chickasaw By Blood Enrollment Cards 1898-1914 Volume I thru V

Cherokee Descendants East An Index to the Guion Miller Applications Volume I
Cherokee Descendants West An Index to the Guion Miller Applications Volume II (A-M)
Cherokee Descendants West An Index to the Guion Miller Applications Volume III (N-Z)

Applications for Enrollment of Seminole Newborn Freedmen, Act of 1905

Eastern Cherokee Census, Cherokee, North Carolina, 1915-1922, Taken by Agent James E. Henderson Volume I (1915-1916)
  Volume II (1917-1918)
  Volume III (1919-1920)
  Volume IV (1921-1922)

Complete Delaware Roll of 1898

Eastern Cherokee Census, Cherokee, North Carolina, 1923-1929, Taken by Agent James E. Henderson Volume I (1923-1924)
  Volume II (1925-1926)
  Volume III (1927-1929)

Applications for Enrollment of Seminole Newborn Act of 1905 Volumes I & II

North Carolina Eastern Cherokee Indian Census 1898-1899, 1904, 1906, 1909-1912, 1914 Revised and Expanded Edition

1932 Hopi and Navajo Native American Census with Birth & Death Rolls (1925-1931) Volume 1 - Hopi
1932 Hopi and Navajo Native American Census with Birth & Death Rolls (1930-1932) Volume 2 - Navajo

Western Navajo Reservation Navajo, Hopi and Paiute 1933 Census with Birth & Death Rolls 1925-1933

Cherokee Citizenship Commission Dockets 1880-1884 and 1887-1889 Volumes I thru V

Copyright © 2013
by Jeff Bowen

ALL RIGHTS RESERVED
No part of this publication may be reproduced
or used in any form or manner whatsoever
without previous written permission from the
copyright holder or publisher.

Originally published:
Baltimore, Maryland
2013

Reprinted by:

Native Study LLC
Gallipolis, OH
www.nativestudy.com
2020

Library of Congress Control Number: 2020917160

ISBN: 978-1-64968-066-2

Made in the United States of America.

This series is dedicated to the descendants of the Chickasaw newborn listed in these applications.

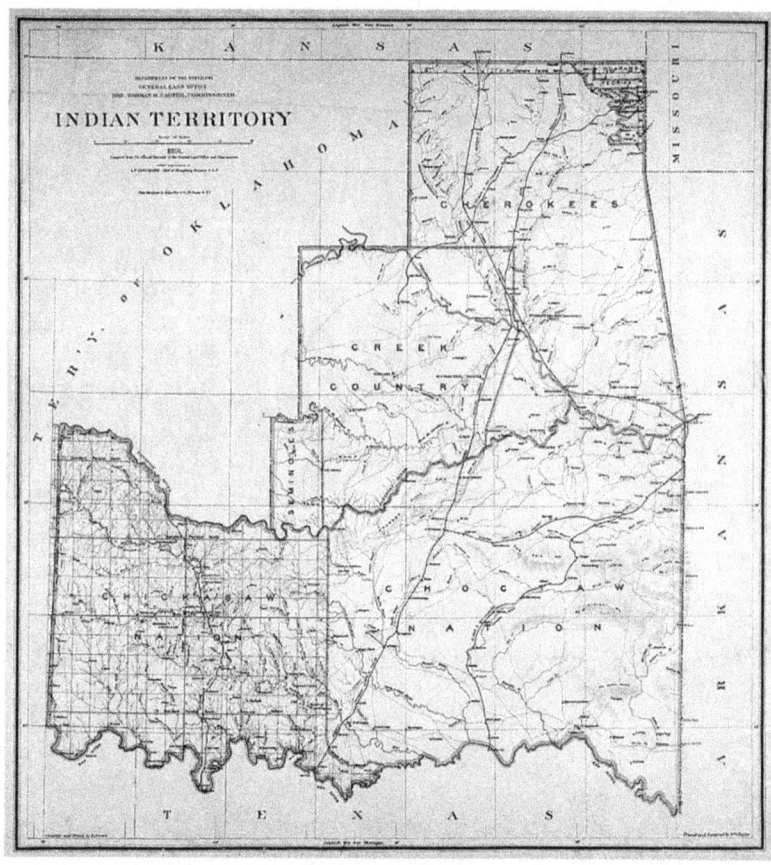

This map of Indian Territory shows how large the Choctaw and Chickasaw Nations' land base was that contained huge deposits of asphalt and coal. Just the size and territory involved was flooded with the "Grafters".

DEPARTMENT OF THE INTERIOR,
Commission to the Five Civilized Tribes.

Rules and Regulations Governing the Selection of Allotments and the Designation of Homesteads in the Choctaw and Chickasaw Nations.

1. Selections of allotments and designations of homesteads for adult citizens and selections of allotments for adult freedmen must be made in person except as herein otherwise provided.
2. Applications to have land set apart and homesteads designated for duly identified Mississippi Choctaws must be made personally before the Commission to the Five Civilized Tribes. Fathers may apply for their minor children and if the father be dead the mother may apply. Husbands may apply for wives. Applications for orphans, insane persons and persons of unsound mind may be made by duly appointed guardian or curator, and for aged and infirm persons and prisoners by agents duly authorized thereunto by power of attorney, in the discretion of said Commission.
3. At the time of the selection of allotment each citizen and duly identified Mississippi Choctaw shall designate as a homestead out of said selection land equal in value to one hundred and sixty acres of the average allottable land of the Choctaw and Chickasaw Nations, as nearly as may be.
4. Each Choctaw and Chickasaw freedman, at the time of selection shall designate as his or her allotment of the lands of the Choctaw and Chickasaw Nations, land equal in value to forty acres of the average allottable land of the Choctaw and Chickasaw Nations.
5. Citizens, freedmen and identified Mississippi Choctaws who are married, whether they have attained their majority or not, will be regarded as of age for the purpose of making selections.
6. Selections may be made by citizen and freedman parents for unmarried male children under twenty-one years of age and for unmarried female children under eighteen years of age, and a male citizen or freedman may make selection for his wife, if she is entitled to make selection, unless she shall, at the time or previously thereto, protest in writing.
7. Where the father of an unmarried minor citizen, freedman or identified Mississippi Choctaw is a non-citizen, the citizen, freedman or identified Mississippi Choctaw mother of such children must make selection in person in behalf of said children.
8. Selections of allotments and designations of homesteads for minor citizens and selections of allotments for minor freedmen may be made by the citizen father or mother or freedman father or mother, as the case may be, or by a guardian, curator, or an administrator having charge of their estate, in the order named.
9. Selections of allotments and designations of homesteads for citizen, and selections of allotment for freedmen, prisoners, convicts, aged and infirm persons and soldiers and sailors of the United States on duty outside of Indian Territory, may be made by duly appointed agents under power of attorney, and for incompetents by guardians, curators, or other suitable person akin to them.
10. Selections may be made and homesteads designated by duly identified Mississippi Choctaws, who have, within one year after the date of their identification as such, made satisfactory proof of bona fide settlement within the Choctaw-Chickasaw country, at any time within six months after the date of their said identification.
11. Persons authorized to make selections by power of attorney, as provided in rules 2 and 9 hereof, must be the husband or wife, or a relative not further removed than a cousin of the first degree of the person for whom such selection is made.
12. It shall be the duty of the Commission to the Five Civilized Tribes to see that selections of allotments and designations of homesteads for the classes of persons mentioned in rules 2, 6, 7, 8 and 9 hereof, are made for the best interests of such persons.
13. Selections of allotments for citizens, freedmen and identified Mississippi Choctaws who have died subsequent to September 25, 1902, and before making a selection of allotment, shall be made by a duly appointed administrator or executor. If, however, such administrator or executor be not duly and expeditiously appointed, or fails to act promptly when appointed, or for any other cause such selections be not so made within a reasonable and practicable time, the Commission to the Five Civilized Tribes shall designate the lands thus to be allotted.
14. In determining the value of a selection the appraised value of the land selected shall be increased by the appraised value of such pine timber on such land as has heretofore been estimated by the Commission to the Five Civilized Tribes.
15. Selections of allotments may be made only by citizens and freedmen whose enrollment has been approved by the Secretary of the Interior, and by persons duly identified by the Commission to the Five Civilized Tribes as Mississippi Choctaws, and by none others.
16. When a selection of land has been made by a citizen, freedman or identified Mississippi Choctaw, and the land so selected is claimed by a person whose rights as a citizen or freedman have not been finally determined, contest for the land so selected may be instituted by the person claiming the land, formal application for the land being first made as is required by the Rules of Practice in Choctaw and Chickasaw allotment contest cases.

THE COMMISSION TO THE FIVE CIVILIZED TRIBES.
Tams Bixby, Chairman.

Muskogee, Indian Territory, March 24, 1903.

The above statement published prior to 1905, was established for what was supposed to be a set of guidelines when it came to allotments. But with supplemental agreements and Congressional legislation, time frames as well as rules and regulations often changed and were not the same for every tribe.

INTRODUCTION

The *Applications for Enrollment of Chickasaw Newborn Act of 1905*, National Archive film M-1301, Rolls 455-458, are found under the heading of Applications for Enrollment of the Commission to the Five Civilized Tribes. For this series, I have transcribed the application forms filled out by individuals applying for enrollment in the Five Civilized Tribes under the Dawes Commission. These applications contain considerably more information than stated on the census cards found in series M-1186. M-1301 possesses its own numerical sequence, separate from M-1186. To find each party's roll number you would have to reference M-1186.

The Chickasaw as well as the Choctaw allotments were likely some of the most sought after properties in Indian Territory. There was supposed to be a 25-year restriction on the sale or lease of any Indian lands so as to insure that the owners wouldn't be swindled, but that isn't what happened. This fact is borne out in the Dawes Commission General Allotment Act, of February 8, 1887, Section 5, which "Provides that after an Indian person is allotted land, the United States will hold the land 'in trust [1] for the sole use and benefit of the Indian' (or his heirs if the Indian landowner dies) for a period of 25 years. (Land held in trust by the United States government cannot be sold or in anyway alienated by the Indian landowner, since the United States government considers the underlying ownership of the land held by itself and not the tribe. After the period of trust ends, the Indian landowner is free to sell the land and is free from any encumbrance from the United States.)"[1] Instead, Native Americans were exploited by the devious. The Chickasaw and Choctaw Districts both had huge asphalt and coal deposits, so there was pressure from outsiders to acquire them from the minute they were discovered. After repeated attacks throughout the years and many legislative changes, President "Roosevelt finally signed the Five Tribes Bill at noon on April 26, 1906, the forces seeking to end all restrictions were disappointed. Section 19 removed restrictions from the sale of all inherited land but directed that no full-bloods could sell their land for twenty-five years. The Act also prohibited leases for more than one year without the approval of the Secretary of the Interior."[2]

Angie Debo described the opportunists that wanted these Native American allotments as, "Grafters". The parents of the newborns enumerated within this series would no sooner receive the approval for their child's allotment than there would be someone there with cash in hand holding a new deed or lease for the parents to sign their child's birthright away. Angie Debo said it best, "As the business incapacity of the allottees became apparent, a horde of despoilers fastened themselves upon their property." According to Debo, "The term 'grafter' was applied as a matter of course to dealers in Indian land, and was frankly accepted by them. The speculative fever also affected Government employees so that it was almost impossible to prevent them from making personal investments."[3]

---

[1] General Allotment Act, Act of Feb. 8, 1887 (24 Stat. 388, ch. 119, 25 USCA 331)
[2] The Dawes Commission and the Allotment of the Five Civilized Tribes, 1893-1914 by Kent Carter, pg. 173
[3] And Still the Waters Run, Angie Debo, p. 92.

INTRODUCTION

According to the Department of Interior in 1905, "It is estimated that there will be added to the final rolls of the citizens and freedmen of the Choctaw and Chickasaw nations the names of 2,000 persons, including 1,500 new-born children to be enrolled under the provisions of the act of Congress approved March 3, 1905."[4]

The quote below explains, in detail, the requirements for qualifying as a newborn Chickasaw, "By the act of Congress approved March 3, 1905 (H.R. 17474), entitled 'An act making appropriations for the current and contingent expenses of the Indian Department and for fulfilling treaty stipulations with various Indian tribes for the fiscal year ending June 30, 1906, and for other purposes,' it was provided as follows:

> 'That the Commission to the Five Civilized Tribes is hereby authorized for sixty days after the date of the approval of this act to receive and consider applications for enrollment of infant children born prior to September twenty-fifth, nineteen hundred and two, and who were living on said date, to citizens by blood of the Choctaw and Chickasaw tribes of Indians whose enrollment has been approved by the Secretary of the Interior prior to the date of the approval of this act; and to enroll and make allotments to such children.'

> 'That the Commission to the Five Civilized Tribes is authorized for sixty days after the date of the approval of this act to receive and consider applications for enrollment of children born subsequent to September twenty-fifth, nineteen hundred and two, and prior to March fourth, nineteen hundred and five, and who were living on said latter date, to citizens by blood of the Choctaw and Chickasaw tribes of Indians whose enrollment has been approved by the Secretary of the Interior prior to the date of the approval of this act; and to enroll and make allotments to such children.'

"Notice is hereby given that the Commission to the Five Civilized Tribes will, up to and inclusive of midnight, May 2, 1905, receive applications for the enrollment of infant children born prior to September 25, 1902, and who were living on said date, to citizens by blood of the Choctaw and Chickasaw tribes of Indians whose enrollment has been approved by the Secretary of the Interior prior to March 3, 1905."[5]

Following is the scope of these transcriptions: Besides the applications themselves, researchers will find the identities of other individuals within these applications -- doctors, lawyers, mid-wives, and other relatives -- that may help with you genealogical research.

Jeff Bowen
Gallipolis, Ohio
NativeStudy.com

---

[4] Annual Reports of the Department of the Interior For the Fiscal Year Ended June 30, 1905, p. 609.
[5] Annual Reports of the Department of the Interior For the Fiscal Year Ended June 30, 1905, p. 593.

Applications for Enrollment of Chickasaw Newborn
Act of 1905 Volume IV

Chic. N.B - 246
   (Viola May Brown
   Born October 12, 1904)

BIRTH AFFIDAVIT.

DEPARTMENT OF THE INTERIOR.
COMMISSION TO THE FIVE CIVILIZED TRIBES.

IN RE APPLICATION FOR ENROLLMENT, as a citizen of the Chickasaw Nation, of Viola May Brown, born on the 12th day of October, 1904

Name of Father: Benson Brown   a citizen of the Chickasaw Nation.
Name of Mother: Cleo Brown   a citizen of the US ~~Nation~~.

Postoffice   Newcastle, I.T.

AFFIDAVIT OF MOTHER.

UNITED STATES OF AMERICA, Indian Territory,
   Southern   DISTRICT.

I, Cleo Brown, on oath state that I am 20 years of age and a citizen by blood, of the US ~~Nation~~; that I am the lawful wife of Benson Brown, who is a citizen, by blood of the Chickasaw Nation; that a female child was born to me on 12th day of October, 1904; that said child has been named Viola May Brown, and was living March 4, 1905.

                                  Cleo Brown
Witnesses To Mark:

Subscribed and sworn to before me this 3rd day of April, 1905

                                  JE Williams
                                  Notary Public.

AFFIDAVIT OF ATTENDING PHYSICIAN OR MID-WIFE.

UNITED STATES OF AMERICA, Indian Territory,
   Southern   DISTRICT.

I, Caroline Hedrick, a midwife, on oath state that I attended on Mrs. Cleo Brown, wife of Benson Brown on the 12th day of October,

Applications for Enrollment of Chickasaw Newborn
Act of 1905   Volume IV

1904; that there was born to her on said date a   female   child; that said child was living March 4, 1905, and is said to have been named   Viola May Brown

Caroline x Hedrick

Witnesses To Mark:
{ George Burkett
{ Maud Barnett

Subscribed and sworn to before me this 3rd   day of   April   , 1905

JE Williams
Notary Public.

Chic. N.B - 247
    (Joseph Hoyt Chitwood
    Born August 3, 1903)

BIRTH AFFIDAVIT.

DEPARTMENT OF THE INTERIOR.
COMMISSION TO THE FIVE CIVILIZED TRIBES.

IN RE APPLICATION FOR ENROLLMENT, as a citizen of the   Chickasaw   Nation, of   Joseph Hoyt Chitwood   , born on the 3rd   day of Aug   , 1903

Name of Father: David P. Chitwood   ~~a citizen of the~~ ....Nation.
Name of Mother: Mary F. Chitwood   a citizen of the   Chickasaw   Nation.

Postoffice   Alex I.T.

AFFIDAVIT OF MOTHER.

UNITED STATES OF AMERICA, Indian Territory, }
    Southern   DISTRICT. }

    I,   Mary F. Chitwood   , on oath state that I am   35   years of age and a citizen by   Blood   , of the   Chickasaw   Nation; that I am the lawful wife of David P. Chitwood   , ~~who is a citizen, by~~ .... ~~of the~~   Non citizen Nation; that a   male   child was born to me on   3rd   day of   Aug   , 1903; that said child has been named   Joseph Hoyt Chitwood   , and was living March 4, 1905.

Mary F. Chitwood

Applications for Enrollment of Chickasaw Newborn
Act of 1905   Volume IV

Witnesses To Mark:
{ A.J. Burch, M.D.
{ F. Polk

Subscribed and sworn to before me this 30 day of   March   , 1905

A.J. Stein
Notary Public.

AFFIDAVIT OF ATTENDING PHYSICIAN OR MID-WIFE.

UNITED STATES OF AMERICA, Indian Territory, }
    Southern   DISTRICT.   }

I, A.J. Burch , a Physician , on oath state that I attended on Mrs. Mary F. Chitwood , wife of David P. Chitwood on the 3rd day of Aug , 1903; that there was born to her on said date a male child; that said child was living March 4, 1905, and is said to have been named Joseph Hoyt Chitwood

A.J. Burch, M.D.

Witnesses To Mark:
{ J.E. Moore
{ J.J. McKinley

Subscribed and sworn to before me this 30 day of   March   , 1905

A.J. Stein
Notary Public.

Chic. N.B - 248
   (Blanche Clopton
   Born March 2, 1904)

Applications for Enrollment of Chickasaw Newborn
Act of 1905   Volume IV

BIRTH AFFIDAVIT.
DEPARTMENT OF THE INTERIOR.
COMMISSION TO THE FIVE CIVILIZED TRIBES.

IN RE APPLICATION FOR ENROLLMENT, as a citizen of the Chickasaw Nation, of Blanche Clopton, born on the 2 day of March, 1904

Name of Father: Rolla M. Clopton   a citizen of the Chickasaw Nation.
Name of Mother: Susan Clopton   a citizen of the Chickasaw Nation.

Postoffice   Newcastle, I.T.

AFFIDAVIT OF MOTHER.

UNITED STATES OF AMERICA, ~~Indian~~ *Okla* Territory, }
Cleveland County   ~~DISTRICT.~~

I, Susan Clopton, on oath state that I am about 38 years of age and a citizen by Blood, of the Chickasaw Nation; that I am the lawful wife of Rolla M. Clopton, who is a citizen, by Marriage of the Chickasaw Nation; that a Female child was born to me on 2nd day of March, 1904, that said child has been named Blanche, and is now ~~living~~. *deceased. That said child died Dec 31ˢᵗ 1904.*

                 her
             Susan x Clopton
Witnesses To Mark: mark
{ L C Allen
   George Burkett

Subscribed and sworn to before me this 15th day of March, 1905.

         J.F. Norman
            Notary Public.

AFFIDAVIT OF ATTENDING PHYSICIAN OR MID-WIFE.

UNITED STATES OF AMERICA, ~~Indian~~ *Okla* Territory, }
Cleveland County   ~~DISTRICT.~~

I, *(Name Illegible)*, a Physician, on oath state that I attended on Mrs. Susan Clopton, wife of Rolla M. Clopton on the 2 day of March, 1904; that there was born to her on said date a Female child; that said child is now ~~living~~ *deceased* and is said to have been named Blanche

Applications for Enrollment of Chickasaw Newborn
Act of 1905   Volume IV

D^r *(Name Illegible)*

Witnesses To Mark:

{

Subscribed and sworn to before me this 15th day of   March , 1905.

J.F. Norman
Notary Public.

No 56

BIRTH AFFIDAVIT.

DEPARTMENT OF THE INTERIOR.
COMMISSION TO THE FIVE CIVILIZED TRIBES.

IN RE APPLICATION FOR ENROLLMENT, as a citizen of the   Chickasaw   Nation, of   Blanche Clopton   , born on the   2nd   day of   March , 1904

Name of Father: Rolla Montgomery Clopton   a citizen of the   Chickasaw Nation.
Name of Mother: Susie Clopton   a citizen of the   Chickasaw Nation.

Postoffice   New Castle, I.T.

AFFIDAVIT OF MOTHER.

Okla
UNITED STATES OF AMERICA, ~~Indian~~ Territory, }
Cleveland County   ~~DISTRICT.~~   }

I,   Susie Clopton   , on oath state that I am   about 40   years of age and a citizen by   Blood   , of the   Chickasaw   Nation; that I am the lawful wife of Rolla Montgomery Clopton   , who is a citizen, by   Marriage   of the Chickasaw   Nation; that a   Female   child was born to me on   second   day of March   , 1904, that said child has been named   Blanche   , and is now living.

             her
           Susan x Clopton
Witnesses To Mark: mark
{ Jas J Phelps
  G.M. Phelps

Subscribed and sworn to before me this 20th day of December , 1904.

J.F. Norman
Notary Public.

Applications for Enrollment of Chickasaw Newborn
Act of 1905   Volume IV

AFFIDAVIT OF ATTENDING PHYSICIAN OR MID-WIFE.

UNITED STATES OF AMERICA, ~~Indian~~ *Okla* Territory,
Cleveland County. ~~DISTRICT.~~

I, (Name Illegible), a Physician, on oath state that I attended on Mrs. Susie Clopton, wife of Rolla Montgomery Clopton on the 2nd day of March, 1......; that there was born to her on said date a Female child; that said child is now living and is said to have been named Blanche

D^r *(Name Illegible)*

Witnesses To Mark:

{

Subscribed and sworn to before me this 20th day of December, 1904.

J.F. Norman
Notary Public.

DEPARTMENT OF THE INTERIOR.
COMMISSION TO THE FIVE CIVILIZED TRIBES.

In the matter of the death of   Blanche Clopton   a citizen of the   Chickasaw   Nation, who formerly resided at or near   New Castle, Ind. Ter., and died on the 31st day of December, 1904

AFFIDAVIT OF RELATIVE.

UNITED STATES OF AMERICA, Indian Territory,
Southern   DISTRICT.

I, Rolla M. Clopton, on oath state that I am Fifty-four years of age and a citizen by Intermarriage, of the Chickasaw Nation; that my postoffice address is New Castle, Ind. Ter.; that I am Father of Blanche Clopton who was a citizen, by blood, of the Chickasaw Nation and that said Blanche Clopton died on the 31st day of December, 1904

Rolla M Clopton

~~Witnesses To Mark~~:
{ *(Name Illegible)*
  Daniel Snell

Applications for Enrollment of Chickasaw Newborn
Act of 1905   Volume IV

Subscribed and sworn to before me this   21st   day of   August , 1905.

                                               (Name Illegible)
            Com Expires 10/17-1908   Notary Public.

AFFIDAVIT OF ACQUAINTANCE.

UNITED STATES OF AMERICA, Indian Territory, ⎫
    Southern   DISTRICT.   ⎬

    I,   James H Waldon   , on oath state that I am   23   years of age, and a citizen by blood   of the   Chickasaw   Nation; that my postoffice address is   Waldon   , Ind. Ter.; that I was personally acquainted with   Blanche Clopton   who was a citizen, by Blood   , of the   Chickasaw   Nation; and that said   Blanche Clopton   died on the   31st   day of   December   , 1904

                                               James H Waldon

~~Witnesses To Mark~~:
   { *(Name Illegible)*
      Daniel Snell

Subscribed and sworn to before me this   21st   day of   August , 1905.

                                             (Name Illegible)
            Com Expires 10/17-1908   Notary Public.

                                                                       9-220

                        Muskogee, Indian Territory, March 24, 1905.

Rolla M. Clopton,
        Newcastle, Indian Territory.

Dear Sir:

    Receipt is hereby acknowledged of your letter of March 15, 1905, stating that on November or December last you forwarded proof of the birth of Blanch Clopton your daughter, born March 2, 1904, but that you have heard nothing from these affidavits; you therefore ask if the same are on file.

    In reply to your letter you are informed that it does not appear from our records that affidavits to the birth of Blanch Clopton, daughter of Rolla M. and Susan Clopton have been filed with this office and for your convenience there is inclosed herewith blank form for the enrollment of an infant child which you should have executed and returned to this office within sixty days from March 3, 1905; receipt is also acknowledged of the affidavits of George Burkett and Rolla M. and Susan Clopton in the matter of the enrollment of George Burkett as a citizen of the Chickasaw Nation, and you are advised

Applications for Enrollment of Chickasaw Newborn
Act of 1905   Volume IV

that it is not known for what purpose these affidavits are forwarded as it appears from our records that George Berkett[sic], his brother Eddie Berkett, and his sister Jennie Berkett, children of Susie Clopton have been enrolled by this Commission as citizens by blood of the Chickasaw Nation and their enrollment as such approved by the Secretary of the Interior, December 12, 1902.

Respectfully,

Chairman.

B. C.

9-NB-248.

Muskogee, Indian Territory, June 29, 1905.

Rolla M. Clopton,
  New Castle, Indian Territory.

Dear Sir:

Referring to the application for the enrollment of your infant child, Blanche Clopton, born March 2, 1904, it is noted from the affidavits heretofore filed in this office that the said applicant died on December 31, 1904. In order that this fact may be made a matter of record you will kindly execute the enclosed proof of death and then return it to this office.

Respectfully,

Chairman.

D.C.

9-NB-248

Muskogee, Indian Territory, August 17, 1905.

Rolla M. Clopton,
  Newcastle, Indian Territory.

Dear Sir:

It appears that your daughter, Blanche Clopton, who was born March 2, 1904, died December 31, 1904, and for the purpose of making her death a matter of record there is inclosed herewith blank form for proof of death which please have executed and returned to this office at once in order that disposition may be made of the application for the enrollment of Blanche Clopton as a citizen of the Chickasaw Nation.

Applications for Enrollment of Chickasaw Newborn
Act of 1905 Volume IV

Respectfully,

D. C.   Acting Commissioner.

9-NB-248

Muskogee, Indian Territory, August 23, 1905.

Rolla M. Clopton,
    Newcastle, Indian Territory.

Dear Sir:

    Receipt is hereby acknowledged of your affidavit and the affidavit of James H. Waldon to the death of Blanche Clopton, which occurred December 31, 1904, and the same have been filed as evidence of the death of the above named child.

Respectfully,

Commissioner.

9-NB-248

Muskogee, Indian Territory, August 26, 1905.

R. M. Clopton,
    Newcastle, Indian Territory.

Dear Sir:

    You are hereby advised that it appearing from the records of this office that your child Blanche Clopton died prior to March 4, 1905, the Commissioner to the Five Civilized Tribes on August 26, 1905, dismissed the application for her enrollment as a citizen by blood of the Chickasaw Nation.

Respectfully,

Commissioner.

Applications for Enrollment of Chickasaw Newborn
Act of 1905   Volume IV

Chic. N.B - 249
    (Walker Theo Pound
    Born January 10, 1903)

BIRTH AFFIDAVIT.

DEPARTMENT OF THE INTERIOR.
COMMISSION TO THE FIVE CIVILIZED TRIBES.

IN RE APPLICATION FOR ENROLLMENT, as a citizen of the Chickasaw Nation, of Walker Theo Pound, born on the 10 day of Jan, 1903

Name of Father: Tom Pound   a citizen of the Chickasaw Nation.
Name of Mother: Mattie Pound   a citizen of the Chickasaw Nation.

                    Postoffice   Alex, I.T.

AFFIDAVIT OF MOTHER.

UNITED STATES OF AMERICA, Indian Territory, }
    Southern   DISTRICT. }

    I, Mattie Pound, on oath state that I am 36 years of age and a citizen by Marriage, of the Chickasaw Nation; that I am the lawful wife of Tom Pound, who is a citizen, by Blood of the Chickasaw Nation; that a male child was born to me on the 10th day of Jan, 1903; that said child has been named Walker Theo Pound, and was living March 4, 1905.

                                    Mattie Pound

Witnesses To Mark:
  { Effie Shepard
     T. Polk

    Subscribed and sworn to before me this 30 day of March, 1905

                                    A. J. Stein
                                      Notary Public.

Applications for Enrollment of Chickasaw Newborn
Act of 1905 Volume IV

AFFIDAVIT OF ATTENDING PHYSICIAN OR MID-WIFE.

UNITED STATES OF AMERICA, Indian Territory, }
Southern DISTRICT.

I, Mary T. Chitwood , a Midwife , on oath state that I attended on Mrs. Mattie Pound , wife of Tom Pound on the 10 day of Jan , 1903; that there was born to her on said date a male child; that said child was living March 4, 1905, and is said to have been named Walker Theo Pound

           Mary T. Chitwood

Witnesses To Mark:
{ J. J. McKinley
  J.E. Moore

   Subscribed and sworn to before me this 30 day of March , 1905

           A. J. Stein
            Notary Public.

Chic. N.B - 250
  (Paul Branum Welch
  Born September 20, 1904)

TRANSCRIPT.

Marriage of   **Robert C. Welch**   *with*   **Affie E. Marsh**

State of Indiana, } *ss:*
LAWRENCE COUNTY.

 𝕭𝖊 𝖎𝖙 𝕽𝖊𝖒𝖊𝖒𝖇𝖊𝖗𝖊𝖉, *That on this* **12th** *day of* **November** *, 1* **1903**, *the following marriage license was issued, to-wit:*

𝕿𝖍𝖊 𝕾𝖙𝖆𝖙𝖊 𝖔𝖋 𝕴𝖓𝖉𝖎𝖆𝖓𝖆:

 𝕿𝖔 𝖆𝖓𝖞 𝖕𝖊𝖗𝖘𝖔𝖓 𝖇𝖞 𝖑𝖆𝖜 𝖊𝖒𝖕𝖔𝖜𝖊𝖗𝖊𝖉 𝖙𝖔 𝖘𝖔𝖑𝖊𝖒𝖓𝖎𝖟𝖊 𝖒𝖆𝖗𝖗𝖎𝖆𝖌𝖊𝖘, 𝕲𝖗𝖊𝖊𝖙𝖎𝖓𝖌:

Applications for Enrollment of Chickasaw Newborn
Act of 1905   Volume IV

You are hereby authorized to join together as husband and wife

   Robert C. Welch   and   **Affie E. Marsh**

and this shall be your warrant for the same.

  Witness my hand and seal of office, at Bedford, this **12th** day
    of **November**   *A. D., 1* **903**

(SEAL)   **Boone Leonard**
           Clerk L. C. C.

  Be it further Remembered, *That on this* **12th** *day of* **November** *1* **903**

  Robert C. Welch   *and*   **Affie E. Marsh**

were joined together as husband and wife by me.

ATTEST:
        R. Scott Hyde.

The State of Indiana, Lawrence County, ss:

  I, **Boone Leonard** , *Clerk of the Lawrence Circuit Court, within and for the County and State aforesaid, sole custodian of the Marriage Records therein, certify that the foregoing is an exact and true copy of the record relating to the marriage of* **Robert C. Welch** *with* **Affie E. Marsh** , *as the same appears of record in my office.*

  Witness my hand and the seal of said Court, at Bedford, this **20** day
    of **April** *190* **5**

        Boone Leonard
        Clerk Lawrence Circuit Court.

BIRTH AFFIDAVIT.

  IN RE-APPLICATION FOR ENROLLMENT*, as a citizen of the* Chickasaw Nation, of Paul Branum Welch , *born on the* 20th *day of* Sept , 190 4

Name of Father: Robert C. Welch   a citizen of the Chickasaw Nation.
Name of Mother: Affie E. Welch   a citizen of the " Nation.

      Postoffice Wister Ind Terr.

Applications for Enrollment of Chickasaw Newborn
Act of 1905   Volume IV

AFFIDAVIT OF MOTHER.

UNITED STATES OF AMERICA, INDIAN TERRITORY, }
   Central   District. }

I,   Affie E. Welch   , on oath state that I am   19   years of age and a citizen by Marriage   , of the   Chickasaw   Nation; that I am the lawful wife of   Robert C. Welch   , who is a citizen, by   Blood   of the   Chickasaw   Nation; that a   Male   child was born to me on   20th day of   Sept   , 1904 , that said child has been named   Paul Branum   , and is now living.

                                           Affie E. Welch

Witnesses To Mark:
{

Subscribed and sworn to before me this   3^d day of   ~~Feb~~   Mch   , 1905.

                                        John C. Wood
                                          Notary Public.

AFFIDAVIT OF ATTENDING PHYSICIAN OR MID-WIFE.

UNITED STATES OF AMERICA, INDIAN TERRITORY, }
   Central   District. }

I,   D^r E E Shippey   , a   Practicing Physician   , on oath state that I attended on Mrs.   Affie E Welch   , wife of   Robert C Welch   on the   20th day of   Sept   , 190 5[sic]; that there was born to her on said date a   Male   child; that said child is now living and is said to have been named   Paul Branum Welch

                                        E.E. Shippey M.D.

Witnesses To Mark:
{

Subscribed and sworn to before me this   3^d day of   March   , 1905.

                                        John C Wood
                                          Notary Public.

Applications for Enrollment of Chickasaw Newborn
Act of 1905   Volume IV

BIRTH AFFIDAVIT.

DEPARTMENT OF THE INTERIOR.
COMMISSION TO THE FIVE CIVILIZED TRIBES.

IN RE APPLICATION FOR ENROLLMENT, as a citizen of the Chickasaw Nation, of Clayton Welch, born on the 19th day of February, 1903

Name of Father: Robert C. Welch   a citizen of the Chickasaw Nation.
Name of Mother: Nellie A Welch   a citizen of the Chickasaw Nation.

Pend·Appv'l

Postoffice ....

AFFIDAVIT OF MOTHER.

UNITED STATES OF AMERICA, Indian Territory,
Central   DISTRICT.

I, Nellie A. Welch, on oath state that I am 30 years of age and a citizen *Pending approval* by inter-marriage, of the Chickasaw Nation; that I ~~am~~ *was* the lawful wife of Robert C. Welch, who is a citizen, by blood of the Chickasaw Nation; that a male child was born to me on 19th day of February, 1903; that said child has been named Clayton Welch, and was living March 4, 1905.

          Nellie A Welch

Witnesses To Mark:
{

Subscribed and sworn to before me this 1st day of April, 1905

          Lacey P Bobo
          Notary Public.

AFFIDAVIT OF ATTENDING PHYSICIAN OR MID-WIFE.

UNITED STATES OF AMERICA, Indian Territory,
Central   DISTRICT.

I, Sarah Jane Mason, a mid-wife, on oath state that I attended on Mrs. Nellie A. Welch, wife of Robert C Welch on the 19th day of February, 1903; that there was born to her on said date a male child; that said child was living March 4, 1905, and is said to have been named Clayton Welch

          Sarah Jane Mason

Applications for Enrollment of Chickasaw Newborn
Act of 1905 Volume IV

Witnesses To Mark:

{

Subscribed and sworn to before me this 1st day of April , 1905

Lacey P Bobo
Notary Public.

9-4614

BIRTH AFFIDAVIT.
DEPARTMENT OF THE INTERIOR.
COMMISSION TO THE FIVE CIVILIZED TRIBES.

IN RE APPLICATION FOR ENROLLMENT, as a citizen of the Chickasaw Nation, of Paul B. Welch , born on the 20 day of September , 1904

Name of Father: Robert C. Welch   a citizen of the Chickasaw Nation.
Name of Mother: Affie E Welch   a citizen of the United States Nation.

Postoffice Wister I.T.

AFFIDAVIT OF MOTHER.

UNITED STATES OF AMERICA, Indian Territory, }
     Central   DISTRICT.

I, Affie E. Welch , on oath state that I am 19 years of age and a citizen by ...., of the United States Nation; that I am the lawful wife of Robert C. Welch , who is a citizen, by blood of the Chickasaw Nation; that a male child was born to me on 20th day of September , 1904; that said child has been named Paul B. Welch , and was living March 4, 1905.

Affie E Welch

Witnesses To Mark:

{

Subscribed and sworn to before me this 22 day of April , 1905

John C Wood
Notary Public.

Applications for Enrollment of Chickasaw Newborn
Act of 1905   Volume IV

AFFIDAVIT OF ATTENDING PHYSICIAN OR MID-WIFE.

UNITED STATES OF AMERICA, Indian Territory,
Central   DISTRICT.

    I, E. E. Shippey, a physician, on oath state that I attended on Mrs. Affie E. Welch, wife of Robert C Welch on the 20th day of September, 1904; that there was born to her on said date a male child; that said child was living March 4, 1905, and is said to have been named Paul B. Welch

                                E.E. Shippey M.D.

Witnesses To Mark:

    Subscribed and sworn to before me this 20 day of April, 1905

                              OL Johnson
                                 Notary Public.

$W^m O.B.$

| COMMISSIONERS:
TAMS BIXBY,
THOMAS B. NEEDLES,
C.R. BRECKINBRIDGE.

WM. O. BEALL
Secretary | DEPARTMENT OF THE INTERIOR,
COMMISSIONER TO THE FIVE CIVILIZED TRIBES. | REFER IN REPLY TO THE FOLLOWING:

9 N B 250 |

ADDRESS ONLY THE
COMMISSION TO THE FIVE CIVILIZED TRIBES.

                        Muskogee, Indian Territory, April 15, 1905.

Robert C. Welch,
    Redoak, Indian Territory.

Dear Sir:

    You are hereby advised that before the application for the enrollment of your infant child, Clayton Welch, can be finally disposed of, it will be necessary for you to furnish the Commission with either the original or a certified copy of the license and certificate of your marriage to his mother, Nellie A. Welch.

    Your early attention in this matter is requested.

                            Respectfully,
                            Tams Bixby
                                Chairman.

Applications for Enrollment of Chickasaw Newborn
Act of 1905   Volume IV

9-NB-250.

Muskogee, Indian Territory, May 15, 1905.

Robert C. Welch,
    Redoak, Indian Territory.

Dear Sir:

    Referring to the application for the enrollment of your infant child, Paul B. Welch, born September 20, 1904, it appears that Affie E. Welch, the mother of the child, is your wife, while the records of the Commission show Nellie A. Welch, who is still living, to be your wife.

    Before this matter can be finally disposed of it will be necessary that you file with the Commission either the original or a certified copy of the decree of divorce between you and your former wife, Nellie A. Welch.

                  Respectfully,

                                Chairman.

---

9 NB 250

Muskogee, Indian Territory, June 10, 1905.

Robert C. Welch,
    Wister, Indian Territory.

Dear Sir:

    Receipt is hereby acknowledged of your letter of June 3, 1905, enclosing certified copy of the record of divorce between Robert C. Welch and Nellie Welch which you offer in support of the application for the enrollment of your child Paul B. Welch and the same has been filed with the record in this case.

                  Respectfully,

                                Chairman.

Applications for Enrollment of Chickasaw Newborn
Act of 1905   Volume IV

Be it remembered that the Circuit Court for the 1st Judicial District Choctaw Nation convened at its February Special Term 1903 At the Circuit Court grounds of said District at Red Oak I.T. on Tuesday Morning February the 3rd 1903 at 9 oclock A.M. It being the time and place for holding said term of court Hon Noel J. Holsom Circuit Judge present and presiding, W. H. Harrison District Attorney, E. W. Benton Sheriff and T. J. Seaton Circuit Clerk were all present.

Wednesday Morning Feb 4th 1903

Court met pursuant to adjournment on February the 4th 1903 at 9 O'clock A.M. Jury roll called all present Officers of the Court present as yesterday minutes of the 3rd Inst. read corrected and approved in open court, the court was declared open and ready for the dispatch of business, the following was had to wit:

Case No 399
R.C. Welch
vs Divorce
Nellie Welch

This cause coming on to be heard and upon motion of C. A. Welch attorney for the plaintiff and the court being sufficiently advised in the premises from the evidence of two witnesses proved the allegations herein set forth are true. The court is of the opinion that the plaintiff is the aggrieved party therefore it is ordered, decreed and adjudged by the court that the bond of matrimony heretofore existing between plaintiff and defendant is forever dissolved and declared null and void.

I do hereby certify that the above is a true and correct copy of the record in in[sic] my office to which I attach my name and official seal this the 27th day of May 1905.

A. P. Harrison
Circuit Clerk
1st District (illegible) Indian Territory

Applications for Enrollment of Chickasaw Newborn
Act of 1905 Volume IV

Chic. N.B - 251
  (Thelma Ray
  Born June 27, 1903)
  (Bernard E. Ray
  Born June 27, 1903)

BIRTH AFFIDAVIT.

IN RE-APPLICATION FOR ENROLLMENT, as a citizen of the   Chickasaw   Nation, of   Thelma Ray   , born on the 27th day of   June , 190 3

Name of Father: Henry L. Ray   a citizen of the   Chickasaw   Nation.
Name of Mother: Mollie Ray   a citizen of the   Chickasaw   Nation.

                Postoffice   Byrne I.T.

AFFIDAVIT OF MOTHER.

UNITED STATES OF AMERICA, INDIAN TERRITORY,
  Central   District.

I,   Mollie Ray   , on oath state that I am   29   years of age and a citizen by Blood   , of the   Chickasaw   Nation; that I am the lawful wife of   Henry L. Ray   , who is a citizen, by   marriage   of the   Chickasaw   Nation; that a   Female   child was born to me on 27th day of   June , 1903 , that said child has been named   Thelma Ray , and is now living.

                             Mollie Ray
Witnesses To Mark:

Subscribed and sworn to before me this 1st day of   April   , 1905.

                             E.J. Ball
                                   Notary Public.

AFFIDAVIT OF ATTENDING PHYSICIAN OR MID-WIFE.

UNITED STATES OF AMERICA, INDIAN TERRITORY,
  Central   District.

I,   M. P. Skeen   , a   physician   , on oath state that I attended on Mrs.   Mollie Ray   , wife of   Henry L Ray   on the   27   day of   June   , 190 3; that there was born to her on said date a   Female   child; that said child is now living and is said to have been named   Thelma Ray

                             M.P. Skeen

Applications for Enrollment of Chickasaw Newborn
Act of 1905   Volume IV

Witnesses To Mark:

{

    Subscribed and sworn to before me this   1st   day of   April   , 1905.

                                       E.J. Ball
                                            Notary Public.

BIRTH AFFIDAVIT.

    IN RE-APPLICATION FOR ENROLLMENT, as a citizen of the   Chickasaw   Nation, of   Bernard E. Ray   , born on the   27th   day of   June   , 190 3

Name of Father: Henry L. Ray   a citizen of the   Chickasaw   Nation.
Name of Mother: Mollie Ray   a citizen of the   Chickasaw   Nation.

                          Postoffice   Byrne I.T.

AFFIDAVIT OF MOTHER.

UNITED STATES OF AMERICA, INDIAN TERRITORY, }
   Central   District.

    I,   Mollie Ray   , on oath state that I am   29   years of age and a citizen by Blood   , of the   Chickasaw   Nation; that I am the lawful wife of   Henry L. Ray   , who is a citizen, by   marriage   of the   Chickasaw   Nation; that a   male   child was born to me on   27th   day of   June   , 1903 , that said child has been named   Bernard E. Ray , and is now living.

                                      Mollie Ray

Witnesses To Mark:

{

    Subscribed and sworn to before me this   1st   day of   April   , 1905.

                                       E.J. Ball
                                            Notary Public.

AFFIDAVIT OF ATTENDING PHYSICIAN OR MID-WIFE.

UNITED STATES OF AMERICA, INDIAN TERRITORY, }
   Central   District.

    I,   M. P. Skeen   , a   physician   , on oath state that I attended on Mrs.   Mollie Ray   , wife of   Henry L Ray   on the   27   day of   June   , 190 3; that there was born to her on said date a   male   child; that said child is now living and is said to have been named   Bernard E. Ray

Applications for Enrollment of Chickasaw Newborn
Act of 1905   Volume IV

M.P. Skeen

Witnesses To Mark:
{

Subscribed and sworn to before me this 1ˢᵗ day of April , 1905.

E.J. Ball
Notary Public.

Chic. N.B - 252
   (Shirley Williamson
   Born January 21, 1905)

BIRTH AFFIDAVIT.

DEPARTMENT OF THE INTERIOR.
COMMISSION TO THE FIVE CIVILIZED TRIBES.

IN RE APPLICATION FOR ENROLLMENT, as a citizen of the   Chickasaw   Nation, of   Shirley Williamson   , born on the 21ˢᵗ day of January , 1905

Name of Father: Edward Williamson   a citizen of the ....Nation.
Name of Mother: Laura Murray now Williamson a citizen of the   Chickasaw   Nation.

Postoffice   Cornish, Pickens Co I.T.

AFFIDAVIT OF MOTHER.

UNITED STATES OF AMERICA, Indian Territory, }
   Southern   DISTRICT.

I,   Laura Murray now Williamson   , on oath state that I am 23   years of age and a citizen by   blood   , of the   Chickasaw   Nation; that I am the lawful wife of   Edward Williamson , who is a citizen, by —— of the ———————Nation; that a male   child was born to me on 21st   day of   January   , 1905; that said child has been named   Shirley Williamson   , and was living March 4, 1905.

Laura Williamson

Witnesses To Mark:
{

Applications for Enrollment of Chickasaw Newborn
Act of 1905   Volume IV

Subscribed and sworn to before me this 30ᵗʰ day of March, 1905.

S.P. Tucker
Notary Public.

AFFIDAVIT OF ATTENDING PHYSICIAN OR MID-WIFE.

UNITED STATES OF AMERICA, Indian Territory,
   Southern   DISTRICT.

     I, L.B. Sutherland, a Physician, on oath state that I attended on Mrs. Laura Williamson, wife of Edward Williamson on the 21st day of January, 1905; that there was born to her on said date a male child; that said child was living March 4, 1905, and is said to have been named Shirley Williamson

L.B. Sutherland M.D.

Witnesses To Mark:
{

Subscribed and sworn to before me this 30ᵗʰ day of March, 1905.

S.P. Tucker
Notary Public.

Chickasaw 512.

Muskogee, Indian Territory, April 8, 1905.

Edward Williamson,
    Cornish, Indian Territory.

Dear Sir:

    Receipt is hereby acknowledged of the affidavits of Laura Williamson and L. B. Sutherland to the birth of Shirley Williamson, son of Edward and Laura Williamson, January 21, 1905, and the same have been filed with our records as an application for the enrollment of said child.

Respectfully,

Commissioner in Charge.

Applications for Enrollment of Chickasaw Newborn
Act of 1905   Volume IV

(The letter below belongs with Chic. N.B. 250.)

Chickasaw 1666.

Muskogee, Indian Territory, April 27, 1905.

Robert C. Welch,
    Wister, Indian Territory.

Dear Sir:

    Receipt is hereby acknowledged of the affidavits of Affie E. Welch and E. E. Shippey to the birth of Paul B. Welch, son of Robert C. and Affie E. Welch, September 20, 1904, and the same have been filed with our records as an application for the enrollment of said child.

    Receipt is also acknowledged of a certified copy of the marriage license and certificate between Robert C. Welch and Affie E. Marsh, which you offer in support of the application for the enrollment of your child, Paul B. Welch, and the same has been filed with the records in this case.

    Respectfully,

    Chairman.

Chic. N.B - 253
    (Dale Eddleman
    Born November 25, 1904)

No 69

BIRTH AFFIDAVIT.

DEPARTMENT OF THE INTERIOR.
COMMISSION TO THE FIVE CIVILIZED TRIBES.

    IN RE APPLICATION FOR ENROLLMENT, as a citizen of the   Chickasaw   Nation, of   Dale Eddleman , born on the 25th   day of Nov , 1904

Name of Father: O.T. Eddleman   ~~a citizen of~~ the   Chickasaw Nation.
Name of Mother: Martha Frances Mead Eddleman   a citizen of the   Chickasaw Nation.

    Postoffice   Ada, I.T.

Applications for Enrollment of Chickasaw Newborn
Act of 1905 Volume IV

AFFIDAVIT OF MOTHER.

UNITED STATES OF AMERICA, Indian Territory,
Southern DISTRICT.

I, Martha Frances Mead Eddleman , on oath state that I am 22 years of age and a citizen by Blood , of the Chickasaw Nation; that I am the lawful wife of O.T. Eddleman , ~~who is a citizen, by~~ *who I married Dec. 7-1905 my maden*[sic] *name being Martha Frances Mead* .... of the .... Nation; that a Male child was born to me on 25th day of Nov , 1904, that said child has been named Dale Eddleman , and is now living.

Martha Frances Mead Eddleman

Witnesses To Mark:
{ WP Doss
{ SM Torbett

Subscribed and sworn to before me this 6 day of Feb , 1905.

(Name Illegible)
Notary Public.

AFFIDAVIT OF ATTENDING PHYSICIAN OR MID-WIFE.

UNITED STATES OF AMERICA, Indian Territory,
Southern DISTRICT.

I, H. Browall M.D. , a physician , on oath state that I attended on Mrs. Martha Frances Mead Eddleman , wife of O. T. Eddleman on the 25 day of Nov , 1904; that there was born to her on said date a Male child; that said child is now living and is said to have been named Dale Eddleman

H. Browall M.D.

Witnesses To Mark:
{ N. Byrd
{ *(Name Illegible)*

Subscribed and sworn to before me this 6 day of Feb , 1905.

(Name Illegible)
Notary Public.

Applications for Enrollment of Chickasaw Newborn
Act of 1905   Volume IV

BIRTH AFFIDAVIT.

DEPARTMENT OF THE INTERIOR.
COMMISSION TO THE FIVE CIVILIZED TRIBES.

IN RE APPLICATION FOR ENROLLMENT, as a citizen of the Chickasaw Nation, of Dale Eddleman , born on the 25th day of November , 1904

Name of Father: O. T. Eddleman   a citizen of the United States Nation.
Name of Mother: Martha Frances Mead (Eddleman) a citizen of the   Chickasaw   Nation.

Postoffice   Ada, Indian Territory.

AFFIDAVIT OF MOTHER.

UNITED STATES OF AMERICA, Indian Territory,
Southern Judicial   DISTRICT.

I, Martha Frances Mead (Eddleman)   , on oath state that I am   22   years of age and a citizen by   blood , of the   Chickasaw   Nation; that I am the lawful wife of   O. T. Eddleman who I married Dec. 27th 1903 , who is a citizen, by ....of the   United States   Nation; that a   male   child was born to me on   25th   day of   November   , 1904; that said child has been named   Dale Eddleman   , and was living March 4, 1905.

Martha Frances Mead Eddleman

Witnesses To Mark:
{ O.T. Eddleman
{ Mrs. J. P. Eddleman

Subscribed and sworn to before me this   25th day of   March   , 1905

R.L. Eddleman
Notary Public.

AFFIDAVIT OF ATTENDING PHYSICIAN OR MID-WIFE.

UNITED STATES OF AMERICA, Indian Territory,
Southern Judicial   DISTRICT.

I,   H. Browall   , a   physician   , on oath state that I attended on Mrs. Martha Frances Mead Eddleman   , wife of O. T. Eddleman   on the 25th   day of November   , 1904; that there was born to her on said date a   male child; that said child was living March 4, 1905, and is said to have been named   Dale Eddleman

H. Browall M.D.

Applications for Enrollment of Chickasaw Newborn
Act of 1905 Volume IV

Witnesses To Mark:
- W.D. Faust
- *(Name Illegible)*

Subscribed and sworn to before me this 25th day of March, 1905

R.L. Eddleman
Notary Public.

AB 7-30

No. 482

Certificate of Record of Marriages.

𝔘𝔫𝔦𝔱𝔢𝔡 𝔖𝔱𝔞𝔱𝔢𝔰 𝔬𝔣 𝔄𝔪𝔢𝔯𝔦𝔠𝔞,
The Indian Territory, } sct.
Central   District.

I,   E. J. Fannin   Clerk
of the United States Court, in the Indian Territory and District aforesaid, do hereby CERTIFY, that the License for and Certificate of the Marriage of

Mr.   O. T. Eddleman   and
M iss Martha F. Mead   was

filed in my office in said Territory and District the
29   day of   December
A.D., 190 3, and duly recorded in Book   1
of Marriage Record, Page   24

WITNESS my hand and Seal of said Court, at
Durant
this   29   day of   December
A.D. 190 3

E.J. Fannin
Clerk.
By   *(Name Illegible)*   Deputy.

P. O. ....

DEPARTMENT OF THE INTERIOR,
COMMISSION TO THE FIVE CIVILIZED TRIBES.
FILED
APR 8 1905
Tams Bixby CHAIRMAN.

Applications for Enrollment of Chickasaw Newborn
Act of 1905   Volume IV

No. 482

MARRIAGE LICENSE

United States of America,   The Indian Territory,
                                               Central   DISTRICT, SS.

To any Person Authorized by Law to Solemnize Marriage, Greeting:

You are hereby commanded to Solemnize the Rite and publish the Banns of Matrimony between Mr.   O. T. Eddleman
of   Ada   in the Indian Territory, aged   27   years,
and M iss Martha F. Mead   of   Sterrett
in the Indian Territory., aged   21   years, according to law, and do you officially sign and return this License to the parties therein named.

WITNESS my hand and official seal, this   26th   day
of   December   A. D. 190 3

E.J. Fannin
Clerk of the United States Court.

(Name Illegible)   Deputy

Certificate of Marriage.

United States of America,
The Indian Territory, } ss.
.................District.

I,   J. B. Bush

a   Minister of Gospel   , do hereby certify, that on the   27   day of   December   A. D. 190 5 , I did, duly and according to law, as commanded in the foregoing License, solemnize the Rite and publish the Banns of Matrimony between the parties therein named.

Witness my hand, this   27   day of   December   A. D. 190 3

My credentials are recorded in the office of the Clerk of
the United States Court in the Indian Territory,   }   J B Bush
Central District, Book   A   , Page   98   a   Minister of the Gospel
Southern

Note—This License and Certificate of Marriage must be returned to the Office of the Clerk of the United States Court of the Indian Territory, from whence it was issued, within sixty days from the date thereof, or the party to whom the License was issued will be liable in the amount of the One Hundred Dollars ($100.00).

Applications for Enrollment of Chickasaw Newborn
Act of 1905   Volume IV

Chic. N.B - 254
   (Charley Elmer Stewart
   Born October 22, 1903)

Pauls Valley   #2116.

CERTIFICATE OF RECORD OF MARRIAGE. UNITED STATES OF AMERICA INDIAN TERRITORY SOUTHERN DISTRICT SCT   I, C.M. Campbell Clerk of the United States Court, in the Indian Territory and District aforesaid DO HEREBY CERTIFY, that the License for and Certificate of Marriage of Mr. John B. Stewart and Miss Maggie Fryar were filed in my office in said Territory and District the 1st day of January A. D. 1903, and duly recorded in Book G of Marriage Record, Page 88,

    Witness my hand and seal of said Court, at Ardmore, this 1st day of January, A. D. 1903.

                                   C. M. Campbell
                                            Clerk.

Return this License to the United States Clerk at Ardmore that it may be recorded, when it will be mailed to the proper address.

    I, Helen C. Miller, Stenographer for the Commission to the Five Civilized Tribes hereby certify that the above is a correct copy of the marriage license and certificate of marriage between John B. Stewart and Maggie Fryar.

                         (Signed) Helen C. Miller.

Subscribed abd[sic] sworn to before me this 3rd day of December, 1903.

                                (Signed)   Fred T. Marr,
                                        Notary Public.

BIRTH AFFIDAVIT.
                           DEPARTMENT OF THE INTERIOR.
            COMMISSION TO THE FIVE CIVILIZED TRIBES.

    IN RE APPLICATION FOR ENROLLMENT, as a citizen of the   Chickasaw   Nation, of   Charley Elmer Stewart   , born on the   22nd   day of   October   , 1903

Name of Father: John Stewart   a citizen of the   Chickasaw   Nation.
Name of Mother: Maggie Fryar Stewart   a citizen of the   Chickasaw   Nation.

                        Postoffice   Wynnewood, Ind. Ter.

Applications for Enrollment of Chickasaw Newborn
Act of 1905 Volume IV

AFFIDAVIT OF MOTHER.

UNITED STATES OF AMERICA, Indian Territory, }
   Southern   DISTRICT.

    I, Maggie Fryar Stewart, on oath state that I am 18 years of age and a citizen by ...., of the Chickasaw Nation; that I am the lawful wife of John Stewart, who is a citizen, by Blood of the Chickasaw Nation; that a male child was born to me on 22nd. day of Oct., 1903; that said child has been named Charley Elmer Stewart, and was living March 4, 1905.

                            Maggie Fryar Stewart

Witnesses To Mark:
{

    Subscribed and sworn to before me this 25th. day of March, 1905

                            J K Rollow
                                Notary Public.

AFFIDAVIT OF ATTENDING PHYSICIAN OR MID-WIFE.

UNITED STATES OF AMERICA, Indian Territory, }
   Southern   DISTRICT.

    I, Tena Smith, a Midwife, on oath state that I attended on Mrs. Maggie Fryar Stewart, wife of John Stewart on the 22nd. day of Oct., 1903; that there was born to her on said date a male child; that said child was living March 4, 1905, and is said to have been named Charley Elmer Stewart

                                her
                        Tena Smith x
Witnesses To Mark: mark
  { TP Rollow
    W T Nisler

    Subscribed and sworn to before me this 25th. day of March, 1905

                            J K Rollow
                              Notary Public.

Applications for Enrollment of Chickasaw Newborn
Act of 1905   Volume IV

9-393

Muskogee, Indian Territory, March 30, 1905.

John Stewart,
    Wynnewood, Indian Territory.

Dear Sir:

    Receipt is hereby acknowledged of the affidavits of Maggie Fryar Stewart and Tena Smith to the birth of Charley Elmer Stewart, son of John and Maggie Stewart, October 22, 1903.

    It is stated in the affidavit of the mother that she is a citizen of the Chickasaw Nation. If she is a citizen by blood of the Chickasaw Nation of the Chickasaw Nation, you are requested to state when, where and under what name application was made for her enrollment, and the names of her parents. If she is a citizen by blood of the Chickasaw Nation you will so state.

    Your early attention is requested in this matter.

        Respectfully,

                Chairman.

(The letter below typed as given.)

        Wynnewood, I. T.
        April 3, 1905.

Hon. Dawes Commission,
    Muskogee I. T.

Dear Sir

    I reply to yours of March the 30. I reply that the mother of Charley Elmer Stewart is not no citizen of the Chickasaw Nation. she is a non citizen.

    Our Notary Public make a mistake it he put her as a citizen of the Chickasaw Nation the Chickasaw Nation.

        Respectfully,

           John Stewart

Applications for Enrollment of Chickasaw Newborn
Act of 1905   Volume IV

9-393

Muskogee, Indian Territory, April 8, 1905.

John Stewart,
    Wynnewood, Indian Territory.

Dear Sir:

    Receipt is hereby acknowledged of your letter of April 3, 1905, in which you state that there is an error in the affidavits recently forwarded to the birth of Charlie Elmer Stewart as the mother is a non citizen instead of a citizen by blood of the Chickasaw Nation.

    In reply to your letter you are informed that the affidavits heretofore forwarded to the birth of Charley Elmer Stewart son of John and Maggie Fryar Stewart have been filed with our records as an application for the enrollment of said child.

    Respectfully,

Commissioner in Charge.

---

9 N B 254

Muskogee, Indian Territory, April 15, 1905.

John Stewart,
    Wynnewood, Indian Territory.

Dear Sir:

    You are hereby advised that before the application for the enrollment of your infant child, Charley Elmer Stewart, can be finally disposed of, it will be necessary for you to furnish the Commission with either the original or a certified copy of the license and certificate of your marriage to his mother, Maggie Fryar Stewart, forwarding same at the earliest practicable date.

    Respectfully,

Chairman.

Applications for Enrollment of Chickasaw Newborn
Act of 1905   Volume IV

Chickasaw N.B.
254.

Muskogee, Indian Territory, April 29, 1905.

John Stewart,
    Wynnewood, Indian Territory.

Dear Sir:

    Receipt is hereby acknowledged of your letter of April 18 in which you state that your license was filed with the Commission at Ardmore in order that you might make your selection of allotment, it appearing that you were under age, but if it is necessary you will secure a certified copy thereof.

    In reply to your letter you are advised that certified copy of your marriage license and certificate has been forwarded to this office, and it will not be necessary for you to secure another copy.

Respectfully,

Chairman.

(The letter below typed as given.)

COPY.

Wynnewood, Ind. ty.

Hon. Dawes Commission

Dear Sir:

    In reply to yours of the 15 I will inform you that my license is at Ardmore I.T. with the Commission if it will be ----- for me to get them notify me and can get them for you, but if you can get them it will be a favor for me. I was under age when I filed and had to leave them there. So hoping a reply at once.

Yours truly,

(Signed) John Stewart.

Applications for Enrollment of Chickasaw Newborn
Act of 1905 Volume IV

Chic. N.B - 255
    (William Henry Armstrong
    Born December 2, 1904)

BIRTH AFFIDAVIT.

DEPARTMENT OF THE INTERIOR.
COMMISSION TO THE FIVE CIVILIZED TRIBES.

    IN RE APPLICATION FOR ENROLLMENT, as a citizen of the   Chickasaw   Nation, of   William Henry Armstrong   , born on the 2 day of Decr , 1904

Name of Father: J.N. Armstrong   a citizen of the   U S   ~~Nation~~.
Name of Mother: Mytle[sic] V. Armstrong   a citizen of the Chickasaw Nation.

    Postoffice   Burneyville Ind. T.

AFFIDAVIT OF MOTHER.

UNITED STATES OF AMERICA, Indian Territory, }
    Southern   DISTRICT.

    I, Myrtle V. Armstrong   , on oath state that I am 17 years of age and a citizen by   Blood   , of the   Chickasaw   Nation; that I am the lawful wife of J. N. Armstrong   , who is a citizen, ~~by~~ .... of the   U S   ~~Nation~~; that a male   child was born to me on 2 day of Decr , 1904; that said child has been named   William Henry Armstrong   , and was living March 4, 1905.

    Myrtle V. Armstrong

Witnesses To Mark:
{

    Subscribed and sworn to before me this 30 day of   Mch   , 1905

    J. E. Wood
        Notary Public.

AFFIDAVIT OF ATTENDING PHYSICIAN OR MID-WIFE.

UNITED STATES OF AMERICA, Indian Territory, }
    Southern   DISTRICT.

    I,   W. T. Welch   , a Physician   , on oath state that I attended on Mrs. Myrtle V. Armstrong   , wife of J. N. Armstrong   on the 2 day of

Applications for Enrollment of Chickasaw Newborn
Act of 1905   Volume IV

Decr   , 1904; that there was born to her on said date a   male   child; that said child was living March 4, 1905, and is said to have been named William Henry Armstrong

W.T. Welch M.D.

Witnesses To Mark:
{

Subscribed and sworn to before me this   31   day of   Mch   , 1905

J. E. Wood
Notary Public.

Burneyville, I. T. March 31, 1905.

Commission to Five Civilized Tribes
    Muskogee, Indian Territory.

Gentlemen:

The attached application for enrollment of child signed by Mrs. Myrtle V. Armstrong, is the same party as is shown on rolls as Myrtle V. Ball would send her roll No. but dont[sic] remember it now.

All three of these parties want to know as soon as possible of the enrollment of their children that they may make their filing.

Respectfully,

J. E. Wood.

Chic. N.B - 256
    (Euna May Alexander
    Born August 24, 1903)

Applications for Enrollment of Chickasaw Newborn
Act of 1905   Volume IV

BIRTH AFFIDAVIT.

DEPARTMENT OF THE INTERIOR.
COMMISSION TO THE FIVE CIVILIZED TRIBES.

IN RE APPLICATION FOR ENROLLMENT, as a citizen of the   Chickasaw   Nation, of   Euna May Alexander   , born on the   24   day of   Aug   , 1903

Name of Father: D. L. Alexander   a citizen of the   U S   ~~Nation~~.
Name of Mother: Ella Alexander   a citizen of the   Chickasaw   Nation.

Postoffice   Pike Ind. T.

AFFIDAVIT OF MOTHER.

UNITED STATES OF AMERICA, Indian Territory, }
    Southern   DISTRICT.

I,   Ella Alexander   , on oath state that I am   22   years of age and a citizen by   Blood   , of the   Chickasaw   Nation; that I am the lawful wife of   D. L. Alexander   , who is a citizen, ~~by~~ .... of the   U. S.   Nation; that a Female   child was born to me on   24   day of   August   , 1903; that said child has been named   Euna May Alexander   , and was living March 4, 1905.

                            Ella Alexander
Witnesses To Mark:
{

Subscribed and sworn to before me this   30   day of   March   , 1905

                            J. E. Wood
                                Notary Public.

AFFIDAVIT OF ATTENDING PHYSICIAN OR MID-WIFE.

UNITED STATES OF AMERICA, Indian Territory, }
    Southern   DISTRICT.

I,   C.A. Beeler   , a Physician   , on oath state that I attended on Mrs.   Ella Alexander   , wife of   D. L. Alexander   on the   24   day of   August   , 1903; that there was born to her on said date a   Female   child; that said child was living March 4, 1905, and is said to have been named   Euna May Alexander

                            C.A. Beeler, M.D.
Witnesses To Mark:
{

Applications for Enrollment of Chickasaw Newborn
Act of 1905   Volume IV

Subscribed and sworn to before me this 30 day of   March   , 1905

                                      J. E. Wood
                                                        Notary Public.

Chic. N.B - 257
    (Cecil Earl Coyle
    Born February 2, 1903)

BIRTH AFFIDAVIT.

DEPARTMENT OF THE INTERIOR.
COMMISSION TO THE FIVE CIVILIZED TRIBES.

IN RE APPLICATION FOR ENROLLMENT, as a citizen of the   Chickasaw   Nation, of   Cecil Earl Coyle   , born on the 2 day of Feb. , 1903

Name of Father: James Thomas Coyle   a citizen of the   Chickasaw Nation.
Name of Mother: Ola Pearl Coyle   a citizen of the   U S   ~~Nation~~.

                         Postoffice   Pike Ind. T.

AFFIDAVIT OF MOTHER.

UNITED STATES OF AMERICA, Indian Territory, }
    Southern   DISTRICT.   }

    I, Ola Pearl Coyle   , on oath state that I am   18   years of age and a citizen ~~by~~ ...., of the   U S   ~~Nation~~; that I am the lawful wife of   James Thomas Coyle   , who is a citizen, by Blood   of the   Chickasaw   Nation; that a male   child was born to me on 2^{ond} day of Feb.   , 1903; that said child has been named   Cecil Earl Coyle   , and was living March 4, 1905.

                                  Ola Pearl Coyle
Witnesses To Mark:
{

    Subscribed and sworn to before me this 30th day of   March   , 1905

                                    J. E. Wood
                                         Notary Public.

Applications for Enrollment of Chickasaw Newborn
Act of 1905   Volume IV

AFFIDAVIT OF ATTENDING PHYSICIAN OR MID-WIFE.

UNITED STATES OF AMERICA, Indian Territory,
Southern   DISTRICT.

I, J. I. Buckmaster, a Physician, on oath state that I attended on Mrs. Ola Pearl Coyle, wife of James Thomas Coyle on the 2^{ond} day of Feb., 1903; that there was born to her on said date a male child; that said child was living March 4, 1905, and is said to have been named Cecil Earl Coyle

J. I. Buckmaster M.D.

Witnesses To Mark:

Subscribed and sworn to before me this 30 day of March, 1905

J. E. Wood
Notary Public.

Certificate of Record of Marriage.

UNITED STATES OF AMERICA,
INDIAN TERRITORY,   sct.
SOUTHERN DISTRICT.

DEPARTMENT OF THE INTERIOR,
COMMISSION TO THE FIVE CIVILIZED TRIBES.

FILED
MAY 10 1905

Tams Bixby CHAIRMAN.

I, C. M. CAMPBELL, Clerk of the United States Court, in the Territory and District aforesaid do hereby certify, that the License for and Certificate of Marriage of

Mr.   Jim Coyl[sic]

AND

Miss Pearl Sands

were filed in my office in said Territory and District the 30 day of April A.D., 190 2 and duly recorded in Book of Marriage Record, Page 327

WITNESS my hand and Seal of said Court, at Ardmore, this 21st day of May A.D. 190 2

C. M. Campbell

FILED
APR 30 1902 8 PM   CLERK.

☞ Return this License/United States Clerk at Ardmore, that it may be recorded, when it will be mailed to the proper address.

C. M. CAMPBELL, Clerk
Southern Dist. Ind. Ter.

Applications for Enrollment of Chickasaw Newborn
Act of 1905 Volume IV

MARRIAGE LICENSE

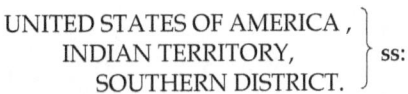

UNITED STATES OF AMERICA,
INDIAN TERRITORY, } ss:
SOUTHERN DISTRICT.

To Any Person Authorized by Law to Solemnize Marriage --- Greeting:

You are hereby commanded *to solemnize the Rite and publish the Banns of Matrimony between Mr.* Jim Coyle *of* Pike *, in the Indian Territory, aged* 17 *years and Miss* Pearl Sands *of* Simon *in the Indian Territory aged* 15 *years according to law, and do you officially sign and return this License to the parties therein named.*

Witness *my hand and official seal at Muscogee Indian Territory this* 29th *day of* April *A.D. 19*02

C. M. Campbell
Clerk of the United States Court

.... *Deputy*

Certificate of Marriage.

United States of America, }
Indian Territory, } ss.   I,   J N Moore
Southern District. }   a   Ordained Minister

do hereby certify, that on the 29" day of Apr , A. D. 190 2 , I did duly and according to law, as commanded in the foregoing License, solemnize the Rite and publish the Banns of Matrimony between the parties therein named.

Witness my hand, this 29" day of Apr , A. D. 190 2

My credentials are recorded in the office of the Clerk of the United States Court, Indian Territory, Southern District, at Ardmore, Indian Territory Book I , Page 2

NOTE:-The person officiating should fill in the   J. N. Moore
spaces for book and page and sign here   a   O.M.

Applications for Enrollment of Chickasaw Newborn
Act of 1905   Volume IV

9-554
9-981
9-600

Muskogee, Indian Territory, April 7, 1905.

J. E. Wood,
    Burneyville, Indian Territory.

Dear Sir:

    Receipt is hereby acknowledged of the affidavits of Ola Pearl Coyle and J. I. Buckmaster to the birth of Cicil[sic] Earl Coyle son of James Thomas and Ola Pearl Coyle, February 2, 1903; also affidavits of Ella Alexander and C. A. Beeler to the birth of Euna May Alexander, daughter of D. L. and Ella Alexander, August 24, 1903; also affidavits of Myrtle V. Armstrong and W. T. Welch to the birth of William Henry Armstrong, son of J. N. and Myrtle V. Armstrong (Ball) December 2, 1904, and the same have been filed with our records as an application for the enrollment of said children.

    Respectfully,

    Commissioner in Charge.

---

9 N B 257

Muskogee, Indian Territory, April 15, 1905.

James Thomas Coyle,
    Pike, Indian Territory.

Dear Sir:

    You are hereby advised that before the application for the enrollment of your infant child, Cecil Earl Coyle, can be finally disposed of, it will be necessary for you to furnish the Commission with either the original or a certified copy of the license and certificate of your marriage to his mother, Ola Pearl Coyle.

    Please give this matter your immediate attention.

    Respectfully,

    Chairman.

Applications for Enrollment of Chickasaw Newborn
Act of 1905 Volume IV

9- N. B. 257.

Muskogee, Indian Territory, May 10, 1905.

James T. Coyle,
    Pike, Indian Territory.

Dear Sir:

    Receipt is hereby acknowledged of your letter of May 2, enclosing marriage license and certificate between yourself and Pearl Sands, which you offer in support of the application for the enrollment of your infant child, Cecil Earl Coyl[sic], and the same have been filed with the records in this case.

                      Respectfully,

                                    Chairman.

Chic. N.B - 258
    (LeRoy Dick
    Born July 3, 1904)

UNITED STATES OF AMERICA

CENTRAL DISTRICT INDIAN TERRITORY.

    Before me the undersigned authority on this day personally appeared Josie Dick, who on oath stated. My name is Josie Dick. I am nineteen years of age and a citizen of the Chickasaw Nation. I am the lawful wife of Taylor Dick who is a citizen of the Choctaw Nation. That a male child was born to me on the 3rd day of July, 1904. Said child has been named Lee Roy Dick, and was living on the 4th day of March, 1905. That I desire said child enrolled as a Chickasaw and that he take and have his allottment[sic] from the Choctaw and Chickasaw public domain.

                              Josephine Dick

    Subscribed and sworn to before me this the 4th day of July, 1905.

                                    AT West
                                    Notary Public.

Applications for Enrollment of Chickasaw Newborn
Act of 1905   Volume IV

UNITED STATES OF AMERICA

CENTRAL DISTRICT INDIAN TERRITORY.

    I Taylor Dick on oath state that I am 24 years of age, and a citizen of the Choctaw Nation. That I am the lawful husband of Josie Dick who is a citizen of the Chickasaw Nation. That a male child was born to us on the 3rd day of July, 1904. That said child has been named Lee Roy Dick, and was living on the 4th day of March, 1905. That we desire said child placed on the Chickasaw roll, and that he take his allottment[sic] from the Choctaw and Chickasaw public domain.

Taylor Dick

    Subscribed and sworn to before me this the 4th day of July, 1905.

AT West
Notary Public.

(The above affidavit of Taylor Dick given again.)

BIRTH AFFIDAVIT.

DEPARTMENT OF THE INTERIOR.
COMMISSION TO THE FIVE CIVILIZED TRIBES.

    IN RE APPLICATION FOR ENROLLMENT, as a citizen of the Chickasaw Nation, of   LeRoy Dick   , born on the 3rd day of July , 1904

Name of Father: Taylor Dick   a citizen of the   Choctaw   Nation.
Name of Mother: Josephine Monroe   a citizen of the   Chickasaw   Nation.

Postoffice   Olney IT

AFFIDAVIT OF MOTHER.

UNITED STATES OF AMERICA, Indian Territory,
   Central   DISTRICT.

    I, Josephine Dick (nee Josephine Monroe) , on oath state that I am   19   years of age and a citizen by   blood   , of the   Chickasaw   Nation; that I am the lawful wife of   Taylor Dick   , who is a citizen, by blood   of the   Choctaw Nation; that a   Male   child was born to me on   3rd day of   July   , 1904; that said child has been named   LeRoy Dick   , and was living March 4, 1905.

Josephine Dick nee Munroe

Applications for Enrollment of Chickasaw Newborn
Act of 1905 Volume IV

Witnesses To Mark:
{

Subscribed and sworn to before me this 3rd day of April , 1905

WH Angell
Notary Public.

AFFIDAVIT OF ATTENDING PHYSICIAN OR MID-WIFE.

UNITED STATES OF AMERICA, Indian Territory, }
Central   DISTRICT.

I, Melia Clark , a Midwife , on oath state that I attended on Mrs. Josephine Dick nee Josephine Monroe , wife of Taylor Dick on the 3rd day of July , 1904; that there was born to her on said date a male child; that said child was living March 4, 1905, and is said to have been named LeRoy Dick

her
Melia x Clark
mark

Witnesses To Mark:
{ WH Martin
{ W^m L Martin

Subscribed and sworn to before me this 3rd day of April , 1905

WH Angell
Notary Public.

BIRTH AFFIDAVIT.

DEPARTMENT OF THE INTERIOR.
COMMISSION TO THE FIVE CIVILIZED TRIBES.

IN RE APPLICATION FOR ENROLLMENT, as a citizen of the Chickasaw Nation, of LeRoy Dick , born on the 3rd day of July , 1904

Name of Father: Taylor Dick   a citizen of the Choctaw Nation.
Name of Mother: Josephine Monroe   a citizen of the Chickasaw Nation.

Postoffice   Olney IT

Applications for Enrollment of Chickasaw Newborn
Act of 1905   Volume IV

AFFIDAVIT OF MOTHER.

UNITED STATES OF AMERICA, Indian Territory,
Central   DISTRICT.

I, Josephine Dick (Monroe) , on oath state that I am .... years of age and a citizen by   blood   , of the   Chickasaw   Nation; that I am the lawful wife of Taylor Dick   , who is a citizen, by blood   of the   Choctaw Nation; that a male   child was born to me on   3rd   day of   July   , 1904; that said child has been named   LeRoy Dick   , and was living March 4, 1905.

Josephine Dick

Witnesses To Mark:
{

Subscribed and sworn to before me this 1st day of May   , 1905

AT West
Notary Public.

AFFIDAVIT OF ATTENDING PHYSICIAN OR MID-WIFE.

UNITED STATES OF AMERICA, Indian Territory,
Central   DISTRICT.

I,   Amelia Clark   , a midwife   , on oath state that I attended on Mrs.   Josephine Dick (Monroe) , wife of   Taylor Dick   on the 3" day of   July , 1904; that there was born to her on said date a   male   child; that said child was living March 4, 1905, and is said to have been named   LeRoy Dick

her
Amelia x Clark
mark

Witnesses To Mark:
{ CH Ewing
  Howard McBride

Subscribed and sworn to before me this 29 day of April   , 1905

CH Ewing
Notary Public.

Applications for Enrollment of Chickasaw Newborn
Act of 1905   Volume IV

9 N B 258

Muskogee, Indian Territory, April 15, 1905.

Taylor Dick,
    Olney, Indian Territory.

Dear Sir:

    There is inclosed you herewith for execution application for the enrollment of your infant child, LeRoy Dick, born July 3, 1904.

    In having these affidavits executed care should be exercised to see that all names are written in full, as they appear in the body of the affidavit, and in the event that either of the persons signing the affidavit are unable to write, signatures by mark must be attested by two witnesses. Each affidavit must be executed before a Notary Public and the notarial seal and signature of the officer must be attached to each separate affidavit.

                Respectfully,

LM 15-165   Chairman.

---

9 N.B. 258.

Muskogee, Indian Territory, May 4, 1905.

Taylor Dick,
    Olney, Indian Territory.

Dear Sir:

    Receipt is hereby acknowledged of the affidavits of Josephine Dick and Amelia Clark to the birth of LeRoy Dick, son of Taylor and Josephine Dick (Monroe), July 3, 1904, and the same have been filed with our records in the matter of the enrollment of said child.

                  Respectfully,

                                                    Chairman.

Applications for Enrollment of Chickasaw Newborn
Act of 1905   Volume IV

9-NB-258.

Muskogee, Indian Territory, May 15, 1905.

Taylor Dick,
    Olney, Indian Territory.

Dear Sir:

    Referring to the application for the enrollment of your infant child, LeRoy Dick, it appears that you are a citizen by blood of the Choctaw Nation, while your wife is a citizen by blood of the Chickasaw Nation.

    Your attention is called to the provision of the Act of Congress approved June 28, 1898, as follows:

    The several tribes may, by agreement, determine the right of persons who for any reason may claim citizenship in two or more tribes, and to allotment of lands and distribution of moneys belonging to each tribe; but if no such agreement be made, then such claimant shall be entitled to such rights in one tribe only, and may elect in which tribe he will take such right; but if he fail or refuse to make such selection in due time, he shall be enrolled in the tribe with whom he has resided, and there be given such allotment and distributions, and not elsewhere.

    It will therefore be necessary for you and your wife to appear before a Notary Public or other officer authorized to administer oaths and by affidavit elect in which nation you desire to have said child enrolled, forwarding same, when properly executed, to the Commission.

                      Respectfully,

[sic]

---

9 NB 258

Muskogee, Indian Territory, June 26, 1905.

Taylor Dick,
    Olney, Indian Territory.

Dear Sir:

    Receipt is hereby acknowledged of your letter of June 23, 1905, asking if you may file for your child Leroy Dick.

    In reply to your letter you are advised that before the application for the enrollment of your child Leroy Dick can be passed upon it will be necessary for you to

Applications for Enrollment of Chickasaw Newborn
Act of 1905   Volume IV

forward the affidavit of yourself and your wife Josephine Dick electing in which nation you desire to have said child enrolled, in compliance with our letter of May 15, 1905. This matter should receive your immediate attention.

                Respectfully,

                              Chairman.

9-NB-258

                Muskogee, Indian Territory, July 21, 1905.

Taylor Dick,
    Olney, Indian Territory.

Dear Sir:

    Receipt is hereby acknowledged of your affidavit and the affidavit of your wife, Josephine Dick, electing to have your child, LeRoy Dick enrolled as a citizen by blood of the Chickasaw Nation, and the same have been filed with the record in this case.

                Respectfully,

                              Commissioner.

9-NB-258

                Muskogee, Indian Territory, September 8, 1905.

Taylor Dick,
    Olney, Indian Territory.

Dear Sir:

    Replying to your letter of September 5th, you are advised that the name of your minor child, LeRoy Dick, was included upon a schedule of new-born citizens by blood of the Chickasaw Nation submitted by the Commissioner to the Secretary of the Interior for approval on August 26, 1905, and when the schedule containing the name of your child has been approved by the Secretary of the Interior you will be notified thereof. Until such approval, no allotment can be selected for the child.

                Respectfully,

                              Acting Commissioner.

Applications for Enrollment of Chickasaw Newborn
Act of 1905   Volume IV

Chic. N.B - 259
    (Jonas Immohotichey
    Born February 27, 1904)

BIRTH AFFIDAVIT.
DEPARTMENT OF THE INTERIOR.
COMMISSION TO THE FIVE CIVILIZED TRIBES.

    IN RE APPLICATION FOR ENROLLMENT, as a citizen of the   Chickasaw   Nation, of   Jonas Immohotichey   , born on the   27   day of   Feb   , 1904

Name of Father: Jesse Immohotichey   a citizen of the   Chickasaw   Nation.
Name of Mother: Lena Immohotichey   a citizen of the   Chickasaw   Nation.

        Postoffice   Fillmore I T

AFFIDAVIT OF MOTHER.

UNITED STATES OF AMERICA, Indian Territory,
    Southern   DISTRICT.

    I,   Lena Immohotichey   , on oath state that I am   22   years of age and a citizen by   Blood   , of the   Chickasaw   Nation; that I am the lawful wife of   Jesse Immohotichey   , who is a citizen, by   Blood   of the   Chickasaw   Nation; that a   male   child was born to me on   27   day of   Feb   , 1904; that said child has been named   Jonas   , and was living March 4, 1905.

                      Lena Immohotichey
Witnesses To Mark:
    Harvey Peter
    Colbert Keel

    Subscribed and sworn to before me this 3   day of   Apr   , 1905

                      J T Gardner
                         Notary Public.

Applications for Enrollment of Chickasaw Newborn
Act of 1905   Volume IV

AFFIDAVIT OF ATTENDING PHYSICIAN OR MID-WIFE.

UNITED STATES OF AMERICA, Indian Territory, }
　　　Southern　　　　　　DISTRICT.

I, Jane Peter , a midwife , on oath state that I attended on Mrs. Jesse Immohotichey , wife of Jesse Immohotichey on the 27 day of Feb , 1904; that there was born to her on said date a male child; that said child was living March 4, 1905, and is said to have been named Jonas

　　　　　　　　　　　　　　Jane Peter

Witnesses To Mark:
　{ Harvey Peter
　 Colbert Keel

Subscribed and sworn to before me this 3 day of Apr , 1905

　　　　　　　　　　　　J T Gardner
　　　　　　　　　　　　　　Notary Public.

Birth Affidavit.　　　　20.　*#137*

Department of the Interior. .....
Commission to the Five Civilized Tribes. ......

IN RE APPLICATION FOR ENROLLMENT, as a citizen of the Chickasaw Nation of JONAS IMMOHOTICHEY, born on the 27th day of February, 1904.

Name of Father: Jesse Immohotichey, a citizen by blood of the Chickasaw Nation.

Name of Mother: Lena Underwood Immohotichey, a citizen by blood of the Chickasaw Nation.

　　　　　　　　　　Postoffice ....Fillmore, I. T.

　　　　　　　Affidavit of Mother. .....

U.S. of America,)
Sou. District,　)
Ind. Territory..)

I, Lena Immohotichey, formerly Lena Underwood, on oath state that I am twenry[sic] two years of age and a citizen by blood of the Chickasaw Nation; that I am the lawful wife of Jesse Immohotichey, who is a citizen by blood of the Chickasaw Nation; that a male child was born to me on the 27th day of February, 1904; that said child has been named JONAS IMMOHOTICHEY, and is now living.

Applications for Enrollment of Chickasaw Newborn
Act of 1905 Volume IV

Lena Imotichey[sic]

Subscribed & sworn to before me this 20th day of February, 1905.

J.B. O'Bryan
Notary Public.

U.S. of America)
Sou. Jud.District)   Affidavit of Mid-wife.
Indian Territory)

I, Jane Peter, on oath state I attended on Mrs. Lena Immohotichey, formerly Lena Underwood, acting as Mid-wife, she being the wife of Jesse Immohotichey, on the 27th day of February, 1904; that there was born to her on said date a male child; that said child is now living and is said to have been named JONAS IMMOHOTICHEY.

Jane Peter

Subscribed & Sworn to before me this 20th day of February, 1905.

J.B. O'Bryan
Notary Public.

Chickasaw 877.

Muskogee, Indian Territory, April 8, 1905.

Jesse Immohotichey,
    Fillmore, Indian Territory.

Dear Sir:

Receipt is hereby acknowledged of the affidavits of Lena Immohotichey and Jane Peter to the birth of Jonas Immohotichey, son of Jesse and Lena Immohotichey, February 27, 1904, and the same have been filed with our records as an application for the enrollment of said child.

Respectfully,

Commissioner in Charge.

Applications for Enrollment of Chickasaw Newborn
Act of 1905   Volume IV

Chic. N.B - 260
   (Bruce Colbert
   Born February 28, 1903)

(The affidavit below typed as given.)

Mill Creek, Ind. Ter.,   April 1st   190 5

United States of America,
   Southern District of Ind. Ter.

on this 1st day of April 1905 before me Personally known as the Persons whose name appears upon the within and foregoing instrument to witt J H English and B. T. King Both of Mill Creek I. T. on oath states that a child was borned to said D. C. Colbert and Netter Colbert on or about February 28th 1903 and said child is now living up to this date; Name of said child is Bruce Colbert

   J H English
   B. T. King

In testimony whereof I have hereunto set my hand and seal as a Notary Public within and for the Southern District of the Ind Ter   W. H. Arnold
   Commission expires Jan 16 1907   Notary Public

DEPARTMENT OF THE INTERIOR.
COMMISSION TO THE FIVE CIVILIZED TRIBES.

In the matter of the death of   Nettie Rowe Colbert
a citizen of the   Chickasaw Nation by Intermarriage   Nation, who formerly resided at or near   Mill Creek   , Ind. Ter., and died on the 31st day of   March   , 1903

AFFIDAVIT OF RELATIVE.

UNITED STATES OF AMERICA, Indian Territory,
   Southern   DISTRICT.

   I,   Robert C. Rowe   , on oath state that I am .... years of age and a citizen by Intermarrige[sic]   , of the Chickasaw   Nation; that my postoffice address is   Mill Creek, Ind. Ter.; that I am   A Brother   of   Nettie Row[sic] Colbert   who was a citizen, by

Applications for Enrollment of Chickasaw Newborn
Act of 1905   Volume IV

Intermarriage   , of the Chickasaw   Nation and that said   Nettie Rowe Colbert   died on the   31st   day of   March   , 1903

Witnesses To Mark:
{

    Subscribed and sworn to before me this   13   day of   July   , 1905.

                            W.H. Arnold
                            Notary Public.

AFFIDAVIT OF ACQUAINTANCE.

UNITED STATES OF AMERICA, Indian Territory, }
    Southern   DISTRICT.   }

    I,   Letitia Rowe   , on oath state that I am   27   years of age, and a citizen by Blood   of the   Chickasaw   Nation; that my postoffice address is   Mill Creek   , Ind. Ter.; that I was personally acquainted with   Nettie Rowe Colbert   who was a citizen, by Intermarriage   , of the   Chickasaw   Nation; and that said   Nettie Rowe Colbert   died on the   31st   day of   March   , 1903

                            Letitia Rowe

Witnesses To Mark:
{

    Subscribed and sworn to before me this   13   day of   July   , 1905.

                            W.H. Arnold
                            Notary Public.

BIRTH AFFIDAVIT.

DEPARTMENT OF THE INTERIOR.
COMMISSION TO THE FIVE CIVILIZED TRIBES.

    IN RE APPLICATION FOR ENROLLMENT, as a citizen of the   Chickasaw   Nation, of   Bruce Colbert   , born on the   28th   day of   February   , 1903

Name of Father: Daugherty C Colbert   a citizen of the   Chickasaw Nation.
Name of Mother: Nettie Colbert   a citizen of the   Chickasaw Nation.

                Postoffice   Mill Creek
                       I.T.

Applications for Enrollment of Chickasaw Newborn
Act of 1905   Volume IV

AFFIDAVIT OF ~~MOTHER~~ *Father*.

UNITED STATES OF AMERICA, Indian Territory, }
Southern   DISTRICT.

I, Daugherty C. Colbert, on oath state that I am 32 years of age and a citizen by Blood, of the Chickasaw Nation; ~~that I am the lawful wife of~~ ———————, who is a citizen, by Blood of the Chickasaw Nation; that a Boy child was born to *her* on 28th day of February, 1903; that said child has been named Bruce Colbert, and was living March 4, 1905.

                                            D.C. Colbert

Witnesses To Mark:
{

Subscribed and sworn to before me this 1st day of April, 1905

                                            WH Arnold
                                            Notary Public.

AFFIDAVIT OF ATTENDING PHYSICIAN OR MID-WIFE.

UNITED STATES OF AMERICA, Indian Territory, }
Southern   DISTRICT.

I, B R Looney M.D., a Physician, on oath state that I attended on Mrs. Nettie Colbert, wife of D.C. Colbert on the 28th day of February, 1903; that there was born to her on said date a male child child; that said child was living March 4, 1905, and is said to have been named Bruce Colbert

                                          B.R. Looney M.D.

Witnesses To Mark:
{

Subscribed and sworn to before me this 1 day of April, 1905

                                        WH Arnold
                                        Notary Public.

Applications for Enrollment of Chickasaw Newborn
Act of 1905   Volume IV

9-163

Muskogee, Indian Territory, April 7, 1905.

D. C. Colbert,
    Millcreek, Indian Territory.

Dear Sir:

    Receipt is hereby acknowledged of your affidavit and the affidavit of B. R. Looney; also joint affidavit of Z. H. English and B. T. King to the birth of Bruce Colbert, Indian Territory son of Dougherty[sic] C. and Nettie Colbert, February 28, 1903, and the same have been filed with our records as an application for the enrollment of said child.

                  Respectfully,

                                Commissioner in Charge.

9-NB-260.

Muskogee, Indian Territory, May 16, 1905.

Dougherty C. Colbert,
    Mill Creek, Indian Territory.

Dear Sir:

    Referring to the application for the enrollment of your infant child, Bruce Colbert, born February 28, 1903, it is noted that you executed the affidavits intended for the mother without giving a reason for so doing. If the mother's affidavit can be secured it will be necessary for you to file it with the Commission before this application can be finally disposed of, but in case the mother is dead, you will kindly have executed and return to this office the enclosed proof of death, in order that this fact may be made a matter of record.

    In having these affidavits executed care should be exercised to see that all names are written in full, as they appear in the body of the affidavit, and in the event that either of the persons signing the affidavit are unable to write, signatures by mark must be attested by two witnesses. Each affidavit must be executed before a Notary Public and the notarial seal and signature of the officer must be attached to each separate affidavit.

                    Respectfully,

                                  Chairman.

Applications for Enrollment of Chickasaw Newborn
Act of 1905   Volume IV

9-NB-260

Muskogee, Indian Territory, July 10, 1905.

D. C. Colbert,
    Millcreek, Indian Territory.

Dear Sir:

    Receipt is hereby acknowledged of your letter of July 4, in which you state that the blanks which were forwarded with office letter of May 16, 1905, were filled out and returned by you June 1, 1905 and must have been misplaced but if they cannot be found you will fill out the blanks and forward the same.

    In reply to your letter you are advised that it does not appear from the records of this office that affidavits which were enclosed with our letter of May 16, 1905, have been returned and you are therefore requested to execute the blanks sent you subsequently and return the same to this office at the earliest practicable date in the inclosed envelope.

                  Respectfully,

Env.   Commissioner.

9-NB-260

Muskogee, Indian Territory, July 12, 1905.

D. C. Colbert,
    Millcreek, Indian Territory.

Dear Sir:

    Receipt is hereby acknowledged of your letter of July 4, 1905, in which you state that the blanks which were forwarded with office letter of May 16, 1905, were filled out and returned by you June 1, 1905, and must have been misplaced but if they cannot be found you will fill out the blanks recently sent you and forward the same.

    In reply to your letter you are advised that it does not appear from the records of this office that affidavits which were enclosed with our letter of May 16, 1905, have been returned and you are therefore requested to execute the blanks sent you subsequently and return the same to this office at the earliest practicable date in the enclosed envelope.

                    Respectfully,

Env.   Commissioner.

Applications for Enrollment of Chickasaw Newborn
Act of 1905   Volume IV

Chic. N.B - 261
    (Matilda Pocahontas Surrell
    Born March 8, 1904)

BIRTH AFFIDAVIT.   *No 3*

DEPARTMENT OF THE INTERIOR.
COMMISSION TO THE FIVE CIVILIZED TRIBES.

IN RE APPLICATION FOR ENROLLMENT, as a citizen of the   Chickasaw   Nation, of   Matilda Pocahontas Surrell   , born on the   8th   day of   March   , 1904

Name of Father: John O Surrell   a citizen of the United States Nation.
Name of Mother: Emily Francis Skeen Surrell   a citizen of the   Chickasaw   Nation.
Roll number 774

                Postoffice   Wapanucka I.T.

AFFIDAVIT OF MOTHER.

UNITED STATES OF AMERICA, Indian Territory, }
    Central   DISTRICT. }

    I, Emily Francis[sic] Skeen Surrell   , on oath state that I am   22   years of age and a citizen by   blood   , of the   Chickasaw   Nation; that I am the lawful wife of   John O Surrell   , who is a citizen, by .... of the   United States Nation; that a   female   child was born to me on   eighth   day of March   , 1904, that said child has been named   Matilda Pocahontas Surrell   , and is now living. *My final Roll number is 774*

                                 Emily Frances Skeen Surrell
Witnesses To Mark:
   { Cicero A Skeen
   { Matilda Skeen

    Subscribed and sworn to before me this   27th day of January   , 1905.

                              (Name Illegible)
                               Notary Public.

Applications for Enrollment of Chickasaw Newborn
Act of 1905   Volume IV

AFFIDAVIT OF ATTENDING PHYSICIAN OR MID-WIFE.

UNITED STATES OF AMERICA, Indian Territory, }
Central   DISTRICT.

I, M.P. Skeen, a Physician, on oath state that I attended on Mrs. Emily Frances Skeen Surrell, wife of John O. Surrell on the eighth day of March, 1904; that there was born to her on said date a female child; that said child is now living and is said to have been named Matilda Pocahontas Surrell

M.P. Skeen

Witnesses To Mark:
{ Cicero A Skeen
{ Matilda Skeen

Subscribed and sworn to before me this 27th day of January, 1905.

(Name Illegible)
Notary Public.

BIRTH AFFIDAVIT.

DEPARTMENT OF THE INTERIOR.
COMMISSION TO THE FIVE CIVILIZED TRIBES.

IN RE APPLICATION FOR ENROLLMENT, as a citizen of the Chickasaw Nation, of Matilda Pocahontas Surrell, born on the 8th day of March, 1904

Name of Father: John O Surrell   a citizen of the United States Nation.
Name of Mother: Emily Francis Surrell   a citizen of the Chickasaw Nation.

Postoffice   Wapanucka I.T.

AFFIDAVIT OF MOTHER.

UNITED STATES OF AMERICA, Indian Territory, }
Central   DISTRICT.

I, Emily Francis Surrell, on oath state that I am 22 years of age and a citizen by blood, of the Chickasaw Nation; that I am the lawful wife of John O Surrell, who is a citizen, ~~by~~ of the United States ~~Nation~~; that a female child was born to me on 8th day of March, 1904; that said child has been named Matilda Pocahontas Surrell, and was living March 4, 1905.

Emily Francis Surrell

Applications for Enrollment of Chickasaw Newborn
Act of 1905 Volume IV

Witnesses To Mark:

{

    Subscribed and sworn to before me this 3d day of   April   , 1905

                                         (Name Illegible)
                                             Notary Public.

AFFIDAVIT OF ATTENDING PHYSICIAN OR MID-WIFE.

UNITED STATES OF AMERICA, Indian Territory, }
   Central   DISTRICT. }

    I, M.P. Skeen   , a Physician   , on oath state that I attended on Mrs. Emily Francis Surrell   , wife of   John O Surrell   on the 8th day of March   , 1904; that there was born to her on said date a .... child; that said child was living March 4, 1905, and is said to have been named Matilda Pocahontas Surrell

                                   M. P. Skeen

Witnesses To Mark:

{

    Subscribed and sworn to before me this 3d day of   April   , 1905

                                         (Name Illegible)
                                           Notary Public.

                            Wapanucka, I. T. 3/405

Commission to the Five Tribes,
    Muskogee, Ind. Ter.

Dear Sirs:

    Enclosed find application and affidavits for the enrollment of Matilda Pocahontas Surrell as a citizen fo[sic] the Chickasaw Nation by blood. You will note that I have endorsed the Allotment Certificate Roll Number of the childs[sic] mother on the back thereof in lead pencil, thinking it might be of aid to you in identifying the child with its mothers[sic] Roll number. Her enrollment may and I think in fact does appear as Emily Francis Skeen, she and I having married after her enrollment. Please acknowledge receipt.

                            Yours truly,

                                  J. O. Surrell.

Applications for Enrollment of Chickasaw Newborn
Act of 1905 Volume IV

9-237

Muskogee, Indian Territory, April 7, 1905.

J. O. Surrell,
    Wapanucka, Indian Territory.

Dear Sir:

    Receipt is hereby acknowledged of your letter of April 4, 1905, enclosing affidavits of Emily Francis Surrell and M. P. Skeen to the birth of Matilda Pocahontas Surrell, March 8, 1904, and the same have been filed with our records as an application for the enrollment of said child.

                    Respectfully,

                                      Commissioner in Charge.

Chic. N.B - 262
    (Georgia Jackson Birdwell
    Born March 3, 1905)

BIRTH AFFIDAVIT.
DEPARTMENT OF THE INTERIOR.
COMMISSION TO THE FIVE CIVILIZED TRIBES.

    IN RE APPLICATION FOR ENROLLMENT, as a citizen of the Chickasaw Nation, of Georgia Jackson Birdwell, born on the 3rd day of March, 1905

Name of Father: H. S. Birdwell   a citizen of the Chickasaw Nation.
                (nee Annie Love)
Name of Mother: Annie Birdwell   a citizen of the Chickasaw Nation.

                  Postoffice   Pauls Valley, I.T.

Applications for Enrollment of Chickasaw Newborn
Act of 1905 Volume IV

AFFIDAVIT OF MOTHER.

UNITED STATES OF AMERICA, Indian Territory, }
   Southern   DISTRICT.

(nee Annie Love)

    I, Annie Birdwell, on oath state that I am Nineteen years of age and a citizen by blood, of the Chickasaw Nation; that I am the lawful wife of H. S. Birdwell, who is a citizen, by intermarriage of the Chickasaw Nation; that a male child was born to me on third day of March, 1905; that said child has been named Georgia Jackson Birdwell, and was living March 4, 1905.

                                        Annie Birdwell

Witnesses To Mark:
{

    Subscribed and sworn to before me this 3rd day of ~~March~~ *April*, 1905

                                        C.J. Davenport
                                              Notary Public.

AFFIDAVIT OF ATTENDING PHYSICIAN OR MID-WIFE.

UNITED STATES OF AMERICA, Indian Territory, }
   Southern   DISTRICT.

    I, J R Callaway, a physician, on oath state that I attended on Mrs. Annie Birdwell, wife of H.S. Birdwell on the 3rd day of March, 1905; that there was born to her on said date a male child; that said child was living March 4, 1905, and is said to have been named Georgia Jackson Birdwell

                                       James R. Callaway, M.D.

Witnesses To Mark:
{

    Subscribed and sworn to before me this 3rd day of April, 1905

                                        C.J. Davenport
                                            Notary Public.

Applications for Enrollment of Chickasaw Newborn
Act of 1905   Volume IV

9-461

Muskogee, Indian Territory, April 7, 1905.

H. S. Birdwell,
    Pauls Valley, Indian Territory.

Dear Sir:

    Receipt is hereby acknowledged of the affidavits of Annie Birdwell and James R. Callaway to the birth of Georgia Jackson Birdwell, son of H. S. and Annie Birdwell, March 3, 1905, and the same have been filed with our records as an application for the enrollment of said child.

        Respectfully,

        Commissioner in Charge.

Chic. N.B - 263
    (Marguerite Priddy
    Born July 21, 1903)

BIRTH AFFIDAVIT.

DEPARTMENT OF THE INTERIOR.
COMMISSION TO THE FIVE CIVILIZED TRIBES.

    IN RE APPLICATION FOR ENROLLMENT, as a citizen of the   Chickasaw   Nation, of   Marguerite Priddy   , born on the 21st day of   July , 1903

Name of Father: Melvin Priddy   a citizen of the   Chickasaw   Nation.
Name of Mother: Siddie Priddy   a citizen of the   Chickasaw   Nation.

        Postoffice   Canadian I.T.

AFFIDAVIT OF MOTHER.

UNITED STATES OF AMERICA, Indian Territory, }
    Central   DISTRICT.

    I,   Siddie Priddy   , on oath state that I am   22   years of age and a citizen by Marriage   , of the   Chickasaw   Nation; that I am the lawful wife of   Melvin Priddy   , who is a citizen, by Blood   of the   Chickasaw   Nation; that a

Applications for Enrollment of Chickasaw Newborn
Act of 1905 Volume IV

Female   child was born to me on the 21st   day of   July   , 1903; that said child has been named   Marguerite Priddy   , and was living March 4, 1905.

Siddie Priddy

Witnesses To Mark:
{ HE Morrison
  Robt F. Turner

Subscribed and sworn to before me this 3rd day of   April   , 1905

Virgil A. Perkins
Notary Public.

AFFIDAVIT OF ATTENDING PHYSICIAN OR MID-WIFE.

UNITED STATES OF AMERICA, Indian Territory,
    Central   DISTRICT.

I,   W. P. Lewallen   , a Physician   , on oath state that I attended on Mrs.   Siddie Priddy   , wife of Melvin Priddy   on the 21st   day of   July   , 1903; that there was born to her on said date a   Female   child; that said child was living March 4, 1905, and is said to have been named Marguerite Priddy

W.P. Lewallen, M.D.

Witnesses To Mark:
{ HE Morrison
  Robt F. Turner

Subscribed and sworn to before me this 3rd day of   April   , 1905

Virgil A. Perkins
Notary Public.

9-1379

Muskogee, Indian Territory, April 7, 1905.

Melvin Priddy,
    Canadian, Indian Territory.

Dear Sir:

Receipt is hereby acknowledged of the affidavits of Siddie Priddy and W. P. Lewallen to the birth of Marguerite Priddy daughter of Melvin and Siddie Priddy, July

Applications for Enrollment of Chickasaw Newborn
Act of 1905 Volume IV

21, 1903, and the same have been filed with our records as an application for the enrollment of said child.

Respectfully,

Commissioner in Charge.

9---1379   *Substitute*
9-NB-263.

Muskogee, Indian Territory, January 12, 1907.

Melvin Priddy,
    Canadian, Indian Territory.

Dear Sir:

    Receipt is hereby acknowledged of your letter of January 2, 1907, stating that you have been notified by C. J. Tisdel, Master in Chancellor, to appear before him within twenty days to be appointed guardian for your children Cecil Lewis Priddy and Marguerite Priddy; you ask to be advised in regard to this matter.

    In reply you are advised that the enrollment of your children Cecil Lewis Priddy and Marguerite Priddy, as citizens by blood of the Chickasaw Nation, has been approved by the Secretary of the Interior and this office has no regulations requiring citizen parents to be appointed guardians of their minor children.

    I have been informed, however, that under the instructions of Honorable William R. Lawrence, Judge of the Western District, C. J. Tisdel Probate Commissioner, is notifying all parents to appear in the matter of appointment of guardians for their minor children.

Respectfully,

Commissioner.

Chic. N.B - 264
    (Henton Lenard Murry
    Born December 1, 1904)

Applications for Enrollment of Chickasaw Newborn
Act of 1905 Volume IV

BIRTH AFFIDAVIT.

DEPARTMENT OF THE INTERIOR.
COMMISSION TO THE FIVE CIVILIZED TRIBES.

IN RE APPLICATION FOR ENROLLMENT, as a citizen of the Chickasaw Nation, of Henton Lenard Murry[sic], born on the 1 day of December, 1904

Name of Father: Henton Murry   a citizen of the Chickasaw Nation.
Name of Mother: Mattie Murry   a citizen of the Chickasaw Nation.

Postoffice Colbert

AFFIDAVIT OF MOTHER.

UNITED STATES OF AMERICA, Indian Territory, }
    Central   DISTRICT.

    I, Mattie Murry, on oath state that I am 25 years of age and a citizen by blood, of the Chickasaw Nation; that I am the lawful wife of Henton Murry, who is a citizen, by blood of the Chickasaw Nation; that a male child was born to me on 1 day of December, 1904, that said child has been named Henton Lenard, and is now living.

                                   Mattie Murray

Witnesses To Mark:
   { M C Murray
     Maye Murray

    Subscribed and sworn to before me this 20 day of February, 1905.

                                   S M Mead
                                        Notary Public.

AFFIDAVIT OF ATTENDING PHYSICIAN OR MID-WIFE.

UNITED STATES OF AMERICA, Indian Territory, }
    ....DISTRICT.

    I,..., a ...., on oath state that I attended on Mrs ...., wife of..on the........... day of ...., 1............; that there was born to her on said date a .... child; that said child is now living and is said to have been named ....

Applications for Enrollment of Chickasaw Newborn
Act of 1905   Volume IV

Witnesses To Mark:
 { M C Murray
   Maye Murray

Subscribed and sworn to before me this.............day of .... , 190....

Notary Public.

BIRTH AFFIDAVIT.

DEPARTMENT OF THE INTERIOR.
COMMISSION TO THE FIVE CIVILIZED TRIBES.

IN RE APPLICATION FOR ENROLLMENT, as a citizen of the   Chickasaw   Nation, of   Henton Lenard Murray   , born on the 3 day of Dec , 1904

Name of Father: Henton Murray   a citizen of the   Chickasaw   Nation.
Name of Mother: Mattie Murray   a citizen of the   Chickasaw   Nation.

Postoffice   Colbert I.T.

AFFIDAVIT OF MOTHER.

UNITED STATES OF AMERICA, Indian Territory, }
       Central   DISTRICT.

I, Mattie Murray , on oath state that I am .... years of age and a citizen by   Blood , of the   Chickasaw   Nation; that I am the lawful wife of   Henton Murray   , who is a citizen, by Blood   of the   Chickasaw   Nation; that a Male   child was born to me on 3   day of December   , 1904; that said child has been named   Henton Lenard Murray   , and was living March 4, 1905.

Mattie Murray

Witnesses To Mark:
 {

Subscribed and sworn to before me this 3 day of   April   , 1905

E K Smith
Notary Public.

Applications for Enrollment of Chickasaw Newborn
Act of 1905   Volume IV

AFFIDAVIT OF ATTENDING PHYSICIAN OR MID-WIFE.

UNITED STATES OF AMERICA, Indian Territory,
Central   DISTRICT.

    I,   WH McCarley   , a Physician   , on oath state that I attended on Mrs. Mattie Murray   , wife of   Henton Murray   on the 3 day of Dec , 1904; that there was born to her on said date a   Male   child; that said child was living March 4, 1905, and is said to have been named   Henton Lenard Murray

                                  W.H. McCarley M.D.

Witnesses To Mark:
{

    Subscribed and sworn to before me this 3 day of   April   , 1905

                                  E K Smith
                                  Notary Public.

                                  Chickasaw 1114.

                Muskogee, Indian Territory, April 7, 1905.

Henton Murray,
    Colbert, Indian Territory.

Dear Sir:

    Receipt is hereby acknowledged of the affidavits of Mattie Murray and W. H. McCarley to the birth of Henton Lenard Murray, son of Henton and Mattie Murray, December 3, 1904, and the same have been filed with our records as an application for the enrollment of said child.

                          Respectfully,

                                        Commissioner in Charge.

Applications for Enrollment of Chickasaw Newborn
Act of 1905   Volume IV

#145

Affidavit.

This is to certify, that I, the undersigned, a practicing Physician of Colbert Indian Territory, on December 3rd., 1904, attended Mrs. Mattie Murray, wife of Hinton Murray, in confinement, at which time she was delivered of a Male child, said child now living to the best of my knowledge and belief.

Signed,   W.H.McCarley M.D.

Central District,
Indian Territory.

    Before me, E. K. Smith, a Notary Public, in and for the Central District, Indian Territory, appeared W. H. McCarley, M. D., to me well known, and acknowledged to me that the above statement, is true and correct in every particular.
    Witness my hand and seal as Notary Public, this the 7th., day of February, 1905.

E K Smith

Chic. N.B. - 265
    (Lela James
    Born August 4, 1904)

Applications for Enrollment of Chickasaw Newborn
Act of 1905   Volume IV

9 NB 265

Certificate of Record of Marriage

United States of America,
  Indian Territory,   } sct.
  Southern District.

  I, C. M. CAMPBELL, Clerk of the United States Court, in the Territory and District aforesaid DO HEREBY CERTIFY, that the License for and Certificate of Marriage of

MR   Turner James   and

M Eliza Buchanan[sic]

were filed in my office in said Territory and District the 1st day of April A.D., 190 3 and duly recorded in Book G of Marriage Record, Page 217

    WITNESS my hand and Seal of said Court, at Ardmore, this 1st day of April   A.D. 190 3

    C. M. Campbell
        CLERK.

FILED
AT ARDMORE.
APR 1 1903 2 PM

C. M. CAMPBELL, Clerk
and Exofficio Recorder.
District No 21 Ind. Ter.

9 NB 265

 MARRIAGE LICENSE

UNITED STATES OF AMERICA ,
 INDIAN TERRITORY, } ss:
 SOUTHERN DISTRICT.

To Any Person Authorized by Law to Solemnize Marriage, Greeting:

  𝔜ou are hereby commanded to solemnize the Rite and publish the Banns of Matrimony between Mr.   Turner James   of   Byrne   in the Indian Territory, aged #18 years, and M iss Eliza Buchannan   of   Byrne   in the Indian Territory, aged 19 years, according to law; and do you officially sign and return this License to the parties therein named.

    𝔚itness my hand and official Seal, this 26th day of   Mch   A. D. 190 3

Applications for Enrollment of Chickasaw Newborn
Act of 1905 Volume IV

C.M. Campbell
Clerk of the United States Court.

Certificate of Marriage.

UNITED STATES OF AMERICA,
INDIAN TERRITORY,   ss:
SOUTHERN DISTRICT.

I,   H. P. Hook _____ do hereby certify that on the 29th day of Mch , A. D. 190 3 , I did duly according to law, as commanded in the foregoing License, solemnize the Rite and publish the Banns of Matrimony between the parties therein named.

Witness my hand this 31st day of Mch A. D. 1903

My credentials are recorded in the office of the Clerk of the United States Court, Indian Territory, ~~Southern~~ Central District, at ~~Ardmore~~ So. M Alester, Book B , Page 166

(NOTE-The person officiating should fill in the spaces for book and page and sign here.)☞

H.P. Hook
a Minister of the Gospel

NOTE (a)-The License and Certificate of Marriage must be returned to the office of the Clerk of the United States Court in the Indian Territory, at Ardmore, within sixty days from the date thereof, or the party to whom the License was issued will be liable in the amount of One Hundred Dollars ($100).

NOTE (b)-No person is authorized to perform the Marriage Ceremony in the Southern District unless the proper credentials have first been recorded in the Clerk's office.

BIRTH AFFIDAVIT.

IN RE-APPLICATION FOR ENROLLMENT, as a citizen of the Chickasaw Nation, of Lela James , born on the 4th day of Aug , 190 4

Name of Father: Turner James   a citizen of the Chickasaw Nation.
Name of Mother: Eliza James   a citizen of the _____ Nation.

Postoffice   Byrne I T

AFFIDAVIT OF MOTHER.

UNITED STATES OF AMERICA, INDIAN TERRITORY,
Central District.

I, Eliza James , on oath state that I am 18 years of age and a citizen by _____, of the United States Nation; that I am the lawful wife of Turner James,

Applications for Enrollment of Chickasaw Newborn
Act of 1905 Volume IV

who is a citizen, by   Blood   of the   Chickasaw   Nation; that a   Female   child was born to me on   4th day of   Aug , 1904 , that said child has been named   Lela James   , and is now living.

Eliza James

Witnesses To Mark:

{

Subscribed and sworn to before me this   24   day of   Feb   , 1905.

E. J. Ball
Notary Public.

AFFIDAVIT OF ATTENDING PHYSICIAN OR MID-WIFE.

UNITED STATES OF AMERICA, INDIAN TERRITORY,
Central   District.}

I,   Minnie James   , a .... , on oath state that I attended on Mrs.   Eliza James   , wife of   Turner James   on the   4th day of   Aug , 190 4; that there was born to her on said date a   Female   child; that said child is now living and is said to have been named   Lela James

Minnie James

Witnesses To Mark:

{

Subscribed and sworn to before me this   24   day of   Feb   , 1905.

E. J. Ball
Notary Public.

BIRTH AFFIDAVIT.

DEPARTMENT OF THE INTERIOR.

COMMISSION TO THE FIVE CIVILIZED TRIBES.

IN RE APPLICATION FOR ENROLLMENT, as a citizen of the   Chickasaw   Nation, of   Lela James   , born on the   4th   day of   August , 1904

Name of Father: Turner James   a citizen of the   Chickasaw   Nation.
Name of Mother: Eliza James   a citizen of the United States   Nation.

Postoffice   Wapanucka I.T.

Applications for Enrollment of Chickasaw Newborn
Act of 1905   Volume IV

AFFIDAVIT OF MOTHER.

UNITED STATES OF AMERICA, Indian Territory, }
   Central   DISTRICT.

I, Eliza James , on oath state that I am 18 years of age and a citizen ~~by~~ ...., of the United States ~~Nation~~; that I am the lawful wife of Turner James , who is a citizen, by blood of the Chickasaw Nation; that a female child was born to me on fourth day of August , 1904; that said child has been named Lela James , and was living March 4, 1905.

                                  Eliza James
Witnesses To Mark:
{

   Subscribed and sworn to before me this 1st day of April , 1905

                              (Name Illegible)
                                Notary Public.

AFFIDAVIT OF ATTENDING PHYSICIAN OR MID-WIFE.

UNITED STATES OF AMERICA, Indian Territory, }
   Central   DISTRICT.

I, M.P. Skeen , a Physician , on oath state that I attended on Mrs. Eliza James , wife of Turner James on the 4th day of August , 1904; that there was born to her on said date a female child; that said child was living March 4, 1905, and is said to have been named Lela James

                                  M.P. Skeen
Witnesses To Mark:
{

   Subscribed and sworn to before me this 1st day of April , 1905

                              (Name Illegible)
                                Notary Public.

Applications for Enrollment of Chickasaw Newborn
Act of 1905   Volume IV

Chickasaw 742.

Muskogee, Indian Territory, April 7, 1905.

Turner James,
    Wapanucka, Indian Territory.

Dear Sir:

    Receipt is hereby acknowledged of the affidavits of Eliza James and M. P. Skeen to the birth of Lela James, daughter of Turner and Eliza James, August 4, 1904, and the same have been filed with our records as an application for the enrollment of said child.

    Respectfully,

    Commissioner in Charge.

---

9 N B 265

Muskogee, Indian Territory, April 15, 1905.

Turner James,
    Wapanucka, Indian Territory.

Dear Sir:

    You are hereby advised that before the application for the enrollment of your infant child, Lela James, can be finally disposed of, it will be necessary for you to furnish the Commission with either the original or a certified copy of the license and certificate of your marriage to her mother, Eliza James.

    Your early attention is requested in this matter.

    Respectfully,

    Chairman.

Applications for Enrollment of Chickasaw Newborn
Act of 1905   Volume IV

Chickasaw NB 265

Muskogee, Indian Territory, April 29, 1905.

Turner James,
    Byrne, Indian Territory.

Dear Sir:

    Receipt is hereby acknowledged of your letter of April 22, inclosing marriage license and certificate between yourself and Miss Eliza Buchanan which you offer in support of the application for the enrollment of your child, Lela James, and the same has been filed with the record in this case.

Respectfully,

Chairman.

Chic. N.B. - 266
    (Edith L. Campbell
    Born March 13, 1903)

BIRTH AFFIDAVIT.

DEPARTMENT OF THE INTERIOR.
COMMISSION TO THE FIVE CIVILIZED TRIBES.

IN RE APPLICATION FOR ENROLLMENT, as a citizen of the Chickasaw Nation, of   Edith L Campbell   , born on the   13   day of   March   , 1903

Name of Father: Montford T Campbell   a citizen of the   Chickasaw   Nation.

Name of Mother: Fannie Campbell   a citizen of the *no* .... Nation.

Postoffice   Minco I.T

Applications for Enrollment of Chickasaw Newborn
Act of 1905   Volume IV

AFFIDAVIT OF MOTHER.

UNITED STATES OF AMERICA, Indian Territory, }
Southern   DISTRICT.

non

I, Fannie Campbell, on oath state that I am 23 years of age and a citizen by Inter marig[sic], of the Chickasaw Nation; that I am the lawful wife of Montford T Campbell, who is a citizen, by Blood of the Chickasaw Nation; that a Female child was born to me on 13th day of March, 1903; that said child has been named Edith L Campbell, and was living March 4, 1905.

Fannie Campbell

Witnesses To Mark:
{

Subscribed and sworn to before me this 4th day of April, 1905.

R M Cochran
Notary Public.

AFFIDAVIT OF ATTENDING PHYSICIAN OR MID-WIFE.

UNITED STATES OF AMERICA, Indian Territory, }
                DISTRICT.

I, E L Dawson, a ...., on oath state that I attended on Mrs. Fannie Campbell, wife of Montford T Campbell on the 13 day of March, 1903; that there was born to her on said date a Female child; that said child was living March 4, 1905, and is said to have been named Edith L Campbell

E.L. Dawson, M.D.

Witnesses To Mark:
{

Subscribed and sworn to before me this 4th day of April, 1905.

R M Cochran
Notary Public.

Applications for Enrollment of Chickasaw Newborn
Act of 1905 Volume IV

APPLICATION FOR ENROLLMENT OF INFANT CHILD, AS MEMBER OF
CHICKASAW TRIBE OF INDIANS.

Edith Louise Campbell, infant child of Montford T. Campbell a citizen of Chickasaw Nation by blood and Francis[sic] C. Campbell, a United States citizen.

Indian Territory.
Southern District. I, Francis C Campbell, having first been duly sworn on oath state that Edith Louise Campbell, a female child, was born to me on the 13th day of March, 1903, and that said child is now living.

            Frances C. Campbell

Subscribed and sworn to before me on this the 7 day of April 1903.

            Reford Bard
            Notary Public.

Indian Territory.
Southern District. I, E. L. Dawson, a practicing physician and a resident of the city of Chickasha Indian Territory, having first been duly sworn state that on the 13th day of March 1903, I attended Mrs Francis C. Campbell, wife of Montford T. Campbell, and on said date there was born to the said Francis C. Campbell a female child and that said child has been named Edith Louise Campbell, and is now living.

            E. L. Dawson

Subscribed and sworn to before me on this the 7 day of April 1903.

            Reford Bard
            Notary Public.

Chic. N.B. - 267
  (Mary Joyce Phillips
  Born September 2, 1903)

Applications for Enrollment of Chickasaw Newborn
Act of 1905 Volume IV

BIRTH AFFIDAVIT.

DEPARTMENT OF THE INTERIOR.
COMMISSION TO THE FIVE CIVILIZED TRIBES.

IN RE APPLICATION FOR ENROLLMENT, as a citizen of the Chickasaw Nation of Mary Joyce Phillips, born on the 2nd day of September, 1903

Name of Father: William Thomas Phillips   a citizen of the Chickasaw Nation.
Name of Mother: Nettie A Phillips   a citizen of the Chickasaw Nation.

Postoffice   Chickasha I.T.

AFFIDAVIT OF MOTHER.

UNITED STATES OF AMERICA, INDIAN TERRITORY,
Southern DISTRICT.

I, Nettie A Phillips, on oath state that I am (24) Twenty four years of age and a citizen by Marriage, of the Chickasaw Nation; that I am the lawful wife of William Thomas Phillips, who is a citizen, by Blood of the Chickasaw Nation; that a Female child was born to me on 2nd day of September, 190 3, that said child has been named Mary Joyce Phillips, and is now living.

                 Nettie A. Phillips

WITNESSES TO MARK:
Mary L. Murphy

Subscribed and sworn to before me this 4th day of April, 1905.

                 Mary L Murphy
                 Notary Public.

AFFIDAVIT OF ATTENDING PHYSICIAN OR MID-WIFE.

UNITED STATES OF AMERICA, INDIAN TERRITORY,
~~Southern~~ *Dallas County* DISTRICT. *State of Texas*

I, Dr. K. W. Field, a Physician, on oath state that I attended on Mrs. W. T. Phillips, wife of William Thomas Phillips on the 2nd day of September, 190 3; that there was born to her on said date a Female child; that said child is now living and is said to have been named Mary Joyce Phillips

                 K.W. Field, M.D.

Applications for Enrollment of Chickasaw Newborn
Act of 1905   Volume IV

WITNESSES TO MARK:
{ J.F. Tierne
{ WY Notley

Subscribed and sworn to before me this 27th   day of   March   , 1905.

          W.E. Foster
            Notary Public.
          Dallas Co Texas

My Commission expires June 1st 1905

Chic. N.B. - 268
  (Roy Oscar Waldon
  Born November 6, 1903)
  (Turner Clyde Waldon
  Born November 23, 1904)

BIRTH AFFIDAVIT.

DEPARTMENT OF THE INTERIOR.
COMMISSION TO THE FIVE CIVILIZED TRIBES.

IN RE APPLICATION FOR ENROLLMENT, as a citizen of the   Chickasaw   Nation, of   Roy Oscar Waldon   , born on the   Sixth   day of   November   , 1903

Name of Father: Hosea Waldon   a citizen of the   Chickasaw   Nation.
Name of Mother: Susie Waldon   a citizen of the   Chickasaw   Nation.

        Postoffice   Tuttle Ind Ter

AFFIDAVIT OF MOTHER.

UNITED STATES OF AMERICA, Indian Territory, }
  Southern DISTRICT. }

  I,   Susie Waldon   , on oath state that I am   38   years of age and a citizen by Blood   , of the   Chickasaw   Nation; that I am the lawful wife of   Hosea Waldon , who is a citizen, by   Blood   of the   Chickasaw   Nation; that a   Male   child was born to me on   6 Sixth   day of   November   , 1903; that said child has been named   Roy Oscar Waldon   , and was living March 4, 1905.

            Susie Waldon

Applications for Enrollment of Chickasaw Newborn
Act of 1905 Volume IV

Witnesses To Mark:

Subscribed and sworn to before me this 23rd day of Mar , 1905

J.H. Carlisle
Notary Public.

AFFIDAVIT OF ATTENDING PHYSICIAN OR MID-WIFE.

UNITED STATES OF AMERICA, Indian Territory,
Southern   DISTRICT.

I, Sophie Waldon , a Midwife , on oath state that I attended on Mrs. Susie Waldon , wife of Hosea Waldon on the 6th day of Nov , 1903; that there was born to her on said date a male child; that said child was living March 4, 1905, and is said to have been named Roy Oscar

Sophie Waldon

Witnesses To Mark:
 B.V. Hartin
 A.S McDaniels

Subscribed and sworn to before me this 23rd day of Mar , 1905

J.H. Carlisle
Notary Public.

My Com Ex - Jan 26th 1907.

BIRTH AFFIDAVIT.

DEPARTMENT OF THE INTERIOR.
COMMISSION TO THE FIVE CIVILIZED TRIBES.

IN RE APPLICATION FOR ENROLLMENT, as a citizen of the Chickasaw Nation, of Turner Clyde Waldon , born on the 23rd day of Nov. , 1904

Name of Father: Hosea Waldon   a citizen of the Chickasaw Nation.
Name of Mother: Susie Waldon   a citizen of the Chickasaw Nation.

Postoffice   Tuttle Ind Ter

Applications for Enrollment of Chickasaw Newborn
Act of 1905   Volume IV

AFFIDAVIT OF MOTHER.

UNITED STATES OF AMERICA, Indian Territory, }
    Southern   DISTRICT.

I, Susie Waldon , on oath state that I am 38 years of age and a citizen by Blood , of the Chickasaw Nation; that I am the lawful wife of Hosea Waldon , who is a citizen, by Blood of the Chickasaw Nation; that a Male child was born to me on 23rd day of Nov , 1904; that said child has been named Turner Clyde Waldon , and was living March 4, 1905.

                                    Susie Waldon

Witnesses To Mark:
{

Subscribed and sworn to before me this 23rd day of Mar , 1905

                                    J.H. Carlisle
                                        Notary Public.

AFFIDAVIT OF ATTENDING PHYSICIAN OR MID-WIFE.

UNITED STATES OF AMERICA, Indian Territory, }
    Southern   DISTRICT.

I, Sophie Waldon , a Midwife , on oath state that I attended on Mrs. Susie Waldon , wife of Hosea Waldon on the 23rd day of Nov , 1904; that there was born to her on said date a male child; that said child was living March 4, 1905, and is said to have been named Turner Clyde

                                    Sophie Waldon

Witnesses To Mark:
{ B.V. Hartin
  A.S McDaniels

Subscribed and sworn to before me this 23rd day of Mar , 1905

                                    J.H. Carlisle
                                        Notary Public.

My Com Ex - Jan 26th 1907.

**Applications for Enrollment of Chickasaw Newborn
Act of 1905   Volume IV**

Chic. N.B. - 269
    (Lousie Maud Collins
    Born February 15, 1904)

BIRTH AFFIDAVIT.

**DEPARTMENT OF THE INTERIOR.
COMMISSION TO THE FIVE CIVILIZED TRIBES.**

IN RE APPLICATION FOR ENROLLMENT, as a citizen of the   Chickasaw   Nation, of   Lousie Maud Collins   , born on the   15   day of   February   , 1904

Name of Father: Ben F Collins   a citizen of the   Chickasaw   Nation.
Name of Mother: Annie Collins   a citizen of the   Chickasaw   Nation.

    Postoffice   Ninnekah, Ind. Ter.

AFFIDAVIT OF MOTHER.

UNITED STATES OF AMERICA, Indian Territory, ⎫
    Southern   DISTRICT. ⎭

    I,   Annie Collins   , on oath state that I am   31   years of age and a citizen by marriage   , of the   Chickasaw   Nation; that I am the lawful wife of   Ben F Collins   , who is a citizen, by birth   of the   Chickasaw   Nation; that a female   child was born to me on   15   day of   February   , 1904; that said child has been named   Lousie Maud Collins   , and was living March 4, 1905.

    Annie Collins

Witnesses To Mark:
{

    Subscribed and sworn to before me this   1   day of   June   , 1905

    Henry Luntz
    Notary Public.

AFFIDAVIT OF ATTENDING PHYSICIAN OR MID-WIFE.

UNITED STATES OF AMERICA, Indian Territory, ⎫
    Southern   DISTRICT. ⎭

    I, Powhatan M. Waltrep   , a   Physician   , on oath state that I attended on Mrs.   Annie Collins   , wife of   Ben F Collins   on the 15th day of   February   ,

Applications for Enrollment of Chickasaw Newborn
Act of 1905   Volume IV

1904; that there was born to her on said date a   Female   child; that said child was living March 4, 1905, and is said to have been named   Lousie Maud Collins

P.M. Waltrep M.D.

Witnesses To Mark:

{

   Subscribed and sworn to before me this 1   day of   June   , 1905

Henry Luntz
Notary Public.

BIRTH AFFIDAVIT.

DEPARTMENT OF THE INTERIOR.
COMMISSION TO THE FIVE CIVILIZED TRIBES.

IN RE APPLICATION FOR ENROLLMENT, as a citizen of the   Chickasaw   Nation, of   Lousie Maud Collins   , born on the   15   day of   Feb 1904   , 1........

Name of Father: Ben F Collins   a citizen of the   Chickasaw   Nation.
Name of Mother: Annie Collins   a citizen of the   Chickasaw   Nation.

Postoffice   Ninnekah

AFFIDAVIT OF MOTHER.

UNITED STATES OF AMERICA, Indian Territory, }
   Southern   DISTRICT.

   I,   Annie Collins   , on oath state that I am   thirty one   years of age and a citizen by   Marriage   , of the   Chickasaw   Nation; that I am the lawful wife of Ben F Collins   , who is a citizen, by Birth   of the   Chickasaw   Nation; that a   Female   child was born to me on   15   day of   Feb 1904   , 1........; that said child has been named   Lousie Maud Collins   , and was living March 4, 1905.

Annie Collins

Witnesses To Mark:

{

   Subscribed and sworn to before me this 1   day of   April   , 1905

Henry Luntz
Notary Public.

Applications for Enrollment of Chickasaw Newborn
Act of 1905   Volume IV

AFFIDAVIT OF ATTENDING PHYSICIAN OR MID-WIFE.

UNITED STATES OF AMERICA, Indian Territory,
Southern   DISTRICT.

I,   P. M. Waltrep   , a   Physician   , on oath state that I attended on Mrs.   Annie Collins   , wife of   Ben F Collins   on the 15   day of   Feb 1904 , 1............; that there was born to her on said date a   Female   child; that said child was living March 4, 1905, and is said to have been named   Lousie Maud Collins

P.M. Waltrep M.D.

Witnesses To Mark:

Subscribed and sworn to before me this 1   day of   June   , 1905

Henry Luntz
Notary Public.

9-NB-269.

Muskogee, Indian Territory, May 20, 1905.

Ben F. Collins,
   Ninnekah, Indian Territory.

Dear Sir:

There is enclosed you herewith for execution application for the enrollment of your infant child, Lousie Maud Collins, born February 15, 1904.

In the affidavits heretofore filed with the Commission the Notary Public failed to affix his seal to the affidavits purported to be executed by the mother. You will therefore execute the enclosed affidavits and return them to this office.

In having these affidavits executed care should be exercised to see that all names are written in full, as they appear in the body of the affidavit, and in the event that either of the persons signing the affidavit are unable to write, signatures by mark must be attested by two witnesses. Each affidavit must be executed before a Notary Public and the notarial seal and signature of the officer must be attached to each separate affidavit.

Respectfully,

VR 20-4.   Chairman.

Applications for Enrollment of Chickasaw Newborn
Act of 1905   Volume IV

9-NB-269

Muskogee, Indian Territory, June 7, 1905.

Ben F. Collins,
    Ninnekah, Indian Territory.

Dear Sir:

    Receipt is hereby acknowledged of the affidavits of Annie Collins and P. M. Waltrep to the birth of Lousie Maud Collins daughter of Ben F. and Annie Collins, February 15, 1904, and the same have been filed with our records as an application for the enrollment of said child.

                    Respectfully,

                                          Chairman.

Chic. N.B. - 270
    (Winnie Elizabeth Shannon
    Born August 22, 1904)

BIRTH AFFIDAVIT.   *No 51*

DEPARTMENT OF THE INTERIOR.
COMMISSION TO THE FIVE CIVILIZED TRIBES.

    IN RE APPLICATION FOR ENROLLMENT, as a citizen of the   Chickasaw   Nation, of Winnie Elizabeth Shannon   , born on the 22nd   day of August , 1904

Name of Father: William T. Shannon   a citizen of the Chickasaw Nation.
Name of Mother: Laura G. Shannon   a citizen of the Chickasaw Nation.

                    Postoffice   Chickasha Ind Terr.

AFFIDAVIT OF MOTHER.

UNITED STATES OF AMERICA, Indian Territory, }
    Southern   **DISTRICT.**

    I, Laura G. Shannon   , on oath state that I am Thirty-Five   years of age and a citizen by   Blood   , of the   Chickasaw   Nation; that I am the lawful wife of   W. T. Shannon   , who is a citizen, by   Inter-Marriage   of the

Applications for Enrollment of Chickasaw Newborn
Act of 1905   Volume IV

Chickasaw Nation; that a Female child was born to me on 22nd day of August, 1904, that said child has been named Winnie Elizabeth Shannon, and is now living.

Laura G Shannon

Witnesses To Mark:
{

Subscribed and sworn to before me this 19 day of December, 1904

Mary L. Murphy
Notary Public.

AFFIDAVIT OF ATTENDING PHYSICIAN OR MID-WIFE.

UNITED STATES OF AMERICA, Indian Territory, }
.... DISTRICT. }

I, W.L. Peters, a Physician, on oath state that I attended on Mrs. William T Shannon, wife of William T. Shannon on the 22 day of August, 1904; that there was born to her on said date a Female child; that said child is now living and is said to have been named Winnie Elizabeth Shannon

W.L. Peters M.D.

Witnesses To Mark:
{

Subscribed and sworn to before me this 19 day of December, 1904

Mary L. Murphy
Notary Public.

BIRTH AFFIDAVIT.

DEPARTMENT OF THE INTERIOR.
COMMISSION TO THE FIVE CIVILIZED TRIBES.

IN RE APPLICATION FOR ENROLLMENT, as a citizen of the Chickasaw Nation of Winnie Elizabeth Shannon, born on the 22nd day of August, 1904

Name of Father: William T Shannon   a citizen of the Chickasaw Nation.
Name of Mother: Laura G Shannon   a citizen of the Chickasaw Nation.

Postoffice   Chickasha IT

Applications for Enrollment of Chickasaw Newborn
Act of 1905   Volume IV

AFFIDAVIT OF MOTHER.

UNITED STATES OF AMERICA, INDIAN TERRITORY,
Southern   DISTRICT.

I, Laura G Shannon, on oath state that I am 35 years of age and a citizen by Blood, of the Chickasaw Nation; that I am the lawful wife of William T Shannon, who is a citizen, by Intermarriage of the Chickasaw Nation; that a Female child was born to me on 22nd day of August, 190 4, that said child has been named Winnie Elizabeth Shannon, and is now living.

Laura G Shannon

WITNESSES TO MARK:

Subscribed and sworn to before me this 3^{d} day of April, 1905.

Ado Melton
Notary Public.

AFFIDAVIT OF ATTENDING PHYSICIAN OR MID-WIFE.

UNITED STATES OF AMERICA, INDIAN TERRITORY,
Southern   DISTRICT.

I, W.L. Peters, a Physician, on oath state that I attended on Mrs. Laura G. Shannon, wife of William T Shannon on the 22nd day of August, 190 4; that there was born to her on said date a Female child; that said child is now living and is said to have been named Winnie Elizabeth Shannon

WITNESSES TO MARK:

Subscribed and sworn to before me this 3^{d} day of April, 1905.

Ado Melton
Notary Public.

Chic. N.B. - 271
  (Edwin Harris Bradley
  Born January 14, 1903)

Applications for Enrollment of Chickasaw Newborn
Act of 1905   Volume IV

Department of the Interior
Commission to the Five Civilized Tribes
Chickasaw Land Office
Ardmore I. T.
March 31, 1905.

In Re Application for enrollment as a citizen of the Chickasaw Nation of Edwin Harris Bradley (Chickasaw Fiedl[sic] card No. 922)

Edwin Bradley after being sworn by Helen C. Miller, Notary Public, testified as follows:

EXAMINATION BY THE COMMISSION:

Q. What is your name? A. Edwin Bradley.
Q. What is your Post Office address? A. Emet, Indian Territory.
Q. What is your age? A. 28.
Q. What is the name of your father? A. William Bradley.
Q. What is the name of your mother? A. Elizabeth Bradley.
Q. Why is it Mr. Bradley, Indian Territory that your wife does not make affidavit relative to the birth of Edwin Harris Bradley?
A. She has a spell of sickness and lost her mind.
Q. Was she insane and unable to make affidavit? A. Yes.
Q. Where is she at the present time? A. In San Antonia, Texas.
Q. She is there in a hospital for treatment? A. Yes.

Shimer P. Boyd after being sworn by H. C. Miller, Notary Public, testified as follows:

EXAMINATION BY THE COMMISSION:

Q. What is your name? A. Shimer P. Boyed[sic].
Q. What is your age? A. 25 years.
Q. What is your Post Office address? A. Tishomingo, I. T.
Q. Mr. Boyd do you know anything about the mental condition of Edwin Bradley's wife, is she unable at this time to make affidavit relative to the birth of her child? A. Yes.
Q. Is she confined in some Insane Asylum or Hospital? A. Yes.

I, Helen A. Smith, after being duly sworn state that as Stenographer to the Commission to the Five Civilized Tribes, I reported the above proceedings on the 31st day of March, 1905, and that sae[sic] is a true and correct transcript of my Stenographic notes.

Helen A Smith

Subscribed and sworn to before me this   5   day of April, 1905.

H.C. Miller
Notary Public.

Applications for Enrollment of Chickasaw Newborn
Act of 1905   Volume IV

attach to testimony

BIRTH AFFIDAVIT.

DEPARTMENT OF THE INTERIOR.
COMMISSION TO THE FIVE CIVILIZED TRIBES.

IN RE APPLICATION FOR ENROLLMENT, as a citizen of the   Chickasaw   Nation, of   Edwin Harris Bradley   , born on the   14th   day of   January   , 1903

Name of Father: Edwin Ruthren Bradley   a citizen of the   Chickasaw   Nation.
Name of Mother: Nettie Bradley   a citizen of the   Chickasaw   Nation.

Postoffice   Emet Ind. Ter.

AFFIDAVIT OF ~~MOTHER~~. *Husband*

UNITED STATES OF AMERICA, Indian Territory,
   Southern   DISTRICT.

I,   Edwin Bradley   , on oath state that I am   28   years of age and a citizen by   blood   , of the   Chickasaw   Nation; that I am the lawful ~~wife~~ *husband* of Nettie Bradley   , who is a citizen, by   blood   of the   Chickasaw   Nation; that a   male   child was born to ~~me~~ *her* on   14th   day of   January   , 1903, that said child has been named   Edwin Harris Bradley   , and is now living.

Edwin Bradley

Witnesses To Mark:

Subscribed and sworn to before me this   31st   day of   March   , 1905.

H.C. Miller
Notary Public.

AFFIDAVIT OF ATTENDING PHYSICIAN OR MID-WIFE.

UNITED STATES OF AMERICA, Indian Territory,
                                DISTRICT.

I,   I. N. Carrell   , a Physician   , on oath state that I attended on Mrs.   Nettie Bradley   , wife of   Edwin R. Bradley   on the   14   day of   January   , 1903; that there was born to her on said date a   male   child; that said child is now living and is said to have been named   Edwin Harris Bradley

I.N. Carrell

Applications for Enrollment of Chickasaw Newborn
Act of 1905   Volume IV

Witnesses To Mark:
{ K. Moorman
{ *(Name Illegible)*

Subscribed and sworn to before me this   23rd   day of   March   , 1905.

G.B. Slater
Notary Public.
My commission expires Jan 5 1908

BIRTH AFFIDAVIT.

DEPARTMENT OF THE INTERIOR.
COMMISSION TO THE FIVE CIVILIZED TRIBES.

IN RE APPLICATION FOR ENROLLMENT, as a citizen of the   Chickasaw   Nation, of   Edwin Harris Bradley   , born on the   14th day of   January   , 1903

Name of Father: Edwin R. Bradley   a citizen of the   Chickasaw   Nation.
Name of Mother: Nettie Bradley   a citizen of the   Chickasaw   Nation.

Postoffice   Emet Ind. Ter.

AFFIDAVIT OF MOTHER.

UNITED STATES OF AMERICA, Indian Territory, }
.... DISTRICT. }

I,   Nettie Bradley   , on oath state that I am   28   years of age and a citizen by   Blood   , of the   Chickasaw   Nation; that I am the lawful wife of   Edwin R Bradley   , who is a citizen, by   Blood   of the   Chickasaw   Nation; that a   Male   child was born to me on   14th day of   January   , 1903; that said child has been named   Edwin Harris Bradley   , and was living March 4, 1905.

her
Nettie x Bradley
mark

Witnesses To Mark:
{ *(Name Illegible)*
{ J.C. Carrell

Subscribed and sworn to before me this   31st day of   May   , 1905.

My Com Expires   A.L. McKinney
   March 14-1908   Notary Public.
                                              Southern Dist IT

Applications for Enrollment of Chickasaw Newborn
Act of 1905   Volume IV

AFFIDAVIT OF ATTENDING PHYSICIAN OR MID-WIFE.

UNITED STATES OF AMERICA, Indian Territory,
Southern   DISTRICT.

    I,   Isaac N. Carrell   , a Physician   , on oath state that I attended on Mrs. Nettie Bradley   , wife of   Edwin R Bradley   on the   14th day of January   , 1903; that there was born to her on said date a   Male   child; that said child was living March 4, 1905, and is said to have been named Edwin Harris Bradley

                                  I.N. Carrell

Witnesses To Mark:

    Subscribed and sworn to before me this 31st day of   May   , 1905

My Com Expires   A.L. McKinney
   March 14-1908   Notary Public.
                                     Southern Dist I.T.

                                                    9-NB -271.

                    Muskogee, Indian Territory, May 16, 1905.

Edwin R. Bradley,
    Emet, Indian Territory.

Dear Sir:

    There is enclosed you herewith for execution application for the enrollment of your infant child, Edwin Harris Bradley, Indian Territory born January 14, 1903.

    It appears from the testimony filed in this office that the mother of the above mentioned applicant is confined in the hospital for treatment and is unable to make affidavit, if this is the case it will be necessary for you to secure the affidavits of two disinterested persons who have actual knowledge of the facts that the child was born, the date of his birth; that he was living on March 4, 1905, and that Nettie Bradley is his mother.

    In having these affidavits executed care should be exercised to see that all names are written in full, as they appear in the body of the affidavit, and in the event that either of the persons signing the affidavit are unable to write, signatures by mark must be attested by two witnesses. Each affidavit must be executed before a Notary Public and the notarial seal and signature of the officer must be attached to each separate affidavit.

Applications for Enrollment of Chickasaw Newborn
Act of 1905   Volume IV

Respectfully,

Chairman.

(The above letter given again, except with date of May 17, 1905.)

9-N.B. 271.

Muskogee, Indian Territory, June 5, 1905.

Edwin R. Bradley,
    Emet, Indian Territory.

Dear Sir:

    Receipt is hereby acknowledged of the affidavits of Nettie Bradley and I. N. Carrell to the birth of Edwin Harris Bradley, son of Edwin R. and Nettie Bradley, January 14, 1903, and the same have been filed with our records in the matter of the enrollment of said child.

Respectfully,

Commissioner in Charge.

Chic. N.B. - 242
    (Frank Ralston Taylor
    Born August 13, 1903)

BIRTH AFFIDAVIT.   *No 80*

DEPARTMENT OF THE INTERIOR.
COMMISSION TO THE FIVE CIVILIZED TRIBES.

    IN RE APPLICATION FOR ENROLLMENT, as a citizen of the   Chickasaw   Nation, of   Frank Ralston Taylor   , born on the   13   day of   Aug   , 1903

Name of Father: Stephen Lee Taylor   a citizen of the   Chickasaw Nation.
Name of Mother: Mary Ann Taylor   a citizen of the   Chickasaw Nation.

Postoffice   Wapanucka IT

Applications for Enrollment of Chickasaw Newborn
Act of 1905   Volume IV

AFFIDAVIT OF MOTHER.

UNITED STATES OF AMERICA, Indian Territory,}
    Central   DISTRICT.}

    I, Mary Ann Taylor, on oath state that I am Twenty five years of age and a citizen by Blood, of the Chickasaw Nation; that I am the lawful wife of Stephen Lee Taylor, who is a citizen, by Marriage of the Chickasaw Nation; that a male child was born to me on 13 day of August, 1903, that said child has been named Frank Roston[sic] Taylor, and is now living.

                                      Mary Ann Taylor

Witnesses To Mark:
{
    Subscribed and sworn to before me this 28 day of January, 1905.

                                      A A Faulk
                                        Notary Public.

AFFIDAVIT OF ATTENDING PHYSICIAN OR MID-WIFE.

UNITED STATES OF AMERICA, Indian Territory,}
    Central   DISTRICT.}

    I, J F Renegar, a Physician, on oath state that I attended on Mrs. Mary Ann Taylor, wife of Stephen Lee Taylor on the 13 day of Aug, 1903; that there was born to her on said date a male child; that said child is now living and is said to have been named Frank Ralston Taylor

                                        J. F. Renegar M.D.

Witnesses To Mark:
{
    Subscribed and sworn to before me this 28 day of January, 1905.

                                      A A Faulk
                                        Notary Public.

Applications for Enrollment of Chickasaw Newborn
Act of 1905 Volume IV

BIRTH AFFIDAVIT.

DEPARTMENT OF THE INTERIOR.
COMMISSION TO THE FIVE CIVILIZED TRIBES.

IN RE APPLICATION FOR ENROLLMENT, as a citizen of the Chickasaw Nation, of Frank R. Taylor , born on the 13th day of August , 1903

Name of Father: Stephen Lee Taylor   a citizen of the Chickasaw Nation.
Name of Mother: Mary Ann Taylor   a citizen of the Chickasaw Nation.

Postoffice   Wapanucka I.T.

AFFIDAVIT OF MOTHER.

UNITED STATES OF AMERICA, Indian Territory,
    Central   DISTRICT.

I, Mary Ann Taylor , on oath state that I am 25 years of age and a citizen by blood , of the Chickasaw Nation; that I am the lawful wife of Stephen Lee Taylor , who is a citizen, by Intermarriage of the Chickasaw Nation; that a male child was born to me on 13th day of August , 1903; that said child has been named Frank R. Taylor , and was living March 4, 1905.

                                               Mary Ann Taylor

Witnesses To Mark:
{

Subscribed and sworn to before me this 1st day of April , 1905

                                       (Name Illegible)
                                               Notary Public.

AFFIDAVIT OF ATTENDING PHYSICIAN OR MID-WIFE.

UNITED STATES OF AMERICA, Indian Territory,
    Central   DISTRICT.

I, J.F. Renegar , a Physician , on oath state that I attended on Mrs. Mary Ann Taylor , wife of Stephen Lee Taylor on the 13th day of August , 1903; that there was born to her on said date a male child; that said child was living March 4, 1905, and is said to have been named Frank R Taylor

                                               J.F. Renegar, M.D.

Witnesses To Mark:
{

Applications for Enrollment of Chickasaw Newborn
Act of 1905   Volume IV

Subscribed and sworn to before me this 3^d day of   April   , 1905

(Name Illegible)
Notary Public.

Chic. N.B. - 273
   *(Ruth Venable
   Born February 2, 1903)*

This is to certify that I was the attending physician of Mrs Dollie Venable the wife of Robert L. Venable in her confinement on the 2nd day of February, 1905[sic] and was born to her a female child and is still living.

Dr. J. M. Childress

This Feb 27-1903
Sworn and subscribed to before me a Notary Public in and for the Central District of the Indian Territory this 27th day of Feb. 1905.

E K Smith
Notary Public

My Commission expires Jan 8, 1907.

BIRTH AFFIDAVIT.

DEPARTMENT OF THE INTERIOR.
COMMISSION TO THE FIVE CIVILIZED TRIBES.

   IN RE APPLICATION FOR ENROLLMENT, as a citizen of the   Chickasaw   Nation, of   Ruth Venable   , born on the 2   day of February , 1903

Name of Father: Robert L Venable   a citizen of the   Chickasaw   Nation.
Name of Mother: Dollie Venable   a citizen of the   Chickasaw   Nation.

Postoffice   Platter, Ind. Ter

Applications for Enrollment of Chickasaw Newborn
Act of 1905   Volume IV

AFFIDAVIT OF MOTHER.

UNITED STATES OF AMERICA, Indian Territory, }
   Central   DISTRICT. }

    I, Dollie Venable , on oath state that I am 28 years of age and a citizen by Blood , of the Chickasaw Nation; that I am the lawful wife of Robert L Venable , who is a citizen, by intermarriage of the Chickasaw Nation; that a Female child was born to me on the 2nd day of February , 1903; that said child has been named Ruth Venable , and was living March 4, 1905.

                          Dollie Venable

Witnesses To Mark:

    Subscribed and sworn to before me this 4 day of   April   , 1905

                          E.Q. Franklin
                              Notary Public.

AFFIDAVIT OF ATTENDING PHYSICIAN OR MID-WIFE.

UNITED STATES OF AMERICA, Indian Territory, }
   Central   DISTRICT. }

    I, Dovie Venable , a midwife , on oath state that I attended on Mrs. Dollie Venable , wife of Robert L Venable on the 2 day of February , 1903; that there was born to her on said date a Female child; that said child was living March 4, 1905, and is said to have been named Ruth Venable

                          Dovie Venable Midwife

Witnesses To Mark:

    Subscribed and sworn to before me this 4 day of   April   , 1905

                          E.Q. Franklin
                            Notary Public.

Applications for Enrollment of Chickasaw Newborn
Act of 1905   Volume IV

BIRTH AFFIDAVIT.

DEPARTMENT OF THE INTERIOR.
COMMISSION TO THE FIVE CIVILIZED TRIBES.

IN RE APPLICATION FOR ENROLLMENT, as a citizen of the   Chickasaw   Nation, of   Ruth Venable   , born on the   2   day of   February   , 1903

Name of Father: Robert L Venable   a citizen of the   Chickasaw Nation.
Name of Mother: Dollie Venable   a citizen of the   Chickasaw Nation.

Postoffice   Platter

AFFIDAVIT OF MOTHER.

UNITED STATES OF AMERICA, Indian Territory,
Central   DISTRICT.

I, Dollie Venable   , on oath state that I am   28   years of age and a citizen by   blood   , of the   Chickasaw   Nation; that I am the lawful wife of   Robert L Venable   , who is a citizen, by   intermarriage   of the   Chickasaw   Nation; that a   female   child was born to me on   2   day of   February   , 1903, that said child has been named   Ruth   , and is now living.

Dollie Venable

Witnesses To Mark:
{ Robert L Venable
{ F.E. Mead

Subscribed and sworn to before me this   27   day of   February   , 1905.

S M Mead
Notary Public.

Chickasaw 1103.

Muskogee, Indian Territory, April 10, 1905.

Robert L. Venable,
    Platter, Indian Territory.

Dear Sir:

Receipt is hereby acknowledged of the affidavits of Dollie Venable and Dovie Venable to the birth of Ruth Venable, daughter of Robert L. and Dollie Venable,

Applications for Enrollment of Chickasaw Newborn
Act of 1905 Volume IV

February 2, 1903, and the same have been filed with our records as an application for the enrollment of said child.

Respectfully,

Commissioner in Charge.

Chic. N.B. - 274

    (Annie Stephenson
    Born January 7, 1904)

BIRTH AFFIDAVIT.

DEPARTMENT OF THE INTERIOR.
COMMISSION TO THE FIVE CIVILIZED TRIBES.

IN RE APPLICATION FOR ENROLLMENT, as a citizen of the Chickasaw Nation, of Annie Stephenson, born on the 7th day of January, 1904.

Name of Father: Philip Stephenson   a citizen of the Chickasaw Nation.
Name of Mother: Victoria Stephenson   a citizen of the Chickasaw Nation.

Postoffice   Springer, Ind Ter

AFFIDAVIT OF MOTHER.

UNITED STATES OF AMERICA, Indian Territory, }
    Southern   DISTRICT. }

    I, Victoria Stephenson, on oath state that I am _____ years of age and a citizen by Blood, of the Chickasaw Nation; that I am the lawful wife of Philip Stephenson, who is a citizen, by Adoption of the Chickasaw Nation; that a female child was born to me on 7th day of January, 1904; that said child has been named Annie Stephenson, and was living March 4, 1905.

Victory[sic] Stephenson

Witnesses To Mark:
  {

    Subscribed and sworn to before me this 27th day of March, 1905.

Edgar *(Illegible)*
Notary Public.

Applications for Enrollment of Chickasaw Newborn
Act of 1905   Volume IV

AFFIDAVIT OF ATTENDING PHYSICIAN OR MID-WIFE.

UNITED STATES OF AMERICA, Indian Territory, }
   Southern   DISTRICT. }

    I,   J.W. Fields   , a   Physician   , on oath state that I attended on Mrs. Victoria Stephenson   , wife of   Philip Stephenson   on the 27th day of January , 1904; that there was born to her on said date a   female   child; that said child was living March 4, 1905, and is said to have been named   Annie Stephenson

                                      J.W. Fields M.D.

Witnesses To Mark:
{

    Subscribed and sworn to before me this   27th day of   March   , 1905

                                        Edgar *(Illegible)*
                                        Notary Public.

---

                                                  9 NB 274

                      Muskogee, Indian Territory, May 18, 1905.

Phillip Stephenson,
    Springer, Indian Territory.

Dear Sir:

    Receipt is hereby acknowledged of your letter of May 11, 1905, in which you state that sometime since you mailed an application for the enrollment of your child Annie Stephenson, and you ask if the same has not been received that you be forwarded another application.

    In reply to your letter you are advised that the affidavits heretofore forwarded to the birth of your child Annie Stephenson have been filed with our records as an application for the enrollment of said child.

                                Respectfully,

                                                 Chairman.

**Applications for Enrollment of Chickasaw Newborn
Act of 1905   Volume IV**

Chic. N.B. - 275
    (John Douglass Brown
    Born February 13, 1904)

101

CERTIFICATE OF
RECORD OF MARRIAGE

UNITED STATES OF AMERICA,
   INDIAN TERRITORY,   } sct.
     SOUTHERN DISTRICT.

   I, C. M. CAMPBELL, Clerk of the United States Court, in the Territory and District aforesaid DO HEREBY CERTIFY, that the License for and Certificate of Marriage of

Mr.   Jno H Brown   and

M   Amelia M Steele

were filed in my office in said Territory and District the   14   day of   Jany   A.D., 190 3   and duly recorded in Book   G   of Marriage Record, Page   122

   WITNESS my hand and Seal of said Court, at Ardmore, this   4   day of   April   A.D. 190 5

       C. M. Campbell
                CLERK.

Return this license to the United States Clerk at Ardmore, that it may be recorded, when it will be mailed to the proper address.

Texas Printing Company, Fort Worth.

DEPARTMENT OF THE INTERIOR,
COMMISSION TO THE FIVE CIVILIZED TRIBES.
FILED
APR 10 1905
Tams Bixby CHAIRMAN.

**Applications for Enrollment of Chickasaw Newborn
Act of 1905   Volume IV**

No person is authorized to perform the Marriage Ceremony in the Indian Territory unless the proper credentials have first been recorded in the Clerk's office.

MARRIAGE LICENSE.
No.   101

UNITED STATES OF AMERICA,
INDIAN TERRITORY,   } SS.   To Any Person Authorized by Law to Solemnize
SOUTHERN DISTRICT.   Marriage, Greeting:

YOU ARE HEREBY COMMANDED to solemnize the Rite and publish the Banns of Matrimony between Mr.   **Jno. H. Brown**   of   Woodville   in the Indian Territory, aged   21   years, and M   Amelia M. Steele   of   Woodville   in the Indian Territory, aged   27   years, according to law; and do you officially sign and return this license to the parties therein named.

WITNESS my hand and official Seal, this   6"   day of   Jany   A. D. 190 3

C.M. Campbell
Clerk of the United States Court.

Certificate of Marriage.

UNITED STATES OF AMERICA,
INDIAN TERRITORY,   } SS.
SOUTHERN DISTRICT.   I,   J. T. Means

_____ do hereby certify that on the   11   day of   Jany   A. D. 190 3 , I did duly and according to law, as commanded in the foregoing License, solemnize the Rite and publish the Banns of Matrimony between the parties therein named.

WITNESS my hand this   12   day of   Jany   A. D. 190 3

My credentials are recorded in the office of the Clerk of the United States Court, Indian Territory, Southern District, at Ardmore, Book   C   , Page   153

J. T. Means
Clergyman

NOTE. (a)- This License and Certificate of Marriages must be returned to the office of the Clerk of the United States Court in the Indian Territory, at Ardmore, within sixty days from the date thereof, or the party to whom the License was issued will be liable in the amount of ONE HUNDRED DOLLARS ($100).

Applications for Enrollment of Chickasaw Newborn
Act of 1905   Volume IV

BIRTH AFFIDAVIT.

IN RE-APPLICATION FOR ENROLLMENT, as a citizen of the   Chickasaw   Nation, of   John Douglass   , born on the   13th   day of   February   , 190 4

Name of Father: John H Brown   a citizen of the   Chickasaw   Nation.
(nee Amelia Steele)
Name of Mother: Amelia Brown   a citizen of the   Chickasaw   Nation.

Postoffice   Woodville Ind Ter

AFFIDAVIT OF MOTHER.

UNITED STATES OF AMERICA, INDIAN TERRITORY,
Southern   District.

I,   Amelia Brown   , on oath state that I am   30   years of age and a citizen by blood   , of the   Chickasaw   Nation; that I am the lawful wife of   John H Brown   , who is a citizen, by   marriage   of the   Chickasaw   Nation; that a   male   child was born to me on   the 13th   day of   February   , 1904 , that said child has been named   John Douglass   , and is now living.

Amelia Brown

Witnesses To Mark: *(Affidavit was folded and blocked the lines down to the notary's signature)*
Robert S Bell
Notary Public.

AFFIDAVIT OF ATTENDING PHYSICIAN OR MID-WIFE.

UNITED STATES OF AMERICA, INDIAN TERRITORY,
Southern   District.

I,   E A Jones   , a   Physician   , on oath state that I attended on Mrs.   Amelia Brown *nee Amelia Steel*   , wife of   John H Brown   on the   13 day of   February   , 190 4; that there was born to her on said date a   male   child; that said child is now living and is said to have been named   John D. Brown

E A Jones M.D.

Witnesses To Mark:

Subscribed and sworn to before me this   2nd   day of   March   , 1905.

Robert S Bell
Notary Public.

Applications for Enrollment of Chickasaw Newborn
Act of 1905   Volume IV

BIRTH AFFIDAVIT.

IN RE-APPLICATION FOR ENROLLMENT, as a citizen of the Chickasaw Nation, of John Douglass Brown, born on the 13th day of February, 1904
Name of Father: John H Brown   a citizen of the ~~Chickasaw~~ United States Nation.
Name of Mother: Amelia Brown   a citizen of the Chickasaw Nation.

Postoffice   Woodville Ind Ter

AFFIDAVIT OF MOTHER.

UNITED STATES OF AMERICA, INDIAN TERRITORY,
Southern   District.

I, Amelia Brown, on oath state that I am 30 years of age and a citizen by blood, of the Chickasaw Nation; that I am the lawful wife of John H Brown, who is a citizen, by ~~marriage~~ of the United States of the Chickasaw Nation; that a male child was born to me on the thirteenth day of Feby, 1904, that said child has been named John Douglass, and is now living.

Amelia Brown

Witnesses To Mark:

Subscribed and sworn to before me this third day of April, 1905.

Robert S Bell
Notary Public.

AFFIDAVIT OF ATTENDING PHYSICIAN OR MID-WIFE.

UNITED STATES OF AMERICA, INDIAN TERRITORY,
Southern   District.

I, E A Jones, a Physician, on oath state that I attended on Mrs. Amelia Brown nee Amelia Steel, wife of John H Brown on the 13th day of Feb, 1904; that there was born to her on said date a male child; that said child is now living and is said to have been named John Douglass Brown

E A Jones M.D.

Witnesses To Mark:

Subscribed and sworn to before me this 31 day of March, 1905.

Robert S Bell
Notary Public.

Applications for Enrollment of Chickasaw Newborn
Act of 1905 Volume IV

9-998

Muskogee, Indian Territory, April 5, 1905.

John H. Brown,
    Woodville, Indian Territory.

Dear Sir:

    Receipt is hereby acknowledged of the affidavits of Amelia Brown and E. A. Jones to the birth of John Douglass Brown, son of John H. and Amelia Brown, February 13, 1904, and the same have been filed with our records as an application for the enrollment of said child.

        Respectfully,

        Commissioner in Charge.

Chickasaw 998.

Muskogee, Indian Territory, April 11, 1905.

H. H. Brown,
    Attorney at Law,
        Ardmore, Indian Territory.

Dear Sir:

    Receipt is hereby acknowledged of your letter of April 4th, enclosing affidavits of Amelia Brown and E. A. Jones to the birth of John Douglas Brown, February 13, 1904. Receipt is also acknowledged of the marriage license and certificate between John H. Brown and Amelia M. Steele, January 11, 1903. The above names papers have been filed with our records as an application for the enrollment of said child.

        Respectfully,

        Commissioner in Charge.

Applications for Enrollment of Chickasaw Newborn
Act of 1905   Volume IV

9-NB-275

Muskogee, Indian Territory, June 17, 1907.

F. P. Kibbey,
    Byars, Indian Territory.

Dear Sir:

    Receipt is hereby acknowledged of your letter of June 11, 1907, in which you ask to be advised if John Brown a new born Chickasaw is on the approved roll.

    In reply to your letter you are advised that John Douglas Brown, child of John H. Brown and Amelia Brown, was approved by the Secretary of the Interior June 21, 1905, as a new born citizen of the Chickasaw Nation under the Act of March 3, 1905.

    If this is not the person to whom you refer and you will give his age, the names of his parents, and any other information you may possess which would lead to his identification the matter of your inquiry will receive further consideration.

        Respectfully,

                            Commissioner.

Chickasaw 276 Newborn
    Clarice Frances Brown
    (Born Feb. 17, 1904)

    Act of Congress Approved
    March 3, 1905

BIRTH AFFIDAVIT.

DEPARTMENT OF THE INTERIOR.
COMMISSION TO THE FIVE CIVILIZED TRIBES.

    IN RE APPLICATION FOR ENROLLMENT, as a citizen of the   Chickasaw   Nation, of   Clarice Frances Brown   , born on the   17   day of   February , 1904

Name of Father: Eben Foster Brown   a citizen of the   Chickasaw   Nation.
Name of Mother: Maude E Brown   a citizen of the   Cherokee   Nation.

Applications for Enrollment of Chickasaw Newborn
Act of 1905   Volume IV

Postoffice   Springer Ind. Ter.

AFFIDAVIT OF MOTHER.

UNITED STATES OF AMERICA, Indian Territory,
Southern DISTRICT.

I, Maude E Brown, on oath state that I am 28 years of age and a citizen by Blood, of the Cherokee Nation; that I am the lawful wife of Eben Foster Brown, who is a citizen, by Blood of the Chickasaw Nation; that a Female child was born to me on 17th day of February, 1904; that said child has been named Clarice Frances Brown, and was living March 4, 1905.

Maude E Brown

Witnesses To Mark:
{ A.L. Adams
{ JH Kuntz

Subscribed and sworn to before me this 25 day of March, 1905

Chas H Eskew
Notary Public.

AFFIDAVIT OF ATTENDING PHYSICIAN OR MID-WIFE.

UNITED STATES OF AMERICA, Indian Territory,
Northern DISTRICT.

I, Mrs Amandy Legate, a midwife, on oath state that I attended on Mrs. Maude E Brown, wife of Eben Foster Brown on the 17th day of Feb, 1904; that there was born to her on said date a Female child; that said child was living March 4, 1905, and is said to have been named Clarice Frances Brown

Mrs. Amandy Legate

Witnesses To Mark:
{ John ? Scott
{ Thomas Rider

Subscribed and sworn to before me this 1st day of April, 1905

John ? Scott
Notary Public.

My term expires
May 20/08

Applications for Enrollment of Chickasaw Newborn
Act of 1905   Volume IV

Indian Territory)
    District   )   *Robert*
Northern   I, Calhoun Parks on my oath, state that I am a duly ordained minister of the Gospel and that I am personally acquainted with Eben Foster Brown, a Chickasaw Indian by blood and his wife Maud E. Brown, a Cherokee by blood. That on the 5th. day of *August*, 1897, at the home of J.B. Brown near Chelsea in the Cherokee Nation, I united in Marriage the said Eben Foster Brown and Maud E. Rider, now Brown.

Robert Calhoun Parks

Subscribed and sworn to before me this 27 day of April 1905.

John T. Ezzard
Notary Public.

---

9 N B 276

Muskogee, Indian Territory, April 17, 1905.

Eben Foster Brown,
    Springer, Indian Territory.

Dear Sir:

    You are hereby advised that before the application for the enrollment of your infant child, Clarice Frances Brown, can be finally disposed of, it will be necessary for you to furnish the Commission with either the original or a certified copy of the license and certificate of your marriage to her mother, Maude E. Brown.

    Please give this matter your immediate attention.

Respectfully,

Chairman.

Applications for Enrollment of Chickasaw Newborn
Act of 1905   Volume IV

9 N.B. 276.

Muskogee, Indian Territory, May 6, 1905.

Chillion Riley,
    Attorney at Law,
        Ardmore, Indian Territory.

Dear Sir:

    Receipt is hereby acknowledged of your letter of May 2, enclosing the affidavit of Robert Calhoun Cox[sic] to the marriage of Eben Foster Brown and Maud E. Brown, which you offer in support of the application for the enrollment of Clarice Frances Brown and the same has been filed with the records in the matter of the enrollment of this child.

    Respectfully,

    Commissioner in Charge.

Chic. N.B. - 277
    (Irene Stella Goforth
    Born July 1, 1903)

BIRTH AFFIDAVIT.
DEPARTMENT OF THE INTERIOR.
COMMISSION TO THE FIVE CIVILIZED TRIBES.

IN RE APPLICATION FOR ENROLLMENT, as a citizen of the Chickasaw Nation, of Irene Stella Goforth, born on the 1st day of July, 1903.

Name of Father: Jos. H. Goforth   a citizen of the Chickasaw Nation.
Name of Mother: Cordelia Goforth   a citizen of the U. S. ~~Nation~~.

    Postoffice   Caddo, I.T.

Applications for Enrollment of Chickasaw Newborn
Act of 1905 Volume IV

AFFIDAVIT OF MOTHER.

UNITED STATES OF AMERICA, Indian Territory,
   Central   DISTRICT.

    I, Cordelia Goforth, on oath state that I am 21 years of age and a citizen by intermarriage, of the Chickasaw Nation; that I am the lawful wife of Joseph H Goforth (deceased), who is a citizen, by blood of the Chickasaw Nation; that a female child was born to me on 1st day of July, 1903; that said child has been named Irene Stella Goforth, and was living March 4, 1905.

                                      Cordelia Goforth

Witnesses To Mark:

    Subscribed and sworn to before me this 25th day of March, 1905

                                       Sol. J. Homer
                                           Notary Public.

AFFIDAVIT OF ATTENDING PHYSICIAN OR MID-WIFE.

UNITED STATES OF AMERICA, Indian Territory,
   Central   DISTRICT.

    I, Mary H. Goforth, a Midwife, on oath state that I attended on Mrs. Cordelia Goforth, wife of Joseph H Goforth on the 1st day of July, 1905[sic]; that there was born to her on said date a female child; that said child was living March 4, 1905, and is said to have been named Irene Stella Goforth

                                          her
                                  Mary H. x Goforth

Witnesses To Mark: mark
    S.J. Homer
    Peter Maytubby Jr

    Subscribed and sworn to before me this 29th day of March, 1905

                                        Sol. J. Homer
                                        Notary Public.

Applications for Enrollment of Chickasaw Newborn
Act of 1905 Volume IV

Chic. N.B. - 278
    (Leona James Lannom
    Born April 5, 1904)

BIRTH AFFIDAVIT.

DEPARTMENT OF THE INTERIOR.
COMMISSION TO THE FIVE CIVILIZED TRIBES.

    IN RE APPLICATION FOR ENROLLMENT, as a citizen of the   Chickasaw   Nation, of   Leona James Lannom   , born on the   5   day of   Apr   , 1904

Name of Father: William R. Lannom   a citizen of the By Intermarriage Nation.
Name of Mother: Cordelia Lannom   a citizen of the   Chickasaw   Nation.

    Postoffice   Hennepin Ind Ter

AFFIDAVIT OF MOTHER.

UNITED STATES OF AMERICA, Indian Territory, ⎫
    Southern   DISTRICT. ⎭

    I,   Cordelia Lannom   , on oath state that I am   21   years of age and a citizen by   Blood   , of the   Chickasaw   Nation; that I am the lawful wife of   William R. Lannom   , who is a citizen, by Intermarriage   of the   Chickasaw   Nation; that a   female   child was born to me on   5   day of   Apr   , 1904; that said child has been named   Leona James Lannom   , and was living March 4, 1905.

    Cordelia Lannom

Witnesses To Mark:
  ⎰ Ardil C. Meeks
  ⎱ J.A.W. Pearson

    Subscribed and sworn to before me this   3   day of   Apr   , 1905

    M. F. Glaze
    Notary Public.

My Com Ex Nov. 29ᵗʰ 1908   *17 District*

Applications for Enrollment of Chickasaw Newborn
Act of 1905   Volume IV

AFFIDAVIT OF ATTENDING PHYSICIAN OR MID-WIFE.

UNITED STATES OF AMERICA, Indian Territory, ⎫
Southern   DISTRICT. ⎭

I,   Annie Poe   , a mid wife   , on oath state that I attended on Mrs.   Cordelia Lannom   , wife of   William R Lannom   on the   5 day of Apr, 1904; that there was born to her on said date a   female   child; that said child was living March 4, 1905, and is said to have been named   Leona James Lannom

Annie Poe

Witnesses To Mark:
{ J.A.W. Pearson
{ Ardil C Meeks

Subscribed and sworn to before me this   3 day of   Apr   , 1905

M. F. Glaze
Notary Public.

My Com Ex Nov. 29ᵗʰ 1908   17 District

Chickasaw 437.

Muskogee, Indian Territory, April 10, 1905.

William R. Lannom,
    Hennepin, Indian Territory.

Dear Sir:

    Receipt is hereby acknowledged of the affidavits of Cordelia Lannom and Annie Poe to the birth of Leona James Lannom, daughter of William R. and Cordelia Lannom, April 5, 1904, and the same have been filed with our records as an application for the enrollment of said child.

Respectfully,

Commissioner in Charge.

<u>Chic. N.B. - 279</u>
    (Josephine Blevins
    Born May 3, 1903)

Applications for Enrollment of Chickasaw Newborn
Act of 1905 Volume IV

BIRTH AFFIDAVIT.

DEPARTMENT OF THE INTERIOR.
COMMISSION TO THE FIVE CIVILIZED TRIBES.

IN RE APPLICATION FOR ENROLLMENT, as a citizen of the Chickasaw Nation, of Josephine Blevins, born on the 3$^{th[sic]}$ day of May, 1903

Name of Father: Lemuel F Blevins   a citizen of the Chickasaw Nation.
Name of Mother: Willie F Blevins   a citizen of the United States ~~Nation~~.

Postoffice   Wynnewood, I.T.

AFFIDAVIT OF MOTHER.

UNITED STATES OF AMERICA, Indian Territory, }
    Southern   DISTRICT.

I, Willie F. Blevins, on oath state that I am Twenty nine years of age and a citizen ~~by~~ _____, of the United States ~~Nation~~; that I am the lawful wife of Lemuel F. Blevins, who is a citizen, by blood of the Chickasaw Nation; that a Female child was born to me on 3th day of May, 1903; that said child has been named Josephine Blevins, and was living March 4, 1905.

                       Willie F. Blevins

Witnesses To Mark:
   { Frank L. Robinson
   { Emma C Packard

Subscribed and sworn to before me this 3rd day of April, 1905

                       Frank L. Robinson
                       Notary Public.

AFFIDAVIT OF ATTENDING PHYSICIAN OR MID-WIFE.

UNITED STATES OF AMERICA, Indian Territory, }
    Southern   DISTRICT.

I, W.E. Settle M.D., a Physician, on oath state that I attended on Mrs. Willie F. Blevins, wife of Lemuel F. Blevins on the 3rd day of May, 1903; that there was born to her on said date a Female child; that said child was living March 4, 1905, and is said to have been named Josephine Blevins

                       W.E. Settle M.D.

Applications for Enrollment of Chickasaw Newborn
Act of 1905 Volume IV

Witnesses To Mark:
{ Frank L. Robinson

Subscribed and sworn to before me this 3rd day of April, 1905

Frank L. Robinson
Notary Public.

Chickasaw 464.

Muskogee, Indian Territory, April 10, 1905.

Lemuel F. Blevins,
Wynnewood, Indian Territory.

Dear Sir:

Receipt is hereby acknowledged of your letter of April 3, transmitting the affidavits of Willie F. Blevins and W. E. Settle to the birth of Josephene[sic] Blevins, daughter of Lemuel F. and Willie F. Blevins, May 3, 1903, and the same have been filed with our records as an application for the enrollment of said child.

Respectfully,

Commissioner in Charge.

Chic. N.B. - 280
    (Janice Pollock
    Born December 21, 1902)
    (Junie Pollock
    Born December 8, 1904)

Applications for Enrollment of Chickasaw Newborn
Act of 1905   Volume IV

BIRTH AFFIDAVIT.

DEPARTMENT OF THE INTERIOR.
COMMISSION TO THE FIVE CIVILIZED TRIBES.

IN RE APPLICATION FOR ENROLLMENT, as a citizen of the   Chickasaw   Nation, of   Junie Pollock   , born on the 8th day of   December , 1904

Name of Father: Lee Pollock   a citizen of the   Chickasaw   Nation.
Name of Mother: Georgie[sic] Pollock   a citizen of the   "   "   Nation.

Postoffice   Kiowa Ind. Ter.

AFFIDAVIT OF MOTHER.

UNITED STATES OF AMERICA, Indian Territory, ⎫
   Central   DISTRICT.   ⎬

I, Georgie Pollock   , on oath state that I am   21   years of age and a citizen by   Blood   , of the   Chickasaw   Nation; that I am the lawful wife of   Lee Pollock   , who is a citizen, by Intermarriage   of the   Chickasaw   Nation; that a   Female   child was born to me on 8th day of December   , 1904; that said child has been named   Junie Pollock   , and was living March 4, 1905.

                                Georgia Pollock

Witnesses To Mark:
  {

Subscribed and sworn to before me this 1st day of   April   , 1905

                                C.E. Culbertson
                                  Notary Public.

AFFIDAVIT OF ATTENDING PHYSICIAN OR MID-WIFE.

UNITED STATES OF AMERICA, Indian Territory, ⎫
   Central   DISTRICT.   ⎬

I,   Dr S. W. Jackson   , a   Physician   , on oath state that I attended on Mrs.   Georgia Pollock   , wife of   Lee Pollock   on the 8th day of December , 1904; that there was born to her on said date a   Female   child; that said child was living March 4, 1905, and is said to have been named   Junie Pollock

                                S.W. Jackson M.D.

Witnesses To Mark:
  {

Applications for Enrollment of Chickasaw Newborn
Act of 1905   Volume IV

Subscribed and sworn to before me this 4th day of   April   , 1905

C.E. Culbertson
Notary Public.

BIRTH AFFIDAVIT.

DEPARTMENT OF THE INTERIOR.
COMMISSION TO THE FIVE CIVILIZED TRIBES.

IN RE APPLICATION FOR ENROLLMENT, as a citizen of the   Chickasaw   Nation, of   Janice Pollock   , born on the 21st day of December , 1902

Name of Father: Lee Pollock   a citizen of the   Chickasaw   Nation.
Name of Mother: Georgie Pollock   a citizen of the   Chickasaw   Nation.

Postoffice   Kiowa Ind. Ter.

AFFIDAVIT OF MOTHER.

UNITED STATES OF AMERICA, Indian Territory, }
Central   DISTRICT.

I, Georgie Pollock   , on oath state that I am   21   years of age and a citizen by   Blood   , of the   Chickasaw   Nation; that I am the lawful wife of   Lee Pollock   , who is a citizen, by Intermarriage   of the   Chickasaw   Nation; that a   Female   child was born to me on   21st   day of December   , 1902; that said child has been named   Janice Pollock   , and was living March 4, 1905.

Georgia Pollock

Witnesses To Mark:
{

Subscribed and sworn to before me this 1st day of   April   , 1905

C.E. Culbertson
Notary Public.

AFFIDAVIT OF ATTENDING PHYSICIAN OR MID-WIFE.

UNITED STATES OF AMERICA, Indian Territory, }
Central   DISTRICT.

I,   Mrs A D Pollock   , a   Midwife   , on oath state that I attended on Mrs.   Georgia Pollock   , wife of   Lee Pollock   on the 21st   day of

Applications for Enrollment of Chickasaw Newborn
Act of 1905   Volume IV

December, 1902; that there was born to her on said date a   Female   child; that said child was living March 4, 1905, and is said to have been named   Janice Pollock

                              Mrs A D Pollock

Witnesses To Mark:

{ Subscribed and sworn to before me this 1st day of   April   , 1905

                              C.E. Culbertson
                                  Notary Public.

                                                Chickasaw 1170.

                   Muskogee, Indian Territory, April 10, 1905.

Lee Pollock,
    Kiowa, Indian Territory.

Dear Sir:

    Receipt is hereby acknowledged of the affidavits of Georgia Pollock and Mrs. A. D. Pollock to the birth of Janice Pollock; also the affidavits of Georgia Pollock and S. W. Jackson to the birth of Junie Pollock, children of Lee and Georgia Pollock, December 21, 1902, and December 8, 1904, respectively, and the same have been filed with our records as applications for the enrollment of said children.

                          Respectfully,

                          Commissioner in Charge.

Chic. N.B. - 281
    (Odis L Brown
    Born November 3, 1903)
    (Josephine Brown
    Born October 8, 1902)

Applications for Enrollment of Chickasaw Newborn
Act of 1905   Volume IV

9-N.B. 281.

DEPARTMENT OF THE INTERIOR,
COMMISSIONER TO THE FIVE CIVILIZED TRIBES.
Muskogee, Indian Territory, Nov. 14, 1905.

In the matter of the application for the enrollment of Odis L. Brown and Josephine Brown, minor children of Joe and Ellen Brown, as citizens of the Chickasaw Nation under the provisions of the Act of Congress approved March 3, 1905 (33 Stats., 1060).

Wirt Franklin of Muskogee, Indian Territory, appearing as Agent for the applicants.

Ellen Brown being first duly sworn testified as follows:
Examination by the Commissioner:
Q What is your name? A Ellen Brown.
Q What is your postoffice address? A Isom Springs, Ind. Ter.
Q How old are you? A Thirty-eight.
Q Are you a white woman? A Yes sir.
Q Do you claim any rights as a citizen of the Chickasaw Nation the Choctaw or Chickasaw Nations[sic]? A No sir.
Q What is the name of your husband? A Joe Brown.
Q Is he a citizen of the Choctaw or Chickasaw Nations[sic]? A Yes sir.
Q Which nation? A Chickasaw Nation.
Q When were you married to Joe Brown? A Last April.
Q April of what year? A 1905.
Q The affidavits that have been filed with this office with reference to the applications for the enrollment of these children, Odis L. Brown and Josephine Brown, show that you swore on April 3, 1905, that you were the mother of Odis L. Brown, born November 3, 1903, and Josephine Brown, born October 8, 1902, and that Joe Brown, a citizen by blood of the Chickasaw Nation, was the father od[sic] said children? A Yes sir.
Q Now you state that you were never lawfully married to him until April, 1905? A No, I was not.
Q Have you been living with Joe Brown as if you had been married to him? A Yes sir.
Q How long? A 1900.
Q And you have been living together for five years without any marriage? A Yes sir.
Q Have you ever lived with anyone else? A No sir.
Q Had you ever been married before you married Joe Brown? A Yes sir.
Q Who had you been married before you married Joe Brown? A Jack Davis.
Q Is he living? A No, he is dead.
Q When did he die? A He died in 1885.
Q When did you begin to live with Joe Brown? A In 1890
Q In 1900? A Yes, in 1900.
Q Have you lived with him continuously since then? A Yes sir.
Q Do you swear that these two children, Odis L. Brown and Josephine Brown are the children of Joe Brown? A Yes sir.
Q Who has supported these children? A Joe Brown.

Applications for Enrollment of Chickasaw Newborn
Act of 1905 Volume IV

Q Have you lived with him all that time? A Yes sir.
Q Has he supported you? A Yes sir.
Q Did Joe Brown ever have any other wife? A No sir.

Examination by Mr. Franklin.
Q During the time that you lived with Joe Brown since 1900, were you considered by your neighbors as husband and wife?
> By the Commissioner: That is inadmissible; there is no question as to what she was considered. They were no married and the question is as to whether these children are citizens or not.

Q During this time he provided for you and the children? A Yes.
Q Did he ever, during this time you have lived with him since 1900, live with any other woman? A No sir.
Q Did you ever live with any other man? A No sir.
Witness excused.

Joe Brown being first duly sworn testifieed[sic] as follows:
Examination by the Commissioner:
Q What is your name? A Joe Brown.
Q What is your age and postoffice address? A Thirty.
Q Where do you live? A Isom Spring.
Q Are you a citizen of the Chickasaw Nation? A Yes sir.
Q Citizen by blood? A Yes sir.
Q How much blood? A Full blood.
> The witness is identified upon the final roll of citizens by blood of the Chickasaw Nation as Joe Brown, opposite No. 2832.

Q Are you the father of these two children Odis L. Brown and Josephine Brown? by a white woman named Ellen Brown? A Yes sir.
Q When were you married to her? A I was married last April.
Q April of the present year? A Yes sir, 1905.
Q When were these children born? A The last one November 3, 1903, Odis; and Josephine was born October 8.
Q What year? A 1902.
Q When were you married to Ellen Brown did you say? April, 1905? A Yes, sir.
Q Had you ever been married before you were married to her? A No.
Q How long have you been living with her? A Been living with her five years.
Q Lived together? A Yes, both together, five years.
Q Supported her and these two children? A Yes sir.
Q Recognized these two children to be your children by this woman? A Yes sir.

Examination by Mr. Franklin:
Q During this time you have lived with this woman continuously? A Yes sir.
Q And in all respects as if you had been lawfully married to her in 1900? A Yes sir.
Q You have represented to the world these children as yours? A Yes sir.
Q And you have so considered them in the neighborhood where you lived? A Yes sir.

Applications for Enrollment of Chickasaw Newborn
Act of 1905   Volume IV

Q How did you happen to get married after living together for five years? What prompted you to get married after having lived with her for five years without marriage?
A Because I had been living with her for a long time and I thought I ought to be married.
Q Because you considered her as your wife? A Yes sir.

Frances R. Lane upon oath states that as stenographer to the Commissioner to the Five Civilized Tribes she correctly reported the testimony in the above entitled cause and that the foregoing is an accurate transcript of her stenographic notes thereof.

Frances R. Lane

Subscribed and sworn to before me this November 14, 1905.

Myran White
Notary Public.

9-N.B. 281.

DEPARTMENT OF THE INTERIOR,
COMMISSIONER TO THE FIVE CIVILIZED TRIBES.
Muskogee, Ind. Ter., Nov. 21, 1905.

In the matter of the application fot[sic] the enrollment of Odis L. Brown and Josephine Brown, minor children of Joe Brown and Ellen Brown, as citizens by blood of the Chickasaw Nation, under the provisions of the Act of Congress approved March 3, 1905.

Apple & Franklin appearing on behalf of the applicant.

Watson Ned being first duly sworn testified as follows:

Examination by the Commissioner.
Q What is your name? A Watson Ned.
Q How old are you? A Twenty-eight.
Q What is your postoffice address? A Madill, Ind. Ter.
Q Are you a citizen of the Chickasaw Nation? A Yes sir.
Q Are you acquainted with Odis L. Brown and Josephine Brown, the minor applicants as citizens by blood of the Chickasaw Nation? A Yes sir.
Q Who is the father of these children? A Joe Brown.
Q Who is the mother of them? A Ellen Brown.
Q Is Joe Brown a citizen of the Chickasaw Nation? A Yes sir.
Q Is Ellen Brown a citizen? A No.
Q Have Joe Brown and Ellen Brown ever been married? A Yes sir.
Q How near do you live to Joe Brown? A I lived in his family for three years.

Applications for Enrollment of Chickasaw Newborn
Act of 1905   Volume IV

Q During what time was this? A I have known them from 1901 to 1904.
Q Known whom? Joe Brown and his wife? A Yes.
Q You were there as a member of his family? during that time from 1901 to 1904?
A Yes sir.
Q Were these children born during that time? A Yes sir.
Q Were Joe Brown and Ellen Brown living together as husband and wife during that time? A Yes sir.
Q Who supported these children since they were born? A Joe Brown.
Q Has he at all times recognized them as his own children? A Yes sir.
Q Are they known in the community in which they live as Joe Brown's children?
A Yes sir.
Q Under what name do they go? A Go by the name of Brown.
Q That is their father's name? A Yes sir.

Examination by Mr. Franklin:
Q How long, to your knowledge, have Joe Brown and Ellen Brown lived together? A I was told the other day five years, but I know Joe Brown about four years.
Q You have known him ever since 1902? A Yes sir.
Q Since you have known him up to the present time have he and Ellen Brown lived together as husband and wife? A Yes sir.
Q Have they been so regarded in the neighborhood in which they live? A Yes sir.
Q Has he at all times held Ellen Brown out to the public and to the community in which he resides as his wife? A Yes sir.
Q Are these children, the applicants in this case, -have they always been regarded in the community in which he lives as his children? A Yes sir.
Q Do the children appear to possess Indian blood? A Yes, they do.
Q To look at them what would you say would be their degree of Indian blood??
A I would say half.
Q At least half? A Yes sir?[sic]
Q Joe Brown is a full blood Chickasaw is he not? A Yes sir.
Witness excused.

Susan Brown Jefferson being first duly sworn testified as follows:
Examination by the Commissioner.
Q What is your name? A Susan Brown Jefferson.
Q How old are you? A Thirty-seven.
Q What is your postoffice address? A Isom Springs.
Q Are you acquainted with Odis L. Brown and Josephine Brown? A Yes sir.
Q Who is the father of these children? A Joe Brown.
Q Who is the mother? A Ellen Brown.
Q Is Joe Brown a citizen of the Chickasaw Nation? A Yes sir.
Q Is Ellen Brown a citizen[sic] [sic] (No answer.
Q Is Ellen Brown a white ewoman[sic]? A Yes sir.
Q Are you related to Joe Brown in any way? A Sister.
Q Do you live in the neighborhood of Joe Brown? A Yes sir.
Q How long has Joe Brown been living with Ellen Brown, the mother of these children?
A Five years.

Applications for Enrollment of Chickasaw Newborn
Act of 1905   Volume IV

Q Continuously, right along? A Yes sir.
Q Have you every reason to believe that these two children are the children of Joe Brown, your brother? A Yes sir.
Q Has he recognized them as his children? Has Joe Brown recognized Odis L. Brown and Josephine Brown as his children? A Yes sir.
Q Supported them all the time since their birth? A Yes sir.
Q And held them out to the community in which he lived as his children? Did his neighbors recognize these children as Joe Brown's children? A Yes sir.

Examination by Mr. Franklin.
Q Mrs. Jefferson, during these five years that you say Joe Brown and Ellen Brown have lived together as husband and wife, how near have you lived to them? A About a mile.
Q During this time were they ever separated? A No sir.
Q Did Ellen Brown ever lived with any other man during this time? A No sir.
Q Did Joe Brown ever live with any other woman during this five years? A No sir.
Q But they have at all times lived together continuously as husband and wife for the last five years? A Yes sir.

Frances R. Lane upon oath states that as stenographer to the Commissioner to the Five Civilized Tribes she correctly reported the testimony in the above entitled cause and that the foregoing is an accurate transcript of her stenographic notes thereof.

                                    Frances R. Lane

Subscribed and sworn to before me this November 21, 1905.

                                    Myron White
                                    Notary Public.

9-NB-281.

DEPARTMENT OF THE INTERIOR,
COMMISSIONER TO THE FIVE CIVILIZED TRIBES.

In the matter of the application for the enrollment of Josephine Brown, et al, as citizens by blood of the Chickasaw Nation.

D E C I S I O N.

It appears from the record in this case that on April 4, 1905, and April 5, 1905, there was filed with the Commission to the Five Civilized Tribes, applications for the enrollment of Josephine Brown and Odis L. Brown, respectively, as citizens by blood of the Chickasaw Nation.

Applications for Enrollment of Chickasaw Newborn
Act of 1905   Volume IV

    It appears from the evidence herein, and from the records of the Commission to the Five Civilized Tribes, that the applicant, Josephine Brown, was born on October 8, 1902; that Odis L. Brown was born on November 4, 1903; that both of said applicants are the illegitimate children of Ellen Brown, a non-citizen white woman, and Joe Brown, a recognized and enrolled citizen by blood of the Chickasaw Nation, whose name appears as number 2832 upon the final roll of citizens by blood of the Chickasaw Nation, approved by the Secretary of the Interior, December 12, 1902, and that both of the said applicants were living on March 4, 1905.

    The Act of Congress approved March 3, 1905 (33 Stats., 1060), provides,

    "That the Commission to the Five Civilized Tribes is authorized for sixty days after the date of the approval of this act to receive and consider applications for enrollment of children born subsequent to September twenty-fifth, nineteen hundred and two, and prior to March fourth, nineteen hundred and five, and who were living on said latter date, to citizens by blood of the Choctaw and Chickasaw tribes of Indians whose enrollment has been approved by the Secretary of the Interior prior to the date of the approval of this act; and to enroll and make allotments to such children."

    I am, therefore, of the opinion that Josephine Brown and Odis L. Brown should be enrolled as citizens by blood of the Chickasaw Nation under the provisions of the act above quoted, and it is so ordered.

                                  Tams Bixby
                                             Commissioner.

Muskogee, Indian Territory.
    MAR 14 1906

BIRTH AFFIDAVIT.

DEPARTMENT OF THE INTERIOR.
COMMISSION TO THE FIVE CIVILIZED TRIBES.

    IN RE APPLICATION FOR ENROLLMENT, as a citizen of the   Chickasaw   Nation, of   Odis L Brown   , born on the 3rd day of Nov , 1903

Name of Father: Joe Brown   a citizen of the   Chickasaw   Nation.
Name of Mother: Ellen Brown   a citizen of the   ———   Nation.

                                Postoffice   Isom I.T.

Applications for Enrollment of Chickasaw Newborn
Act of 1905 Volume IV

AFFIDAVIT OF MOTHER.

UNITED STATES OF AMERICA, Indian Territory,　}
　　Southern　　　　　　　　DISTRICT.

　　I,　Ellen Brown　, on oath state that I am　38　years of age and a citizen by intermarriage　, of the　Chickasaw　Nation; that I am the lawful wife of　Joe Brown　, who is a citizen, by blood　of the　Chickasaw　Nation; that a male　child was born to me on　3rd　day of　Nov　, 1903; that said child has been named　Odis L Brown　, and was living March 4, 1905.

　　　　　　　　　　　　　　　　　Ellen Brown

Witnesses To Mark:

　　Subscribed and sworn to before me this　3rd　day of　April　, 1905

　　　　　　　　　　　　　　　　　DP Johnston
　　　　　　　　　　　　　　　　　　　Notary Public.

AFFIDAVIT OF ATTENDING PHYSICIAN OR MID-WIFE.

UNITED STATES OF AMERICA, Indian Territory,　}
　　Southern　　　　　　　　DISTRICT.

　　I,　J A Leggett　　, a　Physician　, on oath state that I attended on Mrs.　Ellen Brown　, wife of　Joe Brown　on the 3rd　day of November　, 1903; that there was born to her on said date a　male　child; that said child was living March 4, 1905, and is said to have been named　Odis L Brown

　　　　　　　　　　　　　　　　　J A Leggett

Witnesses To Mark:
　　S.W. Mandrell
　　J.R. Pate

　　Subscribed and sworn to before me this　3 day of　April　, 1905

　　　　　　　　　　　　　　　　　M.D. Belt
　　　　　　　　　　　　　　　　　　　Notary Public.

Applications for Enrollment of Chickasaw Newborn
Act of 1905   Volume IV

BIRTH AFFIDAVIT.

DEPARTMENT OF THE INTERIOR.
COMMISSION TO THE FIVE CIVILIZED TRIBES.

IN RE APPLICATION FOR ENROLLMENT, as a citizen of the Chickasaw Nation, of Josephine Brown, born on the 8th day of Oct, 1902.

Name of Father: Joe Brown   a citizen of the Chickasaw Nation.
Name of Mother: Ellen Brown   a citizen of the — Nation.

Postoffice   Isom I.T.

AFFIDAVIT OF MOTHER.

UNITED STATES OF AMERICA, Indian Territory, }
Southern   DISTRICT.

I, Ellen Brown, on oath state that I am 38 years of age and a citizen by intermarriage, of the Chickasaw Nation; that I am the lawful wife of Joe Brown, who is a citizen, by blood of the Chickasaw Nation; that a female child was born to me on 8th day of Oct, 1902; that said child has been named Josephine Brown, and was living March 4, 1905.

Ellen Brown

Witnesses To Mark:
{

Subscribed and sworn to before me this 3rd day of April, 1905.

DR Johnston
Notary Public.

AFFIDAVIT OF ATTENDING PHYSICIAN OR MID-WIFE.

UNITED STATES OF AMERICA, Indian Territory, }
Southern   DISTRICT.

I, Jane Anoatubby, a Midwife, on oath state that I attended on Mrs. Ellen Brown, wife of Joe Brown on the 8th day of Oct, 1902; that there was born to her on said date a female child; that said child was living March 4, 1905, and is said to have been named Josephine Brown

Jane Anoatubby

Witnesses To Mark:
{

Applications for Enrollment of Chickasaw Newborn
Act of 1905   Volume IV

Subscribed and sworn to before me this 3rd day of April , 1905

                            DR Johnston
                                Notary Public.

                    Kingston, I. T., April 20th 1905.

Commission to the Five Civilized Tribes,

        Muskogee, Ind. Ter.,

Dear Sirs:--

        In answer to yours of April 8th 1905, will say my age is thirty, and mother was enrolled Sylvie Okuymbby. My roll # 2832.

                    v Signed   Joe Brown

Indian Territory,

Southern District,

Pickens County.,

        Personally appeared before me, D. R. Johnston, a Notary Public in and for the Southern District of the Indian Territory, one Joe Brown, personally well known by me to be the person signing the above and on oath swore that the above was true to the best of his knowledge.

        Signed and sealed this 20th day of April 1905:

                              D R Johnston
                              Notary Public.

Commission expires March 19th 1907.

Applications for Enrollment of Chickasaw Newborn
Act of 1905   Volume IV

STATE OF TEXAS

MARRIAGE LICENSE
COUNTY OF GRAYSON

To any Judge of the District Court, Judge of the County Court, Ordained or Licensed Minister Jewish Rabbi or Justice of the Peace of Grayson County

GREETING:
YOU ARE HEREBY AUTHORIZED TO CELEBRATE THE
RITES OF MATRIMONY

Between   Joe Brown
and   Mrs Ellen Davis
and make due return to the Clerk of said Court within Sixty days thereafter certifying your action under this License,

     WITNESS *my official signature and seal*
     this 22 *day of* April 190 5

           WE Baird   *Clerk*
     By   (Name Illegible)   *Deputy*

J   J H Baxter   *certify that on the*
   22   *day of*   April   190 5   *I united in Marriage*
         Joe Brown   *and*
   Mrs Ellen Davis   *the parties above named*
Witness my hand this   22   *day of*   April   190 5

          JH Baxter   Minister
          of the Gospel

Returned and filed for record the _____ *day of* _____ *190*__
and recorded the _____ *day of* _____ *190*__

     _____ *Deputy* _____ *County Clerk*

Applications for Enrollment of Chickasaw Newborn
Act of 1905   Volume IV

The State of Texas:
County of Grayson::   I, W. E. Baird, Clerk of the County Court of Grayson County, Texas, do hereby certify that the above and foregoing is a true and correct copy of the original Marriage License issued to Joe Brown and Ellen Davis, as the same appears of record in my office in Book T, Page 491, of the Marriage records of Grayson County, Texas, together with the return thereof.
Given under my hand and seal of office this the 22" day of April 1905.

           W. E. Baird, Clerk.
       Per *(Name Illegible)*   Deputy.

DEPARTMENT OF THE INTERIOR,
COMMISSION TO THE FIVE CIVILIZED TRIBES.
FILED
APR 29 1905
Tams Bixby CHAIRMAN.

№. _____

Marriage License.

_____
AND
_____

Issued the _____ day of _____ 190___
          Clerk County Court, Grayson County.

By _____
              Deputy.

Filed the _____ day

of _____ 190 ___
          Clerk County Court, Grayson County.

By _____
              Deputy.

Recorded in Book   T   Page   491

of Marriage Records.

Applications for Enrollment of Chickasaw Newborn
Act of 1905   Volume IV

Muskogee, Indian Territory, April 8, 1905.

Joe Brown,
    Isom, Indian Territory.

Dear Sir:

    Receipt is hereby acknowledged of the affidavits of Ellen Brown and Jane Anoatubby to the birth of Josephine Brown, daughter of Joe and Ellen Brown, October 8, 1902.

    As there are several persons upon our records by the name of Joe Brown, you are requested to state you age, the names of your parents and your roll number as it appears upon your allotment certificate if practicable.

    This matter should receive immediate attention in order that proper disposition may be made of the application for the enrollment of your child.

Respectfully,

Commissioner in Charge.

Chickasaw 954.

Muskogee, Indian Territory, April 10, 1905.

Joe Brown,
    Isom, Indian Territory.

Dear Sir:

    Receipt is hereby acknowledged of the affidavits of Ellen Brown and J. A. Leggett to the birth of Odis L. Brown, son of Joe and Ellen Brown, November 3, 1903, and the same have been filed with our records as an application for the enrollment of said child.

Respectfully,

Commissioner in Charge.

Applications for Enrollment of Chickasaw Newborn
Act of 1905   Volume IV

9 N B 281

Muskogee, Indian Territory, April 17, 1905.

Joe Brown,
    Isom, Indian Territory.

Dear Sir:

You are hereby advised that before the application for the enrollment of your infant child, Odis L. Brown, can be finally disposed of, it will be necessary for you to furnish the Commission with the original or a certified copy of the license and certificate of your marriage to his mother Ellen Brown.

Please give this matter your immediate attention.

Respectfully,

Chairman.

9-950

Muskogee, Indian Territory, April 26, 1905.

Joe Brown,
    Kingston, Indian Territory.

Dear Sir:

Receipt is hereby acknowledged of your affidavit giving your age, the name of your mother and your Roll Number, and this information has enabled the Commission to identify you u[sic]on its records as an enrolled citizen by blood of the Chickasaw Nation, and the affidavits heretofore forwarded as to the birth of your child, Josephine Brown, have been filed with our records as an application for the enrollment of said child.

Respectfully,

Chairman.

Applications for Enrollment of Chickasaw Newborn
Act of 1905 Volume IV

Chick
~~Choctaw~~
N.B. 281.

Muskogee, Indian Territory, May 1, 1905.

D. P. Johnston,
    Kingston, Indian Territory.

Dear Sir:

    Receipt is hereby acknowledged of your letter of April 24, enclosing certified copy of the marriage license and certificate between Joe Brown and Mrs. Ellen Davis, which you offer in support of the application for the enrollment of your children, Odus[sic] L. and Josephine Brown, and the same have been filed in the matter of the enrollment of said children.

                  Respectfully,

                                      Chairman.

9-NB-281.

Muskogee, Indian Territory, May 20, 1905.

Joe Brown,
    Isom, Indian Territory.

Dear Sir:

    There is returned herewith the certified copy of the license and certificate of your marriage to Ellen Brown in which it appears that you were married on April 22, 1905, while your children, Josephine Brown and Odis L. Brown, in support of whose applications it was filed, were born August 8, 1902, and November 3, 1903, respectively.

    Probably there is an error in the date inserted in the above mentioned certified copy. If so, you will please file a correct copy with this office.

                  Respectfully,

                                      Chairman.

VR 22-1.

Applications for Enrollment of Chickasaw Newborn
Act of 1905   Volume IV

( )[sic]
9-NB-281.

Muskogee, Indian Territory, July 3, 1905.

D. P. Johnston,
    Kingstown[sic], Indian Territory.

Dear Sir:

    In your letter of April 24, 1905, you transmitted a certified copy of the marriage license and certificate between Joe Brown and Mrs. Ella Davis, which you offered in support of the application for the enrollment of Odus L. and Josephine Brown, their infant children. This certified copy was returned to Joe Brown, Isom, Indian Territory, on May 20, 1905, for the reason that it appeared that the marriage ceremony was performed on April 22, 1905, while Josephine Brown and Odus[sic] L. Brown were born August 8, 1902 and November 3, 1903, respectively. It was thought that probably there was an error in the date inserted in this copy.

    Before any further action can be taken for the enrollment of these children, it will be necessary that evidence of the marriage of the children's parents be filed in this office.

                    Respectfully,

                                        Commissioner.

9-NB-281

Muskogee, Indian Territory, August 16, 1905.

Joe Brown,
    Isom, Indian Territory.

Dear Sir:

    On May 20, 1905, this Office returned to you a certified copy of the license and certificate of your marriage to Ellen Brown, in which it appeared that you were married April 2, 1905, while your children, Josephine Brown and Odis L. Brown, in support of whose applications said evidence of marriage was filed, were born October 8, 1902, and November 3, 1903, respectively. The evidence of marriage was returned to you at that time, for the reason that it was found that an error had been made as to the date of your said marriage in making the certified copy of the marriage license and certificate, and you were requested to file with this Office a correct copy of said marriage license and certificate.

    To said letter of May 20, 1905, you have made no reply.

Applications for Enrollment of Chickasaw Newborn
Act of 1905   Volume IV

You are again advised that until you file with this Office a certified copy of the marriage license and certificate, showing marriage between you and Ellen Brown, the non-citizen mother of your said children, this Office cannot determine the rights of your said children as citizens by blood of the Chickasaw Nation.

Respectfully,

Acting Commissioner.

9-NB-281

Muskogee, Indian Territory, March 14, 1906.
COPY

Joe Brown,
   Isom Springs, Indian Territory.

Dear Sir:

Inclosed herewith you will find a copy of the decision of the Commissioner to the Five Civilized Tribes, rendered March 14, 1906, granting the application for the enrollment of your minor children, Josephine and Odis L. Brown as citizens by blood of the Chickasaw Nation.

The attorneys for the Choctaw and Chickasaw Nations have been furnished a copy of this decision and have been allowed fifteen days from the date of this notice within which to file protest against their enrollment. If at the expiration of that time no protest has been filed, the names of Josephine Brown and Odis L. Brown will be placed upon the final roll of citizens by blood of the Chickasaw Nation to be submitted to the Secretary of the Interior for his approval.

Respectfully,

SIGNED
Wm. O. Beall
Acting Commissioner.

Registered.
Incl. 9-NB-281.

Applications for Enrollment of Chickasaw Newborn
Act of 1905   Volume IV

9-NB-281

COPY

Muskogee, Indian Territory, March 14, 1906.

Apple & Franklin,
  Attorneys at Law,
    Muskogee, Indian Territory.

Gentlemen:

  You are hereby notified that the Commissioner to the Five Civilized Tribes, on March 14, 1906, rendered his decision, granting the application for the enrollment of Josephine Brown and Odis L. Brown as citizens by blood of the Chickasaw Nation.

  The attorneys for the Choctaw and Chickasaw Nations have been furnished a copy of this decision and have been allowed fifteen days from the date of this notice within which to file protest against his enrollment. If at the expiration of said time no protest has been filed, the names of Josephine Brown and Odis L. Brown will be placed upon the final roll of Citizens by blood of the Chickasaw Nation to be submitted to the Secretary of the Interior for his approval.

      Respectfully,

      SIGNED
      Wm. O. Beall

Registered.   Acting Commissioner.

REFER IN REPLY TO THE FOLLOWING:

9-NB-281

DEPARTMENT OF THE INTERIOR,
COMMISSIONER TO THE FIVE CIVILIZED TRIBES.

Muskogee, Indian Territory, March 14, 1906.

D. P. Johnston,
  Kingston, Indian Territory.

Dear Sir:

  You are hereby notified that the Commissioner to the Five Civilized Tribes, on March 14, 1906, rendered his decision granting the application for the enrollment of Josephine Brown and Odis L. Brown as citizens by blood of the Chickasaw Nation.

  The attorneys for the Choctaw and Chickasaw Nations have been furnished a copy of this decision and have been allowed fifteen days from the date of this notice within which to file protest against his enrollment. If at the expiration of said time no

Applications for Enrollment of Chickasaw Newborn
Act of 1905 Volume IV

protest has been filed, the names of Josephine Brown and Odis L. Brown will be placed upon the final roll of Citizens by blood of the Chickasaw Nation to be submitted to the Secretary of the Interior for his approval.

                      Respectfully,

                      SIGNED
                      Wm. O. Beall

Registered.   Acting Commissioner.

9-NB-281

                                            COPY
Muskogee, Indian Territory, March 14, 1906.

Mansfield, McMurray & Cornish,
    Attorneys for Choctaw and Chickasaw Nations,
        South McAlester, Indian Territory.

Gentlemen:

    Inclosed herewith you will find a copy of the decision of the Commissioner to the Five Civilized Tribes, rendered March 14, 1906, granting the application for the enrollment of Josephine Brown and Odis L. Brown as citizens by blood of the Chickasaw Nation.

    You are hereby notified that you will be allowed fifteen days from the date of this notice within which to file protest against their enrollment. If at the expiration of that time no protest has been filed, the names of Josephine Brown and Odis L. Brown will be placed upon the final roll of citizens by blood of the Chickasaw Nation to be submitted to the Secretary of the Interior for his approval.

                      Respectfully,

                      SIGNED
                      Wm. O. Beall

Registered.   Acting Commissioner.
Incl. 9-NB-281.

Applications for Enrollment of Chickasaw Newborn
Act of 1905   Volume IV

9-NB-281

Muskogee, Indian Territory, July 18, 1906.

J. F. Ringle,
    Isom Springs, Indian Territory.

Dear Sir:

    Receipt is hereby acknowledged of your letter of June 27, 1906, asking to be advised if Joseph[sic] and Odis L. Brown, children of Joe Brown, have been enrolled.

    In reply you are advised that Odis L. Brown and Josephine Brown, children of Joe Brown and Ellen Brown, have been enrolled as new born citizens of the Chickasaw Nation, and their enrollment as such approved by the Secretary of the Interior July 10, 1906.

                Respectfully,

                              Commissioner.

Chic. N.B. - 282
    (Burney Johnson Fletcher
    Born January 10, 1905)

BIRTH AFFIDAVIT.

DEPARTMENT OF THE INTERIOR.
COMMISSION TO THE FIVE CIVILIZED TRIBES.

    IN RE APPLICATION FOR ENROLLMENT, as a citizen of the Chickasaw Nation, of Burney Johnson Fletcher, born on the 10th day of January, 1905

Name of Father: John Henry Fletcher   a citizen of the Chickasaw Nation.
Name of Mother: Sallie V. Fletcher   a citizen of the Chickasaw Nation.

                Postoffice   Hickory Ind Ter

Applications for Enrollment of Chickasaw Newborn
Act of 1905 Volume IV

AFFIDAVIT OF MOTHER.

UNITED STATES OF AMERICA, Indian Territory,
Southern   DISTRICT.

    I, Sallie V. Fletcher, on oath state that I am Twenty six years of age and a citizen by intermarriage, of the Chickasaw Nation; that I am the lawful wife of John Henry Fletcher, who is a citizen, by blood of the Chickasaw Nation; that a male child was born to me on the 10th day of January, 1905; that said child has been named Burney Johnson Fletcher, and was living March 4, 1905.

                                  Mrs Sallie V Fletcher

Witnesses To Mark:
{

    Subscribed and sworn to before me this 3rd day of April, 1905

                            J M Webster
                            Notary Public.

AFFIDAVIT OF ATTENDING PHYSICIAN OR MID-WIFE.

UNITED STATES OF AMERICA, Indian Territory,
Southern   DISTRICT.

    I, G.W. Slover, a physician, on oath state that I attended on Mrs. Sallie V Fletcher, wife of John Henry Fletcher on the 10th day of January, 1905; that there was born to her on said date a male child; that said child was living March 4, 1905, and is said to have been named Burney Johnson Fletcher

                                G.W. Slover

Witnesses To Mark:
{

    Subscribed and sworn to before me this 3rd day of April, 1905

                            J M Webster
                            Notary Public.

Applications for Enrollment of Chickasaw Newborn
Act of 1905 Volume IV

Chickasaw 927.

Muskogee, Indian Territory, April 10, 1905.

John Henry Fletcher,
    Hickory, Indian Territory.

Dear Sir:

    Receipt is hereby acknowledged of the affidavits of Mrs. Sallie V. Fletcher and G. W. Slover to the birth of Burney Johnson Fletcher, son of John Henry and Sallie V. Fletcher, January 10, 1905, and the same have been filed with our records as an application for the enrollment of said child.

Respectfully,

Commissioner in Charge.

9-NB282

Muskogee, Indian Territory, April 20, 1905.

J. H. Fletcher,
    Hickory, Indian Territory.

Dear Sir:

    Receipt is hereby acknowledged of your letter of April 13, 1905, asking if the application for the enrollment of your child Burney Johnson Fletcher has been received.

    In reply to your letter you are informed that the affidavits heretofore forwarded to the birth of your child Burney Johnson Fletcher have been filed with our records as an application for the enrollment of said child.

Respectfully,

Chairman.

Chic. N.B. - 283
    (Anna Aleen Wilson
    Born October 2, 1902)

Applications for Enrollment of Chickasaw Newborn
Act of 1905 Volume IV

BIRTH AFFIDAVIT.   #106

DEPARTMENT OF THE INTERIOR.
COMMISSION TO THE FIVE CIVILIZED TRIBES.

IN RE APPLICATION FOR ENROLLMENT, as a citizen of the Chickasaw Nation, of Anna Aleen Wilson , born on the 2" day of October , 1902

Name of Father: John D. Wilson   a citizen of the Chickasaw Nation.
Name of Mother: Lillie Luella Wilson   a citizen of the Non-citizen Nation.

Postoffice   Comanche I.T.

AFFIDAVIT OF MOTHER.

UNITED STATES OF AMERICA, Indian Territory,}
   Southern   DISTRICT.

I, Lillie Luella Wilson , on oath state that I am 36 years of age and a citizen by Intermarriage , of the Chickasaw Nation; that I am the lawful wife of John D. Wilson , who is a citizen, by Blood of the Chickasaw Nation; that a female child was born to me on 2nd day of October , 1902, that said child has been named Anna Aleen Wilson , and is now living.

                                      Lillie Luella Wilson

Witnesses To Mark:
{ G.W. Mellish
  H.L. Deaton

Subscribed and sworn to before me this 23 day of February , 1905.

                                      G.W. Mellish
                                      Notary Public.

AFFIDAVIT OF ATTENDING PHYSICIAN OR MID-WIFE.

UNITED STATES OF AMERICA, Indian Territory,}
   Southern District   DISTRICT.

I, J P Bartley , a physician , on oath state that I attended on Mrs. Lillie Luella Willson[sic] , wife of John D Willson on the 2 day of October , 1902; that there was born to her on said date a Female child; that said child is now living and is said to have been named Anna Aleen Willson

                                      J P Bartley MD

Applications for Enrollment of Chickasaw Newborn
Act of 1905   Volume IV

Witnesses To Mark:
{ GW Mellish
  A.B. Weakley

Subscribed and sworn to before me this 23^d day of February, 1905.

G.W. Mellish
Notary Public.

BIRTH AFFIDAVIT.

DEPARTMENT OF THE INTERIOR.
COMMISSION TO THE FIVE CIVILIZED TRIBES.

IN RE APPLICATION FOR ENROLLMENT, as a citizen of the   Chickasaw   Nation, of   Anna Aleen Wilson   , born on the   2   day of   October   , 1902

Name of Father: John D Wilson   a citizen of the   Chickasaw Nation.
Name of Mother: Lillie Louella Wilson   a citizen of the   Chickasaw Nation.

Postoffice   Comanche Ind. Ter

AFFIDAVIT OF MOTHER.

UNITED STATES OF AMERICA, Indian Territory, }
      Southern   DISTRICT.

I, Lillie Louella Wilson, on oath state that I am 36 years of age and a citizen by   Marriage   , of the   Chickasaw   Nation; that I am the lawful wife of John D Wilson   , who is a citizen, by   Blood   of the   Chickasaw Nation; that a   Girl   child was born to me on   second   day of   October   , 1902; that said child has been named   Anna Aleen Wilson   , and was living March 4, 1905.

Lillie Louella Willson[sic]

Witnesses To Mark:
{

Subscribed and sworn to before me this 5th day of April, 1905

J.B. Wilkinson
Notary Public.

Applications for Enrollment of Chickasaw Newborn
Act of 1905   Volume IV

AFFIDAVIT OF ATTENDING PHYSICIAN OR MID-WIFE.

UNITED STATES OF AMERICA, Indian Territory,
Southern   DISTRICT.

I, J. P. Bartley, a Physician, on oath state that I attended on Mrs. Lillie Louella Wilson, wife of John D Wilson on the second day of October, 1902; that there was born to her on said date a Girl child; that said child was living March 4, 1905, and is said to have been named Anna Aleen Wilson

JP Bartley MD

Witnesses To Mark:

Subscribed and sworn to before me this 5th day of April, 1905

J.B. Wilkinson
Notary Public.

Chic. N.B. - 284
(Ira William Hutchins
Born May 24, 1903)

BIRTH AFFIDAVIT.
DEPARTMENT OF THE INTERIOR.
COMMISSION TO THE FIVE CIVILIZED TRIBES.

IN RE APPLICATION FOR ENROLLMENT, as a citizen of the   Chickasaw   Nation, of   Ira William Hutchins , born on the 24 day of May , 1903

Name of Father: William Andrew Hutchins   a citizen of the Chickasaw Nation.
Name of Mother: Lizzie Hutchins   a citizen of the Chickasaw Nation.

Postoffice   Wyatt Ind Terry

Applications for Enrollment of Chickasaw Newborn
Act of 1905 Volume IV

AFFIDAVIT OF MOTHER.

UNITED STATES OF AMERICA, Indian Territory,
Southern DISTRICT.

I, Lizzie Hutchins, on oath state that I am 29 years of age and a citizen by Blood, of the Chickasaw Nation; that I am the lawful wife of William Andrew Hutchins, who is a citizen, by Marriage of the Chickasaw Nation; that a Male child was born to me on 24 day of May, 1903; that said child has been named Ira William Hutchins, and was living March 4, 1905.

Lizzie Hutchins

Witnesses To Mark:

Subscribed and sworn to before me this 6th day of April, 1905

J.R. Hutchins
Notary Public.

AFFIDAVIT OF ATTENDING PHYSICIAN OR MID-WIFE.

UNITED STATES OF AMERICA, Indian Territory,
Southern DISTRICT.

I, Mrs. C. V. Hutchins, a Nurse, on oath state that I attended on Mrs. Lizzie Hutchins, wife of William Andrew Hutchins on the 24 day of May, 1903; that there was born to her on said date a Male child; that said child was living March 4, 1905, and is said to have been named Ira William Hutchins

C.V. Hutchins

Witnesses To Mark:

Subscribed and sworn to before me this 6th day of April, 1905

J.R. Hutchins
Notary Public.

Commission Expires Nov 7-1907

Applications for Enrollment of Chickasaw Newborn
Act of 1905 Volume IV

Chic. N.B. - 285
    (Ola Edith Perry
    Birthdate not given.)

N B 285

CHICKASAW

(Act of March 3, 1905)
Ola Edith Perry.

Transferred to Choctaw
NB 872

Chic. N.B. - 286
    (Grady Elazor Mobley
    Born February 22, 1904)

BIRTH AFFIDAVIT.

DEPARTMENT OF THE INTERIOR.
COMMISSION TO THE FIVE CIVILIZED TRIBES.

    IN RE APPLICATION FOR ENROLLMENT, as a citizen of the   Chickasaw   Nation, of   Grady Elazor Mobley   , born on the 22 day of Feb. , 1904

Name of Father: Benjamin E. Mobley   a citizen of the Chickasaw Nation.
Name of Mother: Tennie Mobley   a citizen of the Chickasaw Nation.

    Postoffice   Eolian I.T.

AFFIDAVIT OF MOTHER.

UNITED STATES OF AMERICA, Indian Territory,
    Southern   **DISTRICT.**

    I, Tennie Mobley   , on oath state that I am 22 years of age and a citizen by   blood   , of the   Chickasaw   Nation; that I am the lawful wife of

Applications for Enrollment of Chickasaw Newborn
Act of 1905   Volume IV

Benjamin E. Mobley, who is a citizen, by Marriage of the Chickasaw Nation; that a Male child was born to me on 22 day of February, 1904; that said child has been named Grady Elazor Mobley, and was living March 4, 1905.

Tennie Mobley

Witnesses To Mark:
{ (Name Illegible)
{ J S Meritt

Subscribed and sworn to before me this 4 day of April, 1905

Geo R Spencer
Notary Public.

AFFIDAVIT OF ATTENDING PHYSICIAN OR MID-WIFE.

UNITED STATES OF AMERICA, Indian Territory, }
Southern   DISTRICT.

I, Lucrecia Worsham, a mid wife, on oath state that I attended on Mrs. Tennie Mobley, wife of Benjamin E Mobley on the 22 day of Feb, 1904; that there was born to her on said date a Male child; that said child was living March 4, 1905, and is said to have been named Grady Elazor Mobley

her
Lucrecia x Worsham
mark

Witnesses To Mark:
{ Jewel Worsham
{ J S Meritt

Subscribed and sworn to before me this 4 day of April, 1905

Geo R Spencer
Notary Public.

9-595

Muskogee, Indian Territory, April 11, 1905.

Benjamin E. Mabley[sic],
    Eolian, Indian Territory.

Dear Sir:

Receipt is hereby acknowledged of the affidavits of Tennie Mabley and Lucrecia Worsham to the birth of Grady Elazor Mobley, son of Benjamin E. and Tennie Mobley,

Applications for Enrollment of Chickasaw Newborn
Act of 1905   Volume IV

February 22, 1902, and the same have been filed with our records as an application for the enrollment of said child.

                                   Respectfully,

                                   Commissioner in Charge.

Chic. N.B. - 287
(Clifton Leeper Goforth
Born February 16, 1904)

CHICKASAW   **287**
NEW BORN
ENROLLMENT

                    Clifton Leeper Goforth
                      (Born Feb. 16, 1904)

Act of Congress Approved March 3, 1905.

287

Chic. N.B. - 288
(Geneva Sittel
Born December 14, 1903)

Applications for Enrollment of Chickasaw Newborn
Act of 1905 Volume IV

Indian Territory } ss
Central District

Scipio I.T.

June 16, 1905

I Edward Sittel do state that I want my Baby Geneva Sittel Put on Chickasaw Rolles.

Edward Sittel

Ind Tery } ss
Cent Dist

Subscribed and sworn to before me a Notary Public for the above District This the 16th day of June 1905

P. S. Coleman
Notary Public

My commission expires Feb 4th 1908

Indian Territory } ss
Central District

Scipio I.T.

June 16, 1905

I Mary Sittel do state that I want my Baby Geneva Sittel to be Put on Chickasaw Rolles.

Mary Sittel

Ind Tery } ss
Cent Dist

Subscribed and sworn to before me a Notary Public for the above District This the 16th day of June 1905

P. S. Coleman
Notary Public

My commission expires Feb 4th 1908

Applications for Enrollment of Chickasaw Newborn
Act of 1905 Volume IV

BIRTH AFFIDAVIT.

DEPARTMENT OF THE INTERIOR.
COMMISSION TO THE FIVE CIVILIZED TRIBES.

IN RE APPLICATION FOR ENROLLMENT, as a citizen of the Chickasaw Nation, of Geneva Sittel, born on the 14th day of Dec., 1903

Name of Father: Edward Sittel   a citizen of the Choctaw Nation.
Name of Mother: Mary Sittel   a citizen of the Chickasaw Nation.

Postoffice Scipio, I.T.

AFFIDAVIT OF MOTHER.

UNITED STATES OF AMERICA, Indian Territory,
Central   DISTRICT.

I, Mary Sittel, on oath state that I am 23 years of age and a citizen by blood, of the Chickasaw Nation; that I am the lawful wife of Edward Sittel, who is a citizen, by blood of the Choctaw Nation; that a female child was born to me on 14th day of December, 1903; that said child has been named Geneva Sittel, and was living March 4, 1905.

           Mary Sittel

Witnesses To Mark:

Subscribed and sworn to before me this 27th day of March, 1905

           P.S. Coleman
           Notary Public.

My commission expires Feb 4th 1908

AFFIDAVIT OF ATTENDING PHYSICIAN OR MID-WIFE.

UNITED STATES OF AMERICA, Indian Territory,
Central   DISTRICT.

I, Malvina Sittel, a mid-wife, on oath state that I attended on Mrs. Mary Sittel, wife of Edward Sittel on the 14th day of December, 1903; that there was born to her on said date a female child; that said child was living March 4, 1905, and is said to have been named Geneva Sittel

           Malvina Sittel

Applications for Enrollment of Chickasaw Newborn
Act of 1905   Volume IV

Witnesses To Mark:
{

Subscribed and sworn to before me this 20th day of March , 1905

Wirt Franklin
Notary Public.

Choctaw 1623.

Muskogee, Indian Territory, April 3, 1905.

Edward Sittel,
Scipio, Indian Territory.

Dear Sir:

Receipt is hereby acknowledged of the affidavits of Mary Sittel and Malvina Sittel to the birth of Geneva Sittel, daughter of Edward and Mary Sittel, December 14, 1903, and the same have been filed with our records as an application for the enrollment of said child.

Respectfully,

Commissioner in Charge.

9-NB-288.

Muskogee, Indian Territory, May 16, 1905.

Edward Sittel,
Scipio, Indian Territory.

Dear Sir:

Referring to the application for the enrollment of your infant child, Geneva Sittel, it appears that you are a citizen by blood of the Choctaw Nation, while your wife is a citizen by blood of the Chickasaw Nation.

Your attention is called to the provision of the Act of Congress approved June 28, 1898, as follows:

The several tribes may, by agreement, determine the right of persons who for any reason may claim citizenship in two or more tribes, and to allotment of lands and distribution of moneys belonging to each tribe; but if no such agreement be made, then such claimant shall be entitled to such rights in one tribe only, and may elect in which

Applications for Enrollment of Chickasaw Newborn
Act of 1905   Volume IV

tribe he will take such right; but if he fail or refuse to make such selection in due time, he shall be enrolled in the tribe with whom he has resided, and there be given such allotment and distributions, and not elsewhere.

It will therefore be necessary for you and your wife to appear before a Notary Public or other officer authorized to administer oaths and by affidavit elect in which nation you desire to have said child enrolled, forwarding same, when properly executed, to the Commission.

Respectfully,

Chairman.

---

9 NB 288

Muskogee, Indian Territory, June 21, 1905.

Edward Sittel,
    Scipio, Indian Territory.

Dear Sir:

Receipt is hereby acknowledged of the affidavits of yourself and Mary Sittel electing to have your child Geneva Sittel enrolled as a citizen by blood of the Chickasaw Nation, and the same have been filed with our records in the matter of the enrollment of said child.

Respectfully,

Chairman.

Chic. N.B. - 289
    (Juanita Willis
    Born December 24, 1902)

Applications for Enrollment of Chickasaw Newborn
Act of 1905   Volume IV

BIRTH AFFIDAVIT.

DEPARTMENT OF THE INTERIOR.
COMMISSION TO THE FIVE CIVILIZED TRIBES.

IN RE APPLICATION FOR ENROLLMENT, as a citizen of the Chickasaw Nation, of Juanita Willis, born on the 24th day of December, 1902

Name of Father: Holmes Willis   a citizen of the Chickasaw Nation.
Name of Mother: Viola Willis   a citizen of the Chickasaw Nation.

Postoffice   Willis Ind. Ter.

AFFIDAVIT OF MOTHER.

UNITED STATES OF AMERICA, ~~Indian Territory,~~
Grayson County Texas   ~~DISTRICT.~~

I, Viola Willis, on oath state that I am 45 years of age and a citizen by Intermarriage, of the Chickasaw Nation; that I am the lawful wife of Holmes Willis, who is a citizen, by blood of the Chickasaw Nation; that a Female child was born to me on 24th day of December, 1902; that said child has been named Juanita Willis, and was living March 4, 1905.

Viola Willis

Witnesses To Mark:

Subscribed and sworn to before me this fifth day of April, 1905

WE Baird *Clerk of County Court Grayson County Texas*

AFFIDAVIT OF ATTENDING PHYSICIAN OR MID-WIFE.

Grayson County Texas
UNITED STATES ~~OF AMERICA, Indian~~ Territory,
                             DISTRICT.

I, R.B. Anderson M.D., a Physician, on oath state that I attended on Mrs. Viola Willis, wife of Holmes Willis on the 24th day of December, 1902; that there was born to her on said date a Female child; that said child was living March 4, 1905, and is said to have been named Juanita Willis

R.B. Anderson M.D.

Applications for Enrollment of Chickasaw Newborn
Act of 1905   Volume IV

Witnesses To Mark:

{

Subscribed and sworn to before me this 5th day of April , 1905

WE Baird *Clerk of County*
Court Grayson County Texas

BIRTH AFFIDAVIT.

DEPARTMENT OF THE INTERIOR.
COMMISSION TO THE FIVE CIVILIZED TRIBES.

IN RE APPLICATION FOR ENROLLMENT, as a citizen of the Chickasaw Nation, of Juanita Willis , born on the 24th day of December , 1902

Name of Father: Holmes Willis a citizen of the Chickasaw Nation.
Name of Mother: Viola Willis a citizen of the Chickasaw Nation.

Postoffice   Willis Ind. Ter.

AFFIDAVIT OF MOTHER.

UNITED STATES OF AMERICA, Indian Territory, }
.... DISTRICT. }

I, Viola Willis , on oath state that I am 45 years of age and a citizen by Intermarriage , of the Chickasaw Nation; that I am the lawful wife of Holmes Willis , who is a citizen, by blood of the Chickasaw Nation; that a female child was born to me on 24th day of December , 1902; that said child has been named Juanita Willis , and was living March 4, 1905.

Viola Willis

Witnesses To Mark:

{

Subscribed and sworn to before me this 27 day of April , 1905

WE Baird *Clerk of Grayson*
County Court Texas

147

Applications for Enrollment of Chickasaw Newborn
Act of 1905 Volume IV

AFFIDAVIT OF ATTENDING PHYSICIAN OR MID-WIFE.

UNITED STATES OF AMERICA, Indian Territory,
....DISTRICT.

I, R.B. Anderson , a Physician , on oath state that I attended on Mrs. Viola Willis , wife of Holmes Willis on the 24th day of December, 1902; that there was born to her on said date a female child; that said child was living March 4, 1905, and is said to have been named Juanita Willis

R.B. Anderson

Witnesses To Mark:

Subscribed and sworn to before me this 27 day of April , 1905

WE Baird *Clerk*
of Grayson County Court Texas

Chickasaw N.B.
289.

Muskogee, Indian Territory, April 26, 1905.

Holmes Willis,
 Willis, Indian Territory.

Dear Sir:

Receipt is hereby acknowledged of your letter of April 14, asking if application for the enrollment of your child, Juanita Willis, has been received.

In reply to your letter you are advised that the affidavits heretofore forwarded to the birth of your child, Juanita Willis, have been filed with our records as an application for the enrollment of said child.

Respectfully,

Chairman.

Applications for Enrollment of Chickasaw Newborn
Act of 1905   Volume IV

9--976.

Muskogee, Indian Territory, May 8, 1905.

Holmes Willis,
    Willis, Indian Territory.

Dear Sir:

    Receipt is hereby acknowledged of your letter of April 27, 1905, enclosing the affidavits of Viola Willis and R. B. Anderson to the birth of Juanita Willis, daughter of Holmes and Viola Willis, December 24, 1902, and the same have been filed with our records as an application for the enrollment of said child.

    Respectfully,

    Commissioner in Charge.

Chic. N.B. - 290
    (Lottie Kate Tussy
    Born February 10, 1904)

BIRTH AFFIDAVIT.

DEPARTMENT OF THE INTERIOR,
COMMISSION TO THE FIVE CIVILIZED TRIBES.

    IN RE Application for Enrollment, as a citizen of the   Chickasaw   Nation, of   Lottie Kate Tussy , born on the   10 day of   February   , 1904

Name of Father: Henry B. Tussy   a citizen of the Chickasaw Nation.
Name of Mother: Lillie Tussy   a citizen of the Chickasaw Nation.

    Post-Office: Tussy, I.T.

Applications for Enrollment of Chickasaw Newborn
Act of 1905 Volume IV

AFFIDAVIT OF MOTHER.

UNITED STATES OF AMERICA, }
    INDIAN TERRITORY.
Southern   District.

I, Lillie Tussy , on oath state that I am 36 years of age and a citizen by Blood , of the Chickasaw Nation; that I am the lawful wife of Henry B. Tussy , who is a citizen, by intermarriage of the Chickasaw Nation; that a Female child was born to me on 10 day of February , 1904 , that said child has been named Lottie Kate Tussy , and is now living.

                              Lilla[sic] Tussy

WITNESSES TO MARK:

{

Subscribed and sworn to before me this 3 day of April , 1905.

                              H.G. Listan
                              NOTARY PUBLIC.

AFFIDAVIT OF ATTENDING PHYSICIAN OR MID-WIFE.

UNITED STATES OF AMERICA, }
    INDIAN TERRITORY.
Southern   District.

I, J I Taylor , a Physician , on oath state that I attended on Mrs. Lillie Tussy , wife of Henry B. Tussy on the 10 day of February , 1904 ; that there was born to her on said date a Female child; that said child is now living and is said to have been named Lottie Kate

                              J.I. Taylor M.D.

WITNESSES TO MARK:

{

Subscribed and sworn to before me this 3 day of April , 1905.

                              H.G. Listan
                              NOTARY PUBLIC.

Applications for Enrollment of Chickasaw Newborn
Act of 1905   Volume IV

9-1291

Muskogee, Indian Territory, April 10, 1905.

Henry B. Tussy,
    Tussy, Indian Territory.

Dear Sir:

    Receipt is hereby acknowledged of the affidavits of Lilla Tussy and J. I. Taylor to the birth of Lottie Kate Tussy daughter of Henry and Lillie Tussy, February 10, 1903, and the same have been filed with our records as an application for the enrollment of said child.

                  Respectfully,

                  Commissioner in Charge.

Chic. N.B. - 291
    (Ida Ray Caraway
    Born December 7, 1904)

BIRTH AFFIDAVIT.

DEPARTMENT OF THE INTERIOR.
COMMISSION TO THE FIVE CIVILIZED TRIBES.

    IN RE APPLICATION FOR ENROLLMENT, as a citizen of the   Chickasaw   Nation, of   Ida Ray Caraway   , born on the   7   day of   December   , 1904

Name of Father: E. J. Caraway   a citizen of the   ———————Nation.
Name of Mother: Mary Caraway   a citizen of the chickasaw[sic] Nation.

                Postoffice   Kemp, Indian Territory.

AFFIDAVIT OF MOTHER.

UNITED STATES OF AMERICA, Indian Territory, ⎫
    Central   DISTRICT. ⎭

    I,   Mary Caraway   , on oath state that I am   20   years of age and a citizen by   blood   , of the   Chickasaw   Nation; that I am the lawful wife of   E.J. Caraway   , who is a citizen, by marriage   of the   chickasaw[sic]   Nation;

Applications for Enrollment of Chickasaw Newborn
Act of 1905   Volume IV

that a   female   child was born to me on   7 day of   December   , 1904; that said child has been named   Ida Ray Caraway   , and was living March 4, 1905.

Mary Caraway

Witnesses To Mark:
{

Subscribed and sworn to before me this 3 day of April   , 1905

O.R. Fowler
Notary Public.

AFFIDAVIT OF ATTENDING PHYSICIAN OR MID-WIFE.

UNITED STATES OF AMERICA, Indian Territory, }
    Central   DISTRICT.

I, Mrs. C.A. Kirby   , a Mid-Wife   , on oath state that I attended on Mrs.   Mary Caraway   , wife of E.J. Caraway   on the 7 day of December , 1904; that there was born to her on said date a   Female   child; that said child was living March 4, 1905, and is said to have been named   Ida Ray Caraway

C A Kirby

Witnesses To Mark:
{

Subscribed and sworn to before me this 3 day of April   , 1905

O.R. Fowler
Notary Public.

Chic. N.B. - 292
   (Roland Troute
   Born November 20, 1902)

Applications for Enrollment of Chickasaw Newborn
Act of 1905   Volume IV

BIRTH AFFIDAVIT.

DEPARTMENT OF THE INTERIOR.
COMMISSION TO THE FIVE CIVILIZED TRIBES.

    IN RE APPLICATION FOR ENROLLMENT, as a citizen of the   Chickasaw   Nation, of   Roland Troute   , born on the   20   day of   Nov , 1902

Name of Father: Buck Troute   a citizen of the .... Nation.
Name of Mother: Ada Trout[sic]   a citizen of the   Chickasaw   Nation.

                          Postoffice   Purcell I.T.

AFFIDAVIT OF MOTHER.

UNITED STATES OF AMERICA, Indian Territory, }
    Southern   DISTRICT.

    I,   Ada Troute   , on oath state that I am   21   years of age and a citizen by blood   , of the   Chickasaw   Nation; that I am the lawful wife of   Buck Trout[sic]   , who is a citizen, by —— of the —— Nation; that a   male   child was born to me on   20th   day of   November   , 1902, that said child has been named   Roland Trout[sic]   , and is now living.

                          Ada Phillips Troute

Witnesses To Mark:
{

    Subscribed and sworn to before me this   27th   day of   March   , 1905.

                          Dorset Carter
                              Notary Public.

AFFIDAVIT OF ATTENDING PHYSICIAN OR MID-WIFE.

UNITED STATES OF AMERICA, Indian Territory, }
    Southern   DISTRICT.

    I,   J. S. Childs   , a Physician   , on oath state that I attended on Mrs.   Ada Troute   , wife of   Buck Troute   on the   20th   day of November , 1902; that there was born to her on said date a   male   child; that said child is now living and is said to have been named   Roland Trout[sic]

                          J.S. Childs

Witnesses To Mark:
{

Applications for Enrollment of Chickasaw Newborn
Act of 1905 Volume IV

Subscribed and sworn to before me this 4th day of April , 1905.

                                                       Dorset Carter
                                                       Notary Public.

                                                                   Chickasaw 26.

                       Muskogee, Indian Territory, April 10, 1905.

Dorsett[sic] Carter,
    Attorney at Law,
        Purcell, Indian Territory.

Dear Sir:

      Receipt is hereby acknowledged of your letter of March 30, transmitting the affidavits of Ada Phillips Troute and J. S. Childs to the birth of Roland Troute, son of Ada and Buck Troute, November 20, 1902, and the same have been filed with our records as an application for the enrollment of said child.

                                Respectfully,

                                                Commissioner in Charge.

Chic. N.B. - 293
      (Rosalee Levina Watkins
      Born February 10, 1904)

BIRTH AFFIDAVIT.
                            DEPARTMENT OF THE INTERIOR.
                COMMISSION TO THE FIVE CIVILIZED TRIBES.

      IN RE APPLICATION FOR ENROLLMENT, as a citizen of the Chickasaw Nation, of Rosalee Levina Watkins , born on the 10 day of February , 1904

Name of Father: George W Watkins   a citizen of the Chickasaw Nation.
Name of Mother: Emma A Watkins   a citizen of the Chickasaw Nation.

                                  Postoffice   Madill, Ind. Ter.

Applications for Enrollment of Chickasaw Newborn
Act of 1905 Volume IV

AFFIDAVIT OF MOTHER.

UNITED STATES OF AMERICA, Indian Territory, }
Southern DISTRICT. }

I, Emma A Watkins , on oath state that I am 34 years of age and a citizen by blood , of the Chickasaw Nation; that I am the lawful wife of George W Watkins , who is a citizen, by intermarriage of the Chickasaw Nation; that a female child was born to me on 10 day of February , 1904; that said child has been named Rosalee Levina Watkins , and was living March 4, 1905.

Emma A Watkins

Witnesses To Mark:
{

Subscribed and sworn to before me this 4 day of April , 1905

Geo. E. Rider
Notary Public.

AFFIDAVIT OF ATTENDING PHYSICIAN OR MID-WIFE.

UNITED STATES OF AMERICA, Indian Territory, }
Southern DISTRICT. }

I, J. S. Welch , a Physician , on oath state that I attended on Mrs. Emma A Watkins , wife of George W Watkins on the 10 day of February , 1905[sic]; that there was born to her on said date a female child; that said child was living March 4, 1905, and is said to have been named Rosalee Levina Watkins

J.S. Welch M.D.

Witnesses To Mark:
{

Subscribed and sworn to before me this 4 day of April , 1905

Geo. E. Rider
Notary Public.

Applications for Enrollment of Chickasaw Newborn
Act of 1905   Volume IV

BIRTH AFFIDAVIT.

DEPARTMENT OF THE INTERIOR.
COMMISSION TO THE FIVE CIVILIZED TRIBES.

IN RE APPLICATION FOR ENROLLMENT, as a citizen of the   Chickasaw   Nation, of   Rosalee Levina Watkins   , born on the   10   day of   February   , 1904

Name of Father: George W Watkins   a citizen of the   Chickasaw Nation.
Name of Mother: Emma A Watkins   a citizen of the   Chickasaw Nation.

Postoffice   Madill, Ind. Ter.

AFFIDAVIT OF MOTHER.

UNITED STATES OF AMERICA, Indian Territory,
Southern   DISTRICT.

I,   Emma A Watkins   , on oath state that I am   34   years of age and a citizen by   blood   , of the   Chickasaw   Nation; that I am the lawful wife of George W Watkins   , who is a citizen, by inter-marriage   of the   Chickasaw   Nation; that a   female   child was born to me on   10   day of   February   , 1904; that said child has been named   Rosalee Levina Watkins   , and was living March 4, 1905.

Emma A Watkins

Witnesses To Mark:

Subscribed and sworn to before me this   25   day of   April   , 1905

Geo. E. Rider
Notary Public.

AFFIDAVIT OF ATTENDING PHYSICIAN OR MID-WIFE.

UNITED STATES OF AMERICA, Indian Territory,
Southern   DISTRICT.

I,   J. S. Welch   , a Physician   , on oath state that I attended on Mrs.   Emma A Watkins   , wife of   George W Watkins   on the   10   day of February   , 1904; that there was born to her on said date a   female   child; that said child was living March 4, 1905, and is said to have been named   Rosalee Levina Watkins

J.S. Welch M.D.

Witnesses To Mark:

Applications for Enrollment of Chickasaw Newborn
Act of 1905   Volume IV

Subscribed and sworn to before me this 25 day of   April   , 1905

Geo. E. Rider
Notary Public.

Chickasaw N.B. 293.

Muskogee, Indian Territory, April 21, 1905.

George E. Rider,
    Attorney at Law,
        Madill, Indian Territory.

Dear Sir:

    Receipt is hereby acknowledged of your letter of April 17, referring to the application for the enrollment of Rosalee Levina Watkins, in which you state that the correct date of the birth of this child is February 10, 1904, and you ask if it appears in the application as February 10, 1905, as stated in our letter of April 10, 1905.

    In reply to your letter you are informed that the affidavit of the mother to the birth of Rosalee Levina Watkins gives the date of the birth of said child as February 10, 1904, while the affidavit of the physician gives it as February 10, 1905.

    For the purpose of showing the correct date of the birth of this child there is enclosed herewith a blank which please have executed and returned to this office as early as practicable.

                        Respectfully,

1 B.C.   Chairman.

Chickasaw 738.

Muskogee, Indian Territory, April 10, 1905.

George E. Rider,
    Attorney at Law,
        Madill, Indian Territory.

Dear Sir:

    Receipt is hereby acknowledged of your letter of April 4, transmitting the affidavits of Emma A. Watkins and J. S. Welch to the birth of Rosalee Levina Watkins, daughter of George W. and Emma A. Watkins, February 10, 1905[sic], and the same have been filed with our records as an application for the enrollment of said child.

Applications for Enrollment of Chickasaw Newborn
Act of 1905   Volume IV

Respectfully,

Commissioner in Charge.

9-738.

Muskogee, Indian Territory, April 28 1905.

George E. Rider,
    Attorney at Law,
        Madill, Indian Territory.

Dear Sir:

Receipt is hereby acknowledged of your letter of April 25, 1905 enclosing affidavits of Emma A. Watkins and J. S. Welch to the birth of Rosalee Levina Watkins, daughter of George W. and Emma A. Watkins, February 10, 1904, and the same have been filed with our records as an application for the enrollment of said child.

Respectfully,

Chairman.

Chic. N.B. - 294
    (Charles Cruce Thomas
    Born November 2, 1901)

BIRTH AFFIDAVIT.

DEPARTMENT OF THE INTERIOR,
COMMISSION TO THE FIVE CIVILIZED TRIBES.

IN RE Application for Enrollment, as a citizen of the   Chickasaw   Nation, of   Charles Cruce Thomas , born on the   2nd   day of   November   , 1901

Name of Father: Chas W. Thomas   a citizen of the   Chickasaw   Nation.
Name of Mother: Minnie G Thomas   a citizen of the   Chickasaw   Nation.

Post-Office: *(Illegible)* Ind Ter

158

Applications for Enrollment of Chickasaw Newborn
Act of 1905   Volume IV

AFFIDAVIT OF MOTHER.

UNITED STATES OF AMERICA,
    INDIAN TERRITORY.
  Southern   District.

I,   Minnie G Thomas   , on oath state that I am   Thirty seven   years of age and a citizen by   blood   , of the   Chickasaw   Nation; that I am the lawful wife of   Charles W. Thomas   , who is a citizen, by   marriage   of the Chickasaw Nation; that a   male   child was born to me on   2nd   day of   November   , 1901 , that said child has been named   Charles Cruce Thomas   , and is now living.

Minnie G. Thomas

WITNESSES TO MARK:

{

Subscribed and sworn to before me this   22   *day of*   November   , 1901

W.P. Bleakmore
NOTARY PUBLIC.

AFFIDAVIT OF ATTENDING PHYSICIAN OR MID-WIFE.

UNITED STATES OF AMERICA,
    INDIAN TERRITORY.
  Southern   District.

I,   W.T. Gardner   , a physician   , on oath state that I attended on Mrs.   Minnie G Thomas   , wife of   Charles W Thomas   on the   2nd   day of November   , 1901 ; that there was born to her on said date a   male   child; that said child is now living and is said to have been named   Charles Cruce Thomas

W.T. Gardner MD

WITNESSES TO MARK:

{

Subscribed and sworn to before me this   24th   *day of*   November   , 1901

W.P. Bleakmore
NOTARY PUBLIC.

Applications for Enrollment of Chickasaw Newborn
Act of 1905   Volume IV

(The letter below does not belong with the current applicant.)

Chickasaw 1311.

Muskogee, Indian Territory, April 10, 1905.

W. H. Thompson,
    Chickasha, Indian Territory.

Dear Sir:

    Receipt is hereby acknowledged of your letter of April 4, transmitting the affidavits of Della May Thompson and G. R. Gerard to the birth of Virginia May Thompson, daughter of William H. and Della May Thompson, September 25, 1903, and the same have been filed with our records as an application for the enrollment of said child.

    Respectfully,

Commissioner in Charge.

Chic. N.B. - 295
    (Nicy Hawkins
    Born January 2, 1904)

BIRTH AFFIDAVIT.

DEPARTMENT OF THE INTERIOR.
COMMISSION TO THE FIVE CIVILIZED TRIBES.

    IN RE APPLICATION FOR ENROLLMENT, as a citizen of the Chickasaw Nation, of Nicy Hawkins, born on the 2nd day of Jan, 1904

Name of Father: Nelson Hawkins   a citizen of the Chickasaw Nation.
Name of Mother: Millie Hawkins   a citizen of the Chickasaw Nation.

    Postoffice   Stonewall, I.T.

Applications for Enrollment of Chickasaw Newborn
Act of 1905   Volume IV

AFFIDAVIT OF MOTHER.

UNITED STATES OF AMERICA, Indian Territory, }
Southern   DISTRICT.

I, Millie Hawkins, on oath state that I am 30 years of age and a citizen by blood, of the Chickasaw Nation; that I am the lawful wife of Nelson Hawkins, who is a citizen, by Blood of the Chickasaw Nation; that a Female child was born to me on 2nd day of January, 1904; that said child has been named Nicy Hawkins, and was living March 4, 1905.

                                            her
                                   Millie x Hawkins
Witnesses To Mark: mark
{ Marion J Burris
  G. F. Byrd

Subscribed and sworn to before me this 6th day of April, 1905

                                  W.F. Harrison
                                  Notary Public.

AFFIDAVIT OF ATTENDING PHYSICIAN OR MID-WIFE.

UNITED STATES OF AMERICA, Indian Territory, }
Southern   DISTRICT.

I, Salanie Thom, a Midwife, on oath state that I attended on Mrs. Millie Hawkins, wife of Nelson Hawkins on the 2nd day of Jan, 1904; that there was born to her on said date a Female child; that said child was living March 4, 1905, and is said to have been named Nicy Hawkins

                                            her
                                   Salanie x Thom
Witnesses To Mark: mark
{ Marion J Burris
  G. F. Byrd

Subscribed and sworn to before me this 6th day of April, 1905

                                  W.F. Harrison
                                  Notary Public.

Applications for Enrollment of Chickasaw Newborn
Act of 1905   Volume IV

BIRTH AFFIDAVIT.   *No. 46*
DEPARTMENT OF THE INTERIOR.
COMMISSION TO THE FIVE CIVILIZED TRIBES.

IN RE APPLICATION FOR ENROLLMENT, as a citizen of the   Chickasaw   Nation, of   Nicy Hawkins   , born on the   8   day of Feb , 1904

Name of Father: Nelson Hawkins   a citizen of the   Chickasaw Nation.
Name of Mother: Millie Hawkins   a citizen of the   Chickasaw Nation.

Postoffice   Franks

AFFIDAVIT OF MOTHER.

UNITED STATES OF AMERICA, Indian Territory, }
   Southern   DISTRICT.

I, Millie Hawkins , on oath state that I am 30   years of age and a citizen by   blood   , of the   Chickasaw   Nation; that I am the lawful wife of   Nelson Hawkins , who is a citizen, by   blood   of the   Chickasaw   Nation; that a female   child was born to me on 8   day of February , 1904, that said child has been named   Nicy Hawkins   , and is now living.

                                     her
                               Millie x Hawkins
Witnesses To Mark: mark
{ Jno. P. Crawford
  Charley Folsum

Subscribed and sworn to before me this 17" day of   December , 1904

                               Jno. P. Crawford
                                  Notary Public.

AFFIDAVIT OF ATTENDING PHYSICIAN OR MID-WIFE.

UNITED STATES OF AMERICA, Indian Territory, }
   Southern   DISTRICT.

I,   Salene Thom   , a midwife   , on oath state that I attended on Mrs. Millie Hawkins , wife of   Nelson Hawkins   on the 8   day of Feb , 1904; that there was born to her on said date a   female   child; that said child is now living and is said to have been named Nicy Hawkins
                                       her
                                 Salene x Thom
                                   mark

Applications for Enrollment of Chickasaw Newborn
Act of 1905   Volume IV

Witnesses To Mark:
 { Jno. P. Crawford
   Charley Folsum

   Subscribed and sworn to before me this 17" day of   December , 1904

   Jno. P. Crawford
   Notary Public.

———

9-158

Muskogee, Indian Territory, April 11, 1905.

Nelson Hawkins,
   Stonewall, Indian Territory.

Dear Sir:

   Receipt is hereby acknowledged of the affidavits of Millie Hawkins and Salanie Thom to the birth of Nicy Hawkins, daughter of Nelson and Millie Hawkins January 2, 1904, and the same have been filed with our records as an application for the enrollment of said child.

   Respectfully,

   Commissioner in Charge.

———

Chic. N.B. - 296
   (Florence Marzett Frye
   Born January 30, 1903)

———

BIRTH AFFIDAVIT.
DEPARTMENT OF THE INTERIOR.
COMMISSION TO THE FIVE CIVILIZED TRIBES.

———

   IN RE APPLICATION FOR ENROLLMENT, as a citizen of the   Chickasaw   Nation, of   Florence Marzett Frye   , born on the   30 day of January   , 1903

Name of Father: Samuel J Frye   a citizen of the   Chickasaw   Nation.
Name of Mother: Bertha Frye   a citizen of the   Chickasaw   Nation.

Applications for Enrollment of Chickasaw Newborn
Act of 1905 Volume IV

Postoffice   Springer Ind Ter

___

AFFIDAVIT OF MOTHER.

UNITED STATES OF AMERICA, Indian Territory, }
  Southern   DISTRICT.

I,   Bertha Frye   , on oath state that I am   24   years of age and a citizen by ...., of the   United States   Nation; that I am the lawful wife of Samuel J Frye   , who is a citizen, by Blood   of the   Chickasaw   Nation; that a   Female   child was born to me on   30   day of   January   , 1903; that said child has been named   Florence Marzett Frye   , and was living March 4, 1905.

Bertha Frye

Witnesses To Mark:
{

Subscribed and sworn to before me this 5th day of April   , 1905

D H Cass
Notary Public.

___

AFFIDAVIT OF ATTENDING PHYSICIAN OR MID-WIFE.

UNITED STATES OF AMERICA, Indian Territory, }
  Southern   DISTRICT.

I,   Mrs B.F. Cox   , a midwife   , on oath state that I attended on Mrs.   Bertha Frye   , wife of   Samuel J Frye   on the 30 day of January , 1903; that there was born to her on said date a   Female   child; that said child was living March 4, 1905, and is said to have been named Florence Marzett Frye

B.F. Cox

Witnesses To Mark:
{

Subscribed and sworn to before me this 5th day of April   , 1905

D H Cass
Notary Public.

___

164

Applications for Enrollment of Chickasaw Newborn
Act of 1905 Volume IV

CERTIFICATE OF
RECORD OF MARRIAGE

United States of America, }
   Indian Territory,   } sct.
   Southern District. }

I, C. M. Campbell, Clerk of the United States Court, in the Territory and District aforesaid Do Hereby Certify, that the License for and Certificate of Marriage of

Mr.   S. J. Frye   and

M   Bertha Cox

were filed in my office in said Territory and District the   11th   day of   Dec.   A.D., 190 1   and duly recorded in Book   F   of Marriage Record, Page   124

DEPARTMENT OF THE INTERIOR,
COMMISSION TO THE FIVE CIVILIZED TRIBES.
FILED
APR 11 1905

Tams Bixby CHAIRMAN.

Witness my hand and Seal of said Court, at Ardmore, this   11th   day of   Dec.   A.D. 190 1

         C. M. Campbell   (SEAL)
                         Clerk.

Return this license to the United States Clerk at Ardmore, that it may be recorded, when it will be mailed to the proper address.

Texas Printing Company, Fort Worth.

Indian Territory,
Southern District.

       I, C. M. Campbell, Clerk of the United States Court, Southern District, Indian Territory, do hereby certify that the above and foregoing is a true and correct copy of the Marriage License and Certificate of Marriage of S.J. Frye and Bertha Cox, as the same appears of record in my office at Ardmore in Marriage Record F, page 124.   IN TESTIMONY WHEREOF, I have hereunto set my hand and affixed the seal of said Court, at my office in Ardmore, this 5th day of April, A.D. 1905.

                         C. M. Campbell, Clerk,

               By   *(Name Illegible)*   Deputy.

Applications for Enrollment of Chickasaw Newborn
Act of 1905   Volume IV

No person is authorized to perform the Marriage Ceremony in the Indian Territory unless the proper credentials have first been recorded in the Clerk's office.

MARRIAGE LICENSE.
No.   1727

UNITED STATES OF AMERICA,
  INDIAN TERRITORY,   } SS.   To Any Person Authorized by Law to Solemnize
  SOUTHERN DISTRICT.   Marriage, Greeting:

YOU ARE HEREBY COMMANDED to solemnize the Rite and publish the Banns of Matrimony between Mr.   S. J. Frye   in the Indian Territory, aged   21   years, and of   Ardmore   M   Bertha Cox   of   Ardmore   in the Indian Territory, aged   21   years, according to law; and do you officially sign and return this license to the parties therein named.

WITNESS my hand and official Seal, this   7th   day of   Dec.   A. D. 190 1

(SEAL)   C. M. Campbell
                                     Clerk of the United States Court.

Certificate of Marriage.

UNITED STATES OF AMERICA,
  INDIAN TERRITORY,   } SS.
  SOUTHERN DISTRICT.   *I,*   John L. Williams

Ardmore   *do hereby certify that on the*   7th   *day of*   Dec.   A. D. 190 1   *, I did duly and according to law, as commanded in the foregoing License, solemnize the Rite and publish the Banns of Matrimony between the parties therein named.*

WITNESS my hand this   7th   day of   Dec.   A. D. 190 1

My credentials are recorded in the office of the Clerk of the United States Court, Indian Territory, Southern District, at Ardmore, Book   C   , Page   37

                              John L. Williams
                              Pastor M.E.C.So.

NOTE. (a)- This License and Certificate of Marriages must be returned to the office of the Clerk of the United States Court in the Indian Territory, at Ardmore, within sixty days from the date thereof, or the party to whom the License was issued will be liable in the amount of ONE HUNDRED DOLLARS ($100).

Applications for Enrollment of Chickasaw Newborn
Act of 1905 Volume IV

9-517

Muskogee, Indian Territory, April 11, 1905.

Samuel J. Frye,
    Springer, Indian Territory.

Dear Sir:

    Receipt is hereby acknowledged of the affidavits of Bertha Frye and B. F. Cox to the birth of Florence Maryett[sic] Frye daughter of Samuel and Bertha Frye, January 30, 1903, and the same have been filed with our records as an application for the enrollment of said child.

    Receipt is also acknowledged of certified copy of marriage license and certificate between Samuel J. Frye and Bertha Cox and the same has been filed in the matter of the enrollment of the child herein named.

                    Respectfully,

                                Commissioner in Charge.

Chic. N.B. - 297
    (Lucy May Harkins
    Born November 22, 1903)

BIRTH AFFIDAVIT.

DEPARTMENT OF THE INTERIOR.
COMMISSION TO THE FIVE CIVILIZED TRIBES.

    IN RE APPLICATION FOR ENROLLMENT, as a citizen of the   Chickasaw   Nation, of   Lucy May Harkins   , born on the 22 day of Nov , 1903

Name of Father: Charley Harkins   a citizen of the Chickasaw Nation.
Name of Mother: Lula Harkins   a citizen of the Chickasaw Nation.

                    Postoffice   Emet I.T.

Applications for Enrollment of Chickasaw Newborn
Act of 1905   Volume IV

AFFIDAVIT OF MOTHER.

UNITED STATES OF AMERICA, Indian Territory,
Southern DISTRICT.

I, Lula Harkins, on oath state that I am 32 years of age and a citizen by Blood, of the Chickasaw Nation; that I am the lawful wife of Charley Harkins, who is a citizen, by Blood of the Chickasaw Nation; that a Female child was born to me on 22 day of Nov, 1903; that said child has been named Lucy May Harkins, and was living March 4, 1905.

Lula Harkins

Witnesses To Mark:
 { Lucy Cheadle
 { Mary Harkins

Subscribed and sworn to before me this 4 day of April, 1905

John H Dobson
Notary Public.

AFFIDAVIT OF ATTENDING PHYSICIAN OR MID-WIFE.

UNITED STATES OF AMERICA, Indian Territory,
Southern DISTRICT.

I, Pegy[sic] Colbert, a Midwife, on oath state that I attended on Mrs. Lula Harkins, wife of Charley Harkins on the 22 day of Nov, 1903; that there was born to her on said date a Female child; that said child was living March 4, 1905, and is said to have been named Lucy May Harkins

her
Peggy x Colbert
mark

Witnesses To Mark:
 { A L Jany
 { *(Name Illegible)*

Subscribed and sworn to before me this 4 day of April, 1905

John H Dobson
Notary Public.

Applications for Enrollment of Chickasaw Newborn
Act of 1905 Volume IV

9-773

Muskogee, Indian Territory, April 11, 1905.

Charlie Harkins,
    Emet, Indian Territory.

Dear Sir:

    Receipt is hereby acknowledged of the affidavits of Lula Harkins and Peggy Colbert to the birth of Lucy May Harkins, daughter of Charley and Lula Harkins, November 22, 1903, and the same have been filed with our records as an application for the enrollment of said child.

                  Respectfully,

                                      Commissioner in Charge.

Chic. N.B. - 298
    (Morine Ward
    Born January 12, 1903)

Indian Territory }
Southern District }

    Before me a Notary Public in and for the Southern District of the Indian Territory, this day personally appeared T. M. Merchant, who being by me duly sworn upon his oath states that he is the father of Frances Ward, formerly Frances Merchant; that her Christian name is Frances and that an error was made in the marriage license stating her name as "Florence"; that she is the wife of Houston Ward, a citizen by blood of the Chickasaw Nation, and the mother of Morine Ward; for whom application for enrollment was made some time since; also appeared Houston Ward, husband of the said Frances Ward who also makes affidavit that the facts are as above stated.

                                      T.M. Merchant
                                      Houston Ward

Applications for Enrollment of Chickasaw Newborn
Act of 1905   Volume IV

Subscribed and sworn to before me at Woodville, Ind. Ter. this 19th day of June - 1905

Robert S Bell
Notary Public

Commission till Feb. 8-1909

Certificate of Record of Marriage.

UNITED STATES OF AMERICA, ⎫
INDIAN TERRITORY,   ⎬ sct.
SOUTHERN DISTRICT.   ⎭

DEPARTMENT OF THE INTERIOR,
COMMISSION TO THE FIVE CIVILIZED TRIBES.

FILED
JUN 5 1905

Tams Bixby CHAIRMAN.

I, C. M. CAMPBELL, Clerk of the United States Court, in the Territory and District aforesaid do hereby certify, that the License for and Certificate of Marriage of

MR.   Huston[sic] Ward
            AND
M   Florence[sic] Merchant

were filed in my office in said Territory and District the   28   day of   June   A.D., 190 2   and duly recorded in Book   F.   of Marriage Record, Page   327

WITNESS my hand and Seal of said Court, at Ardmore, this   5th day of   July   A.D. 190 2

C. M. Campbell
CLERK.

☞ Return this License to the United States Clerk at Ardmore, that it may be recorded, when it will be mailed to the proper address.

FILED
JUN 28 1902 8 AM

C. M. CAMPBELL Clerk.
Southern Dist. Ind. Ter.

Applications for Enrollment of Chickasaw Newborn
Act of 1905   Volume IV

MARRIAGE LICENSE

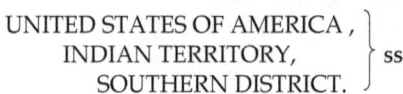

UNITED STATES OF AMERICA,
   INDIAN TERRITORY,   } ss:
     SOUTHERN DISTRICT.

To Any Person Authorized by Law to Solemnize Marriage --- Greeting:

You are hereby commanded to solemnize the Rite and publish the Banns of Matrimony between Mr. Houston Ward *of* Isom Springs *, in the Indian Territory, aged* 22 *years and M* Florence Merchant *of* Isom Springs *in the Indian Territory aged* 21 *years according to law, and do you officially sign and return this License to the parties therein named.*

Witness my hand and official seal this 30 *day of* April *A.D. 190* 2

CM Campbell
Clerk of the United States Court

...................................*Deputy*

Certificate of Marriage.

United States of America,   }
  Indian Territory,   } ss.
    Southern District. }

I, united Mr. Huston
a Ward and Flora Merchant

do hereby certify, that on the 25 day of June , A. D. 190 2 , I did duly and according to law, as commanded in the foregoing License, solemnize the Rite and publish the Banns of Matrimony between the parties therein named.

Witness my hand, this 25 day of June , A. D. 190 2

My credentials are recorded in the office of the Clerk of the United States Court, Indian Territory, Southern District, at Ardmore, Indian Territory Book C , Page 127

NOTE:-The person officiating should fill in the spaces for book and page and sign here   a   J. R. Flowers

NOTE (a)-The License and Certificate of Marriage must be returned to the office of the Clerk of the United States Court in the Indian Territory, at Ardmore, within sixty days from the date thereof, or the party to whom the License was issued will be liable in the amount of One Hundred Dollars ($100).

NOTE (b)-No person is authorized to perform the Marriage Ceremony in the Southern District unless the proper credentials have first been recorded in the Clerk's office.

Applications for Enrollment of Chickasaw Newborn
Act of 1905 Volume IV

BIRTH AFFIDAVIT.

DEPARTMENT OF THE INTERIOR.
COMMISSION TO THE FIVE CIVILIZED TRIBES.

IN RE APPLICATION FOR ENROLLMENT, as a citizen of the Chickasaw Nation, of Morine Ward, born on the 12 day of Jan, 1903

Name of Father: Houston Ward   a citizen of the Chickasaw Nation.
Name of Mother: Frances Ward   a citizen of the Chickasaw Nation.

Postoffice   Isom Springs

AFFIDAVIT OF MOTHER.

UNITED STATES OF AMERICA, Indian Territory,
Southern   DISTRICT.

I, Frances Ward, on oath state that I am 27 years of age and a citizen by Marriage, of the Chickasaw Nation; that I am the lawful wife of Houston Ward, who is a citizen, by Birth of the Chickasaw Nation; that a Girl child was born to me on 12 day of Jan, 1903, that said child has been named Morine Ward, and is now living.

                           Frances Ward

Witnesses To Mark:
   { D.J. Belt
     W[sic]

Subscribed and sworn to before me this 18 day of Mch, 1905.

                           M.D. Belt
                           Notary Public.

AFFIDAVIT OF ATTENDING PHYSICIAN OR MID-WIFE.

UNITED STATES OF AMERICA, Indian Territory,
Southern   DISTRICT.

I, M.D. Belt M.D., a Physician, on oath state that I attended on Mrs. Frances Ward, wife of Houston Ward on the 12 day of Jan, 1903; that there was born to her on said date a Female child; that said child is now living and is said to have been named Morine Ward

                           M.D. Belt

Applications for Enrollment of Chickasaw Newborn
Act of 1905 Volume IV

Witnesses To Mark:
{ *(Name Illegible)*
{ *(Name Illegible)*

    Subscribed and sworn to before me this 22 day of March , 1905.

                                    T. L. Wright
                                            Notary Public.

Wm O.B.

COMMISSIONERS:
TAMS BIXBY,
THOMAS B. NEEDLES,
C.R. BRECKINBRIDGE.

DEPARTMENT OF THE INTERIOR,
COMMISSIONER TO THE FIVE CIVILIZED TRIBES.

REFER IN REPLY TO THE FOLLOWING:

9-975

WM. O. BEALL
Secretary

ADDRESS ONLY THE
COMMISSION TO THE FIVE CIVILIZED TRIBES.

                                Muskogee, Indian Territory, April 10, 1905.

Houston Ward,
    Ironbridge, Indian Territory.

Dear Sir:

    Receipt is hereby acknowledged of the affidavits of Frances Ward and M. D. Belt to the birth of Morine Ward, daughter of Houston and Frances Ward, January 12, 1903, and the same have been filed with our records as an application for the enrollment of said child.

                                      Respectfully,
                                      T.B. Needles
                                      Commissioner in Charge.

                                                      9-N.B. 298.

                                Muskogee, Indian Territory, May 9, 1905.

Houston Ward,
    Isom Springs, Indian Territory.

Dear Sir:

    Your letter of May 3rd addressed to the United States Indian Agent has been by him referred to this Commission for appropriate action. Therein you ask if the application which was forwarded for the enrollment of your child has been received.

Applications for Enrollment of Chickasaw Newborn
Act of 1905   Volume IV

In reply to your letter you are advised that the affidavits to the birth of Morine Ward, child of Houston and Frances Ward, have been filed with our records as an application for the enrollment of said child.

Replying to that portion of your letter in which you ask if you can have land selected for your child, you are advised that no reservation of land or selection of allotment can be permitted for children for whom application has been made under the provisions of the act of Congress of March 3, 1905, until their enrollment has been approved by the Secretary of the Interior.

                Respectfully,

                              Commissioner in Charge.

                              9-NB-298.

                Muskogee, Indian Territory, May 16, 1905.

Houston Ward,
    Isom Springs, Indian Territory.

Dear Sir:

Referring to the application for the enrollment of your infant child, Morine Ward, born January 12, 1903, it is noted that the applicant claims through you.

In this event it will be necessary for you to file with the Commission either the original or a certified copy of the license and certificate of your marriage to the applicant's mother, Frances Ward.

                Respectfully,

                              Chairman.

Applications for Enrollment of Chickasaw Newborn
Act of 1905 Volume IV

7 NB 298

Muskogee, Indian Territory, June 7, 1905.

Houston Ward,
    Woodville, Indian Territory.

Dear Sir:

    Receipt is hereby acknowledged of your letter of May 29, 1905, enclosing license and certificate between Houston Ward and Florence Merchant which you offer in support of the application for the enrollment of your child Morine Ward and the same have been filed with the record in this case.

    It appears, however, that the name of your wife is given in the affidavits to the birth of your child Morine Ward as Frances Ward while her name is given in the marriage license and certificate as Florence Ward. You are therefore requested to forward an affidavit explaining this discrepance[sic] and stating if the Florence Ward referred to in the marriage license and certificate is identical with Frances Ward, mother of your child Morine Ward. This matter should receive immediate attention.

                  Respectfully,

                  Commissioner in Charge.

Chic. N.B. - 299
    (Sam Louis Colbert
    Born May 17, 1903)

BIRTH AFFIDAVIT.

    IN RE-APPLICATION FOR ENROLLMENT, as a citizen of the Chickasaw Nation, of Sam Louis Colbert, born on the 17th. day of May. , 190 3

Name of Father: Sam Tildon Colbert   a citizen of the Chickasaw Nation.
Name of Mother: Alberta Colbert   a citizen of the United States Nation.

            Postoffice   Duncan, I.T.

Applications for Enrollment of Chickasaw Newborn
Act of 1905   Volume IV

AFFIDAVIT OF MOTHER.

UNITED STATES OF AMERICA, INDIAN TERRITORY,
Southern District   District.

I, Alberta Colbert, on oath state that I am 22 years of age and a citizen by ~~blood~~, of the United States Nation; that I am the lawful wife of Sam Tildon Colbert, who is a citizen, by blood of the Chickasaw Nation; that a Male child was born to me on 17th. day of May, 1903, that said child has been named Sam Louis Colbert, and is now living.

Alberta Colbert

Witnesses To Mark:

Subscribed and sworn to before me this 13th day of March, 1905.

John Vaughn
Notary Public.

AFFIDAVIT OF ATTENDING PHYSICIAN OR MID-WIFE.

UNITED STATES OF AMERICA, INDIAN TERRITORY,
Southern   District.

I, Dr. B.J. Plunkett, a Physician, on oath state that I attended on Mrs. Alberta Colbert, wife of Sam Tildon Colbert on the 17th. day of May, 1903; that there was born to her on said date a Male child; that said child is now living and is said to have been named Sam Louis Colbert

Benj. J. Plunkett MD

Witnesses To Mark:

Subscribed and sworn to before me this 13th day of March, 1905.

John Vaughn
Notary Public.

**Applications for Enrollment of Chickasaw Newborn
Act of 1905 Volume IV**

CERTIFICATE OF
RECORD OF MARRIAGE

UNITED STATES OF AMERICA,
INDIAN TERRITORY, } sct.
SOUTHERN DISTRICT.

DEPARTMENT OF THE INTERIOR,
COMMISSION TO THE FIVE CIVILIZED TRIBES.
FILED
MAY 25 1905
Tams Bixby CHAIRMAN

I, C. M. CAMPBELL, Clerk of the United States Court, in the Territory and District aforesaid DO HEREBY CERTIFY, that the License for and Certificate of Marriage of

Mr. Samuel T. Colbert and

M Alberta Witt

were filed in my office in said Territory and District the 4th day of Nov. A.D., 190 2 and duly recorded in Book F of Marriage Record, Page 600

WITNESS my hand and Seal of said Court, at Ardmore, this 4th day of Nov. A.D. 190 2

C. M. Campbell
CLERK.

Return this license to the United States Clerk at Ardmore, that it may be recorded, when it will be mailed to the proper address.

Texas Printing Company, Fort Worth.

Indian Territory,
Southern District.

    I, C. M. Campbell, Clerk of the United States Court, Southern District, Indian Territory, do hereby certify that the above and foregoing is a true and correct copy of the Marraige[sic] License and Certificate of Marriage, filed for record in my office at Ardmore, on the 4th day of November, A.D. 1902 and duly recorded in Vol. F, page 600, of Marriage Records.

    In testimony whereof, I have hereunto set my hand and affixed the seal of said Court at my office in Ardmore, Indian Territory this 20th day of May, A.D. 1905.

C. M. Campbell, Clerk,

By N H McCoy Chief Deputy.

**Applications for Enrollment of Chickasaw Newborn
Act of 1905   Volume IV**

No person is authorized to perform the Marriage Ceremony in the Indian Territory unless the proper credentials have first been recorded in the Clerk's office.

MARRIAGE LICENSE.
No.   1644

UNITED STATES OF AMERICA,
  INDIAN TERRITORY, } SS.   To Any Person Authorized by Law to Solemnize
  SOUTHERN DISTRICT.   Marriage, Greeting:

YOU ARE HEREBY COMMANDED to solemnize the Rite and publish the Banns of Matrimony between Mr.   Samuel T. Colbert
of   Duncan   in the Indian Territory, aged   26   years, and
M   Alberta Witt   of   Duncan   in the Indian Territory, aged
    19   years, according to law; and do you officially sign and return this license to the parties therein named.

WITNESS my hand and official Seal, this   2nd   day
of   November   A. D. 190 2

C. M. Campbell
Clerk of the United States Court.

Certificate of Marriage.

UNITED STATES OF AMERICA,
  INDIAN TERRITORY, } SS.
  SOUTHERN DISTRICT.   I,   N. R. Waters

_____ do hereby certify that on the   2nd   day
of   November   A. D. 190 2 , I did duly and according to law, as commanded in the foregoing License, solemnize the Rite and publish the Banns of Matrimony between the parties therein named.

WITNESS my hand this   2nd   day of   November   A. D. 190 2

My credentials are recorded in the office of the Clerk of the United States Court, Indian Territory, Southern District, at Ardmore, Book   C   , Page   20

N. R. Waters
Minister

NOTE. (a)- This License and Certificate of Marriages must be returned to the office of the Clerk of the United States Court in the Indian Territory, at Ardmore, within sixty days from the date thereof, or the party to whom the License was issued will be liable in the amount of ONE HUNDRED DOLLARS ($100).

Applications for Enrollment of Chickasaw Newborn
Act of 1905   Volume IV

9-1284

Muskogee, Indian Territory, March 22, 1905.

Sam T. Colbert,
    Duncan, Indian Territory.

Dear Sir:

    Receipt is hereby acknowledged of your letter of March 17, 1905, enclosing affidavits of Alberta Colbert and Benjamin J. Plunkett to the birth of Sam Louis Colbert, son of Sam Tildon and Alberta Colbert, May 17, 1903, and the same have been filed with our records as an application for the enrollment of said child.

    Replying to that part of your letter in which you request to be advised when you can file for your child you are informed that no selection of allotment can be made for children born subsequent to September 25, 1902, until their enrollment has been approved by the Secretary of the Interior.

Respectfully,

Chairman.

COMMISSIONERS:
TAMS BIXBY,
THOMAS B. NEEDLES,
C.R. BRECKINBRIDGE.

DEPARTMENT OF THE INTERIOR,
COMMISSIONER TO THE FIVE CIVILIZED TRIBES.

WM. O. BEALL
Secretary

ADDRESS ONLY THE
COMMISSION TO THE FIVE CIVILIZED TRIBES.

$W^m O.B.$

REFER IN REPLY TO THE FOLLOWING:

9-NB-299.

Muskogee, Indian Territory, May 16, 1905.

Sam Tildon Colbert,
    Duncan, Indian Territory.

Dear Sir:

    Referring to the application for the enrollment of your infant child, Sam Louis Colbert, born May 17, 1903, it is noted that the applicant claims through you.

    In this event it will be necessary for you to file with the Commission either the original or a certified copy of the license and certificate of your marriage to the applicant's mother, Alberta Colbert.

Applications for Enrollment of Chickasaw Newborn
Act of 1905 Volume IV

Respectfully,
Tams Bixby
Chairman.

---

9 N.B. 299.

Muskogee, Indian Territory, May 26, 1905.

Sam Tilden[sic] Colbert,
    Duncan, Indian Territory.

Dear Sir:

    Receipt is hereby acknowledged of certified copy of the marriage license and certificate between Samuel T. Colbert and Alberta Witt, which you offer in support of the application for the enrollment of your child, Sam Louis Colbert, and the same has been filed with the records in this case.

Respectfully,

Chairman.

Chic. N.B. - 300
    (Josephine Lucy Goins
    Born February 7, 1903)
    (Charles Reuben Goins
    Born July 27, 1904)

BIRTH AFFIDAVIT.

DEPARTMENT OF THE INTERIOR.
COMMISSION TO THE FIVE CIVILIZED TRIBES.

IN RE APPLICATION FOR ENROLLMENT, as a citizen of the Chickasaw Nation, of Josephine Lucy Goins, born on the 7th day of February, 1903.

Name of Father: Charles Calvin Goins   a citizen of the Chickasaw Nation.
Name of Mother: Sally Goins   a citizen of the United States Nation.

Postoffice   Purcell Indian Territory

Applications for Enrollment of Chickasaw Newborn
Act of 1905   Volume IV

AFFIDAVIT OF MOTHER.

UNITED STATES OF AMERICA, Indian Territory, }
   Southern   DISTRICT.

   I, Sally Goins   , on oath state that I am 18 years of age and a citizen ~~by~~ of the United States — — ~~Nation~~; that I am the lawful wife of   Charley Calvin Goins , who is a citizen, by blood   of the   Chickasaw   Nation; that a female   child was born to me on 7th day of February   , 1903; that said child has been named   Josephine Lucy Goins   , and was living March 4, 1905.

Sally Goins

Witnesses To Mark:
{

   Subscribed and sworn to before me this 5th day of   April   , 1905

O H Loomis
Notary Public.

AFFIDAVIT OF ATTENDING PHYSICIAN OR MID-WIFE.

UNITED STATES OF AMERICA, Indian Territory, }
   Southern   DISTRICT.

   I,   Susan Goins   , a midwife   , on oath state that I attended on Mrs.   Sally Goins   , wife of   Charles Calvin Goins   on the 7th day of February , 1903; that there was born to her on said date a   female   child; that said child was living March 4, 1905, and is said to have been named   Josephine Lucy Goins

Susan Goins

Witnesses To Mark:
{

   Subscribed and sworn to before me this 5th day of   April   , 1905

O H Loomis
Notary Public.

Applications for Enrollment of Chickasaw Newborn
Act of 1905 Volume IV

BIRTH AFFIDAVIT.

DEPARTMENT OF THE INTERIOR.
COMMISSION TO THE FIVE CIVILIZED TRIBES.

IN RE APPLICATION FOR ENROLLMENT, as a citizen of the Chickasaw Nation, of Charles Reuben Goins , born on the 27 day of July , 1904

Name of Father: Charles Calvin Goins   a citizen of the Chickasaw Nation.
Name of Mother: Sally Goins   a citizen of the United States Nation.

Postoffice   Purcell Indian Territory

AFFIDAVIT OF MOTHER.

UNITED STATES OF AMERICA, Indian Territory,
Southern   DISTRICT.

I, Sally Goins , on oath state that I am 18 years of age and a citizen ~~by~~ of the United States —— —— ~~Nation~~; that I am the lawful wife of Charley Calvin Goins , who is a citizen, by blood of the Chickasaw Nation; that a male child was born to me on 27 day of July , 1904; that said child has been named Charles Reuben Goins , and was living March 4, 1905.

Sally Goins

Witnesses To Mark:
{

Subscribed and sworn to before me this 5th day of April , 1905

O H Loomis
Notary Public.

AFFIDAVIT OF ATTENDING PHYSICIAN OR MID-WIFE.

UNITED STATES OF AMERICA, Indian Territory,
Southern   DISTRICT.

I, J. H. Colby , a physician , on oath state that I attended on Mrs. Sally Goins , wife of Charles Calvin Goins on the 27 day of July , 1904; that there was born to her on said date a male child; that said child was living March 4, 1905, and is said to have been named Charley Reuben Goins

J.H. Colby M.D.

Witnesses To Mark:
{

Applications for Enrollment of Chickasaw Newborn
Act of 1905 Volume IV

Subscribed and sworn to before me this 5th day of April , 1905

O H Loomis
Notary Public.

Marriage Certificate

Territory of Oklahoma, Cleveland County, ss.

THIS IS TO CERTIFY THAT I, THE UNDERSIGNED, DID, ON THE 24th DAY OF September , A. D. 190 2 , JOIN IN MARRIAGE, ACCORDING TO THE LAWS OF SAID TERRITORY, Charles C. Goins AND Miss Sallie Goins IN THE PRESENCE OF W.L. Goins AND S. Goins , OF Chickasaw Nation AS WITNESSES THERETO.

GIVEN UNDER MY HAND THIS 24th DAY OF September A. D. 190 2

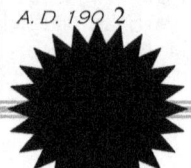

Charles L. Botsford
Probate Judge

9-1301

Muskogee, Indian Territory, April 10, 1905.

J. F. Sharp,
    Attorney at Law,
        Purcell, Indian Territory.

Dear Sir:

    Receipt is hereby acknowledged of your letter of April 5, 1905, enclosing the affidavits of Sally Goins and Susan Goins to the birth of Josephine Lucy Goins, daughter of Charles Calvin and Sally Goins, February 7, 1903; also affidavits of Sally Goins and J. H. Colby to the birth of Charles Reuben Goins, son of Charles Calvin and Sally Goins, July 27, 1904, and the same have been filed with our records as an application for the enrollment of said child.

Respectfully,

Commissioner in Charge.

Applications for Enrollment of Chickasaw Newborn
Act of 1905 Volume IV

COMMISSIONERS:
TAMS BIXBY,
THOMAS B. NEEDLES,
C.R. BRECKINBRIDGE.

WM. O. BEALL
Secretary

DEPARTMENT OF THE INTERIOR,
COMMISSIONER TO THE FIVE CIVILIZED TRIBES.

$W^m O.B.$

REFER IN REPLY TO THE FOLLOWING:

9 N B 300

ADDRESS ONLY THE
COMMISSION TO THE FIVE CIVILIZED TRIBES.

Muskogee, Indian Territory, April 17, 1905.

Charles Calvin Goins,
   Purcell, Indian Territory.

Dear Sir:

    You are hereby advised that before the applications for the enrollment of your infant children, Josephine Lucy Goins and Charles Reuben Goins, can be finally disposed of, it will be necessary that you furnish the original or a certified copy of the license and certificate of your marriage to their mother, Sally Goins.

    Please give this matter your immediate attention.

                Respectfully,
                    Tams Bixby
                          Chairman.

9 NB 300

Muskogee, Indian Territory, April 26, 1905.

Charles Calvin Goins,
   Purcell, Indian Territory.

Dear Sir:

    Receipt is hereby acknowledged of the marriage license and certificate between Charles C. Goins and Sallie Goins which you offer in support of the application for the enrollment of your children, Charles R. and Josephine Goins and the same has been filed with the records in this case.

                Respectfully,

                          Chairman.

Applications for Enrollment of Chickasaw Newborn
Act of 1905 Volume IV

Chic. N.B. - 301
    (Lena May True
    Born April 22, 1903)
    (Lottie Belle True
    Born February 5, 1905)

BIRTH AFFIDAVIT.

DEPARTMENT OF THE INTERIOR.
COMMISSION TO THE FIVE CIVILIZED TRIBES.

IN RE APPLICATION FOR ENROLLMENT, as a citizen of the Chickasaw Nation, of Lena May True, born on the 22nd day of April, 1903

Name of Father: John L. True   a citizen of the United States Nation.

Name of Mother: Melinda Alzina True *nee Goins*   a citizen of the Chickasaw Nation.

Postoffice   Purcell, I.T.

AFFIDAVIT OF MOTHER.

UNITED STATES OF AMERICA, Indian Territory,
   Southern   DISTRICT.

    I, Melinda Alzina True *nee Goins*, on oath state that I am 20 years of age and a citizen by Blood, of the Chickasaw Nation; that I am the lawful wife of John L True, who is a citizen, by —— of the United States ~~Nation~~; that a Female child was born to me on 22nd day of April, 1903, that said child has been named Lena May True, and is now living.

     Signature   Melinda Alzina True nee Goins
Witnesses To ~~Mark~~:
  { M.R. Pugh
     O.H. Loomis

    Subscribed and sworn to before me this 8th day of March, 1905.

                               O.H. Loomis
                               Notary Public.

Applications for Enrollment of Chickasaw Newborn
Act of 1905   Volume IV

AFFIDAVIT OF ATTENDING PHYSICIAN OR MID-WIFE.

UNITED STATES OF AMERICA, Indian Territory, }
  Southern   DISTRICT.

I, Susan Goins, a Mid-wife, on oath state that I attended on Mrs. Melinda Alzina True nee Goins, wife of John L True on the 22nd day of April, 1903; that there was born to her on said date a Female child; that said child is now living and is said to have been named Lena May True

Susan Goins

Witnesses To Mark:
{ M.R. Pugh
  O.H. Loomis

Subscribed and sworn to before me this 8th day of March, 1905.

O.H. Loomis
Notary Public.

BIRTH AFFIDAVIT.

DEPARTMENT OF THE INTERIOR.
COMMISSION TO THE FIVE CIVILIZED TRIBES.

IN RE APPLICATION FOR ENROLLMENT, as a citizen of the Chickasaw Nation, of Lottie Belle True, born on the 7th day of February, 1905

Name of Father: John L. True   a citizen of the United States Nation.

nee Goins

Name of Mother: Melinda Alzina True   a citizen of the Chickasaw Nation.

Postoffice   Purcell, I.T.

AFFIDAVIT OF MOTHER.

UNITED STATES OF AMERICA, Indian Territory, }
  Southern   DISTRICT.

I, Mrs Melinda Alzina True *nee Goins*, on oath state that I am 20 years of age and a citizen by Blood, of the Chickasaw Nation; that I am the lawful wife of John L True, who is a citizen, by ....of the United States ~~Nation~~; that a Female child was born to me on 7th day of February, 1905, that said child has been named Lottie Belle True, and is now living.

186

Applications for Enrollment of Chickasaw Newborn
Act of 1905   Volume IV

Signature   Melinda Alzina True nee Goins
Witnesses To ~~Mark~~:
{ M.R. Pugh
{ O.H. Loomis

     Subscribed and sworn to before me this 8th day of March , 1905.

                                   O.H. Loomis
                                   Notary Public.

AFFIDAVIT OF ATTENDING PHYSICIAN OR MID-WIFE.

UNITED STATES OF AMERICA, Indian Territory, }
    Southern   DISTRICT. }

     I, Susan Goins , a Mid-wife , on oath state that I attended on Mrs. Melinda Alzina True nee Goins , wife of John L True on the 7th day of February , 1905; that there was born to her on said date a Female child; that said child is now living and is said to have been named Lottie Belle True

Signature   Susan Goins
Witnesses To ~~Mark~~:
{ M.R. Pugh
{ O.H. Loomis

     Subscribed and sworn to before me this 8th day of February[sic] , 1905.

                                   O.H. Loomis
                                   Notary Public.

                                                 9-1301

                Muskogee, Indian Territory, March 13, 1905.

J. L. True,
     Purcell, Indian Territory.

Dear Sir:

     Receipt is hereby acknowledged of the affidavits of Melinda Alzina True and Susan Goins to the birth of Lena May True and Lottie Belle True, children of John L. and Melinda Alzina True nee Goins, April 22, 1903, and February 7, 1905, respectively, and the same have been filed with our records as an application for the enrollment of said child.

Applications for Enrollment of Chickasaw Newborn
Act of 1905   Volume IV

Respectfully,

Chairman.

Chic. N.B. - 302
    (Bessie Annie Godfrey
    Born November 24, 1904)
    (Addie Mary Godfrey
    Born November 11, 1902)

BIRTH AFFIDAVIT.

DEPARTMENT OF THE INTERIOR.
COMMISSION TO THE FIVE CIVILIZED TRIBES.

IN RE APPLICATION FOR ENROLLMENT, as a citizen of the   Chickasaw   Nation, of   Bessie Annie Godfrey   , born on the 24th day of   November , 1904

Name of Father: Ed Godfrey   a citizen of the Non Citizen Nation.
Name of Mother: Annie Godfrey   a citizen of the Chickasaw Nation.

Postoffice   Kiowa, Ind. Ter.

AFFIDAVIT OF MOTHER.

UNITED STATES OF AMERICA, Indian Territory,
    Central   DISTRICT.

I, Annie Godfrey , on oath state that I am 22 years of age and a citizen by   Blood , of the   Chickasaw   Nation; that I am the lawful wife of   Ed Godfrey , who is a citizen, by .... of the   Non-Citizen   ~~Nation~~; that a   Female   child was born to me on 24th day of November , 1904; that said child has been named   Bessie Annie Godfrey , and was living March 4, 1905.

Annie Godfrey

Witnesses To Mark:

Subscribed and sworn to before me this 5th day of   April   , 1905

My commission expires
Feb 28, 1907

WA Foyil
    Notary Public.

Applications for Enrollment of Chickasaw Newborn
Act of 1905   Volume IV

AFFIDAVIT OF ATTENDING PHYSICIAN OR MID-WIFE.

UNITED STATES OF AMERICA, Indian Territory, }
  Central   DISTRICT.

    I,   Lee W. McMorries   , a   Physician   , on oath state that I attended on Mrs.   Annie Godfrey   , wife of   Ed Godfrey   on the 24th day of   November , 1904; that there was born to her on said date a   Female   child; that said child was living March 4, 1905, and is said to have been named   Bessie Annie Godfrey

                                          Lee W McMorries

Witnesses To Mark:

{

    Subscribed and sworn to before me this 5th day of   April   , 1905

My commission expires
Feb 28-1907
                                    WA Foyil
                                    Notary Public.

AFFIDAVIT OF MOTHER.

UNITED STATES OF AMERICA, }
  INDIAN TERRITORY,
  Central   District.

    I,   Annie Godfrey   , on oath state that I am   20   years of age and a citizen by   blood   , of the   Chickasaw   Nation; that I am the lawful wife of   Ed Godfrey   , who is a citizen, by Marriage of the   Chickasaw   Nation; that a   female   child was born to me on   11   day of   November   , 1902 , that said child has been named   Addie Mary Godfrey   , and is now living.

                                      her
                                 Annie x Godfrey
WITNESSES TO MARK: mark
{ E.E. Davis
  R E McDaniel

    Subscribed and sworn to before me this   22 day of   May , 1903

                                    H B Rowley
                                    NOTARY PUBLIC.

Applications for Enrollment of Chickasaw Newborn
Act of 1905   Volume IV

AFFIDAVIT OF ATTENDING PHYSICIAN OR MID-WIFE.

UNITED STATES OF AMERICA,
   INDIAN TERRITORY,
   Central   District.

I, Addie Godfrey, a midwife, on oath state that I attended on Mrs. Annie Godfrey, wife of Ed Godfrey on the 11 day of November, 1902; that there was born to her on said date a female child; that said child is now living and is said to have been named Addie Mary Godfrey

                        Addie Godfrey

WITNESSES TO MARK:

Subscribed and sworn to before me this 22 day of May, 1903

                        H B Rowley
                              NOTARY PUBLIC.

BIRTH AFFIDAVIT.

DEPARTMENT OF THE INTERIOR.
COMMISSION TO THE FIVE CIVILIZED TRIBES.

IN RE APPLICATION FOR ENROLLMENT, as a citizen of the Chickasaw Nation, of Addie Mary Godfrey, born on the 11th day of November, 1902

Name of Father: Ed Godfrey   a citizen of the Non Citizen Nation.
Name of Mother: Annie Godfrey   a citizen of the Chickasaw Nation.

                Postoffice   Kiowa, Ind. Ter.

AFFIDAVIT OF MOTHER.

UNITED STATES OF AMERICA, Indian Territory,
   Central   **DISTRICT.**

I, Annie Godfrey, on oath state that I am 22 years of age and a citizen by Blood, of the Chickasaw Nation; that I am the lawful wife of Ed Godfrey, who is ~~a citizen, by~~ of the Non-Citizen Nation; that a Female child was born to me on 11th day of November, 1902; that said child has been named Addie Mary Godfrey, and was living March 4, 1905.

                        Annie Godfrey

Applications for Enrollment of Chickasaw Newborn
Act of 1905   Volume IV

Witnesses To Mark:

{

Subscribed and sworn to before me this 5th   day of   April   , 1905

My commission expires   WA Foyil
Feb 28th 1907   Notary Public.

AFFIDAVIT OF ATTENDING PHYSICIAN OR MID-WIFE.

UNITED STATES OF AMERICA, Indian Territory, }
   Central   DISTRICT.

I,   Lee W. McMorries   , a   Physician   , on oath state that I attended on Mrs.   Annie Godfrey   , wife of   Ed Godfrey   on the 11th   day of   November , 1902; that there was born to her on said date a   Female   child; that said child was living March 4, 1905, and is said to have been named   Addie Mary Godfrey

Lee W McMorries

Witnesses To Mark:

{

Subscribed and sworn to before me this 5th   day of   April   , 1905

My commission expires   WA Foyil
Feb 28-1907   Notary Public.

9-1089

Muskogee, Indian Territory, April 10, 1905.

Ed Godfrey,
   Kiowa, Indian Territory.

Dear Sir:

Receipt is hereby acknowledged of the affidavits of Annie Godfrey and Lee W. McMorries to the birth of Bessie Annie Godfrey and Addie Mary Godfrey, children of Ed and Annie Godfrey, November 24, 1904, and November 11, 1902, and the same have been filed with our records as an application for the enrollment of said child.

Respectfully,

Commissioner in Charge.

Applications for Enrollment of Chickasaw Newborn
Act of 1905   Volume IV

Chic. N.B. - 303
   (Edith Audrey Tinsley
   Born December 25, 1903)

BIRTH AFFIDAVIT.

DEPARTMENT OF THE INTERIOR.
COMMISSION TO THE FIVE CIVILIZED TRIBES.

IN RE APPLICATION FOR ENROLLMENT, as a citizen of the   Chickasaw   Nation, of   Edith Audrey Tinsley   , born on the 25th day of December , 1903

Name of Father: Vester T Tinsley   a citizen of the .... Nation.
Name of Mother: Eula Tinsley (nee Barker)   a citizen of the   Chickasaw   Nation.

Postoffice   Yuba I.T.

AFFIDAVIT OF MOTHER.

UNITED STATES OF AMERICA, Indian Territory, }
   Central   DISTRICT. }

I,   Eula Tinsley nee Barker   , on oath state that I am   21   years of age and a citizen by   Blood   , of the   Chickasaw   Nation; that I am the lawful wife of Vester T Tinsley   , who is a citizen, by mariag[sic]   of the   Chickasaw   Nation; that a   Girl   child was born to me on 25 day of   December   , 1903; that said child has been named   Edith Audrey Tinsley   , and was living March 4, 1905.

                    Eula Tinsley
Witnesses To Mark:
{

Subscribed and sworn to before me this 3 day of April   , 1905

                    Chas P Walker
                    Notary Public.

AFFIDAVIT OF ATTENDING PHYSICIAN OR MID-WIFE.

UNITED STATES OF AMERICA, Indian Territory, }
   Central   DISTRICT. }

I,   C. O. Lively   , a Physician   , on oath state that I attended on Mrs.   Eula Tinsley nee Barker   , wife of   V.T. Tinsley   on the   25   day of

Applications for Enrollment of Chickasaw Newborn
Act of 1905 Volume IV

December   , 1903; that there was born to her on said date a   female   child; that said child was living March 4, 1905, and is said to have been named Edith Audrey Tinsley

C.O. Lively M.D.

Witnesses To Mark:
{

  Subscribed and sworn to before me this 31st day of   March   , 1905

P.L. Cain
Notary Public.

9-1090

Muskogee, Indian Territory, April 10, 1905.

Vester T. Tinsley,
  Yuba, Indian Territory.

Dear Sir:

  Receipt is hereby acknowledged of the affidavits of Eula Tinsley and C. O. Lively to the birth of Edith Audrey Tinsley, daughter of Vester F[sic] and Eula Tinsley, December 25, 1905[sic], and the same have been filed with our records as an application for the enrollment of said child.

Respectfully,

Commissioner in Charge.

Chic. N.B. - 304
  (Frances May McGill
  Born May 13, 1903)

Applications for Enrollment of Chickasaw Newborn
Act of 1905   Volume IV

BIRTH AFFIDAVIT.

DEPARTMENT OF THE INTERIOR.
COMMISSION TO THE FIVE CIVILIZED TRIBES.

IN RE APPLICATION FOR ENROLLMENT, as a citizen of the Chickasaw Nation, of Frances May McGill , born on the 13 day of May , 1903

Name of Father: Noah McGill   a citizen of the Chickasaw Nation.
Name of Mother: Eliza McGill   a citizen of the Chickasaw Nation.

Postoffice   Tishomingo I.T.

AFFIDAVIT OF MOTHER.

UNITED STATES OF AMERICA, Indian Territory,
    Southern   DISTRICT.

I, Eliza McGill , on oath state that I am about 40 years of age and a citizen by blood , of the Chickasaw Nation; that I am the lawful wife of Noah McGill , who is a citizen, by blood of the Chickasaw Nation; that a Female child was born to me on 13 day of May , 1903; that said child has been named Frances May McGill , and was living March 4, 1905.

Eliza McGill

Witnesses To Mark:
 { Rosa McGill
   Mach McGill

Subscribed and sworn to before me this 6 day of April , 1905

W.M. Lucas
Notary Public.

AFFIDAVIT OF ATTENDING PHYSICIAN OR MID-WIFE.

UNITED STATES OF AMERICA, Indian Territory,
    Southern   DISTRICT.

I, Mary Herring , a mid-wife , on oath state that I attended on Mrs. Eliza McGill , wife of Noah McGill on the 13 day of May , 1903; that there was born to her on said date a Female child; that said child was living March 4, 1905, and is said to have been named Frances May McGill

her
Mary   x   Herring
mark

Applications for Enrollment of Chickasaw Newborn
Act of 1905 Volume IV

Witnesses To Mark:
  { W F Herring
  { Hugh Herring

  Subscribed and sworn to before me this 6 day of   April   , 1905

W.M. Lucas
Notary Public.

9-920

Muskogee, Indian Territory, April 10, 1905.

Noah McGill,
  Tishomingo, Indian Territory.

Dear Sir:

  Receipt is hereby acknowledged of the affidavits of Eliza McGill and Mary Herring to the birth of Frances Mary McGill daughter of Noah and Eliza McGill, May 13, 1903, and the same have been filed with our records as an application for the enrollment of said child.

Respectfully,

Commissioner in Charge.

Chic. N.B. - 305
  (Daisy Monette Byrd
  Born February 26, 1903)

BIRTH AFFIDAVIT.

DEPARTMENT OF THE INTERIOR.
COMMISSION TO THE FIVE CIVILIZED TRIBES.

IN RE APPLICATION FOR ENROLLMENT, as a citizen of the Chickasaw Nation, of Daisy Monette , born on the 26 day of Feb , 1903

Name of Father: Benj. F Byrd   a citizen of the Chickasaw Nation.
Name of Mother: Mamie E. Byrd   a citizen of the Chickasaw Nation.

Postoffice   Franks, Ind. Ter.

Applications for Enrollment of Chickasaw Newborn
Act of 1905 Volume IV

AFFIDAVIT OF MOTHER.

UNITED STATES OF AMERICA, Indian Territory, }
    Sou   DISTRICT. }

    I, Mamie E. Byrd, on oath state that I am thirty nine years of age and a citizen by blood, of the Chickasaw Nation; that I am the lawful wife of Benj. F. Byrd, who is a citizen, by blood of the Chickasaw Nation; that a female child was born to me on 26th day of Feby, 1903; that said child has been named Daisy Monette Byrd, and was living March 4, 1905.

                              Mamie E. Byrd

Witnesses To Mark:
{

    Subscribed and sworn to before me this 3rd day of April, 1905

                              W.H. Burdeshaw
                                  Notary Public.

AFFIDAVIT OF ATTENDING PHYSICIAN OR MID-WIFE.

UNITED STATES OF AMERICA, Indian Territory, }
    Sou   DISTRICT. }

    I, Victoria Schiele, a Midwife, on oath state that I attended on Mrs. Mamie Byrd, wife of B. F. Byrd on the 26 day of Feb, 1903; that there was born to her on said date a female child; that said child was living March 4, 1905, and is said to have been named Daisy Monette

                              Victoria Schiele

Witnesses To Mark:
{

    Subscribed and sworn to before me this 3 day of April, 1905

                              W.H. Burdeshaw
                                  Notary Public.

Applications for Enrollment of Chickasaw Newborn
Act of 1905   Volume IV

No 60

BIRTH AFFIDAVIT.

DEPARTMENT OF THE INTERIOR.
COMMISSION TO THE FIVE CIVILIZED TRIBES.

IN RE APPLICATION FOR ENROLLMENT, as a citizen of the   Chickasaw   Nation, of   Daisy Monette Byrd   , born on the   26   day of   Feb   , 1903

Name of Father: B. F. Byrd   a citizen of the   Chickasaw   Nation.
Name of Mother: Mamie Byrd   a citizen of the   Chickasaw   Nation.

Postoffice   Franks

AFFIDAVIT OF MOTHER.

UNITED STATES OF AMERICA, Indian Territory,
Southern   DISTRICT.

I,   Mamie Byrd   , on oath state that I am   39   years of age and a citizen by blood   , of the   Chickasaw   Nation; that I am the lawful wife of   B. F. Byrd   , who is a citizen, by   blood   of the   Chickasaw   Nation; that a   female   child was born to me on   26   day of   Feb   , 1903, that said child has been named   Daisy Monette Byrd   , and is now living.

Mamie E Byrd

Witnesses To Mark:

Subscribed and sworn to before me this   31   day of   Dec.   , 1904

W.H. Burdeshaw
Notary Public.

AFFIDAVIT OF ATTENDING PHYSICIAN OR MID-WIFE.

UNITED STATES OF AMERICA, Indian Territory,
Southern   DISTRICT.

I,   Victoria Schiele   , a   Midwife   , on oath state that I attended on Mrs.   Mamie Byrd   , wife of   B F Byrd   on the   26   day of   Feb   , 1903; that there was born to her on said date a   female   child; that said child is now living and is said to have been named   Daisy Monette Byrd

Victoria Schiele

Applications for Enrollment of Chickasaw Newborn
Act of 1905   Volume IV

Witnesses To Mark:

{

Subscribed and sworn to before me this 31st day of   Dec. , 1904

W.H. Burdeshaw
Notary Public.

9-499

Muskogee, Indian Territory, April 11, 1905.

B. F. Byrd,
Franks, Indian Territory.

Dear Sir:

Receipt is hereby acknowledged of your letter of April 3, 1905, enclosing affidavits of Mamie E. Byrd and Victoria Schule[sic] to the birth of Daisy Monette Byrd, daughter of Benjamin F. and Mamie E. Byrd, February 26, 1903, and the same have been filed with our records as an application for the enrollment of said child.

Replying to that portion of your letter in which you ask if it will be necessary for you to present a blank similar to the one enclosed by you to the Choctaw Enrolling party at Ada, you are advised that it will not be necessary for you to appear before the enrolling party unless you so desire. If further evidence is necessary to determine the right of your child to enrollment you will be duly notified.

Respectfully,

Commissioner in Charge.

Chic. N.B. - 306
    (Viola Iona Harden
    Born May 18, 1903)

Applications for Enrollment of Chickasaw Newborn
Act of 1905   Volume IV

BIRTH AFFIDAVIT.

DEPARTMENT OF THE INTERIOR.
COMMISSION TO THE FIVE CIVILIZED TRIBES.

IN RE APPLICATION FOR ENROLLMENT, as a citizen of the   Chickasaw   Nation, of   Viola Iona   , born on the   18   day of   May   , 1903

Name of Father: Andrew J Harden   a citizen of the   Chickasaw   Nation.
Name of Mother: Elizabeth Harden   a citizen of the   Chickasaw   Nation.

Postoffice   Franks

AFFIDAVIT OF MOTHER.

UNITED STATES OF AMERICA, Indian Territory,
    Sou   DISTRICT.

I,   Elizabeth Harden   , on oath state that I am   38   years of age and a citizen by   blood   , of the   Chickasaw   Nation; that I am the lawful wife of   Andrew J Harden   , who is a citizen, by   intermarriage   of the   Chickasaw   Nation; that a   female   child was born to me on   18   day of   May   , 1903, that said child has been named   Viola Iona   , and is now living.

Elizabeth Harden

Witnesses To Mark:
{

Subscribed and sworn to before me this   3rd day of   Apr   , 1905.

W.H. Burdeshaw
Notary Public.

AFFIDAVIT OF ATTENDING PHYSICIAN OR MID-WIFE.

UNITED STATES OF AMERICA, Indian Territory,
    Sou   DISTRICT.

I,   J S Keener   , a Physician   , on oath state that I attended on Mrs.   Elizabeth Harden   , wife of   A. J. Harden   on the   18   day of May , 1903; that there was born to her on said date a   female   child; that said child is now living and is said to have been named Viola Iona

J.S. Keener

Witnesses To Mark:
{

Applications for Enrollment of Chickasaw Newborn
Act of 1905 Volume IV

Subscribed and sworn to before me this 3rd day of Apr , 1905.

W.H. Burdeshaw
Notary Public.

9-1746

Muskogee, Indian Territory, April 11, 1905.

Andrew J. Harden,
    Franks, Indian Territory.

Dear Sir:

    Receipt is hereby acknowledged of your letter of April 3, 1905, enclosing affidavits of Elizabeth Hardin[sic] and J. S. Keener to the birth of Viola Iona Hardin daughter of Andrew and Elizabeth Hardin, May 18, 1903, and the same have been filed with our records as an application for the enrollment of said child.

Respectfully,

Commissioner in Charge.

Chic. N.B. - 307
    (Mickie or Mica Stout
    Born April 22, 1904)

BIRTH AFFIDAVIT. *47*

DEPARTMENT OF THE INTERIOR.
COMMISSION TO THE FIVE CIVILIZED TRIBES.

IN RE APPLICATION FOR ENROLLMENT, as a citizen of the Chickasaw Nation, of Mickie Stout , born on the 22nd day of April , 1904

Name of Father: Jeff Stout   a citizen of the Chickasaw Nation.
Name of Mother: Tennie Stout   a citizen of the Chickasaw Nation.

Postoffice   Franks

Applications for Enrollment of Chickasaw Newborn
Act of 1905 Volume IV

AFFIDAVIT OF MOTHER.

UNITED STATES OF AMERICA, Indian Territory,
Southern DISTRICT.

I, Tennie Stout, on oath state that I am 32 years of age and a citizen by blood, of the Chickasaw Nation; that I am the lawful wife of Jeff Stout, who is a citizen, by blood of the Chickasaw Nation; that a female child was born to me on 22nd day of April, 1904, that said child has been named Mickie Stout, and is now living.

                                                              her
Witnesses To Mark: Tennie x Stout
  { J.W. Wallace   mark
  { R P Dudley

Subscribed and sworn to before me this 20 day of Dec, 1904

                                    W.H. Burdeshaw
                                      Notary Public.

AFFIDAVIT OF ATTENDING PHYSICIAN OR MID-WIFE.

UNITED STATES OF AMERICA, Indian Territory,
Southern DISTRICT.

I, Mandy Cohee, a midwife, on oath state that I attended on Mrs. Tennie Stout, wife of Jeff Stout on the 22nd day of April, 1904; that there was born to her on said date a female child; that said child is now living and is said to have been named Mickie Stout

                                                              her
                                                 Mandy x Cohee
Witnesses To Mark: mark
  { J.W. Wallace
  { R P Dudley

Subscribed and sworn to before me this 20 day of Dec, 1904

                                    W.H. Burdeshaw
                                      Notary Public.

Applications for Enrollment of Chickasaw Newborn
Act of 1905 Volume IV

BIRTH AFFIDAVIT.

DEPARTMENT OF THE INTERIOR.
COMMISSION TO THE FIVE CIVILIZED TRIBES.

IN RE APPLICATION FOR ENROLLMENT, as a citizen of the Chickasaw Nation, of Mica Stout, born on the 22nd day of April, 1904

Name of Father: Jeff Stout   a citizen of the Chickasaw Nation.
Name of Mother: Tennie Stout   a citizen of the Chickasaw Nation.

Postoffice Franks

AFFIDAVIT OF MOTHER.

UNITED STATES OF AMERICA, Indian Territory,
Sou   DISTRICT.

I, Tennie Stout, on oath state that I am 34 years of age and a citizen by blood, of the Chickasaw Nation; that I am the lawful wife of Jeff Stout, who is a citizen, by blood of the Chickasaw Nation; that a female child was born to me on 22nd day of April, 1904; that said child has been named Mica, and was living March 4, 1905.

                                                       her
                                          Tennie x Stout
Witnesses To Mark: mark
    Jim Carpenter
    J.P. Hodges

Subscribed and sworn to before me this 6 day of April, 1905

                                         W.H. Burdeshaw
                                         Notary Public.

AFFIDAVIT OF ATTENDING PHYSICIAN OR MID-WIFE.

UNITED STATES OF AMERICA, Indian Territory,
Sou   DISTRICT.

I, Elsie Porter, a midwife, on oath state that I attended on Mrs. Tennie Stout, wife of Jeff Stout on the 22nd day of April, 1904; that there was born to her on said date a female child; that said child was living March 4, 1905, and is said to have been named Mica

                                                her
                                       Elsie x Porter
                                           mark

Applications for Enrollment of Chickasaw Newborn
Act of 1905 Volume IV

Witnesses To Mark:
- Jim Carpenter
- J.P. Hodges

Subscribed and sworn to before me this 6 day of April , 1905

W.H. Burdeshaw
Notary Public.

9-95

Muskogee, Indian Territory, April 11, 1905.

Jeff Stout,
    Franks, Indian Territory.

Dear Sir:

    Receipt is hereby acknowledged of the affidavits of Tennie Stout and Elsie Porter to the birth of Mica Stout, daughter of Jeff and Tennie Stout, April 22, 1904, and the same have been filed with our records as an application for the enrollment of said child.

Respectfully,

Commissioner in Charge.

Chic. N.B. - 308
(Thomas Errol Bates
Born January 8, 1903)
(Orman Leycester Bates
Born December 2, 1904)

Applications for Enrollment of Chickasaw Newborn
Act of 1905 Volume IV

BIRTH AFFIDAVIT.

#94

IN RE-APPLICATION FOR ENROLLMENT, as a citizen of the   Chickasaw   Nation, of   Thomas Errol Bates   , born on the Eighth ^{8} day of January , 190 3

Name of Father: William A. Bates   a citizen of the   Chickasaw   Nation.
Name of Mother: M. Pearle Bates   a citizen of the   Chickasaw   Nation.

Postoffice   Robber Roost I.T.

AFFIDAVIT OF MOTHER.

UNITED STATES OF AMERICA, INDIAN TERRITORY,
  Central   District.

I,   M Pearle Bates   , on oath state that I am Twenty two ^{22} years of age and a citizen by   Blood   , of the   Chickasaw   Nation; that I am the lawful wife of   William A Bates   , who is a citizen, by   Blood   of the   Chickasaw   Nation; that a   Male   child was born to me on Eighth ^{8th} day of   January , 1903 , that said child has been named   Thomas Errol Bates   , and is now living.

M Pearle Bates

Witnesses To Mark:
  { J M Sharp
  { Lillie Sharp

Subscribed and sworn to before me this 13th day of   February   , 1905.

C.T. Luttrell
Notary Public.

AFFIDAVIT OF ATTENDING PHYSICIAN OR MID-WIFE.

UNITED STATES OF AMERICA, INDIAN TERRITORY,
  Central   District.

I,   G.W. Green   , a   Physician   , on oath state that I attended on Mrs.   M. Pearle Bates   , wife of   William A Bates   on the ^{8th} Eighth day of   January , 190 3; that there was born to her on said date a   Male   child; that said child is now living and is said to have been named   Thomas Errol Bates

G.W. Green M.D.

Witnesses To Mark:
  { J M Sharp
  { Lillie Sharp

Applications for Enrollment of Chickasaw Newborn
Act of 1905   Volume IV

Subscribed and sworn to before me this 13th day of February , 1905.

C.T. Luttrell
Notary Public.

BIRTH AFFIDAVIT.

Department of the Interior,
COMMISSION TO THE FIVE CIVILIZED TRIBES.

IN RE APPLICATION FOR ENROLLMENT, as a citizen of the Chickasaw Nation, of Orman Leycester Bates , born on the 2nd day of Dec , 190 4

Name of Father: William A Bates   a citizen of the Chickasaw Nation.
Name of Mother: M. Pearle Bates   a citizen of the Chickasaw Nation.

Post-Office: Robbers Roost I.T.

AFFIDAVIT OF MOTHER.

UNITED STATES OF AMERICA, ⎫
   INDIAN TERRITORY, ⎬
  Central   District. ⎭

I, M. Pearle Bates , on oath state that I am 22 years of age and a citizen by Blood , of the Chickasaw Nation; that I am the lawful wife of William A. Bates , who is a citizen, by Blood of the Chickasaw Nation; that a Male child was born to me on 2nd day of Dec , 190 4, that said child has been named Orman Leycester Bates , and is now living.

M. Pearle Bates

WITNESSES TO MARK:
  { J W Brown
    L F Brown

Subscribed and sworn to before me this 23rd day of February , 190 5

C.T. Luttrell
Notary Public.

Applications for Enrollment of Chickasaw Newborn
Act of 1905   Volume IV

AFFIDAVIT OF ATTENDING PHYSICIAN OR MID-WIFE.

UNITED STATES OF AMERICA,
INDIAN TERRITORY,
Central   District.

I,   Mrs Emma Bates   , a Midwife   , on oath state that I attended on Mrs.   M Pearle Bates   , wife of   William A. Bates   on the 2nd day of   Dec   , 1904 ; that there was born to her on said date a   Male   child; that said child is now living and is said to have been named   Orman Leycester Bates

Emma Bates

WITNESSES TO MARK:
{ D.H. Hanna
  Fannie Luttrell

Subscribed and sworn to before me this 23rd day of   February   , 190 5

C.T. Luttrell
Notary Public.

BIRTH AFFIDAVIT.

DEPARTMENT OF THE INTERIOR.
COMMISSION TO THE FIVE CIVILIZED TRIBES.

IN RE APPLICATION FOR ENROLLMENT, as a citizen of the   Chickasaw   Nation, of   Thomas Errol Bates   , born on the   8   day of   Jan   , 1903

Name of Father: William A Bates   a citizen of the   Chickasaw   Nation.
Name of Mother: M. Pearle Bates   a citizen of the   Chickasaw   Nation.

Postoffice   Robbers Roost, I.T.

AFFIDAVIT OF MOTHER.

UNITED STATES OF AMERICA, Indian Territory,
Central   DISTRICT.

I,   M. Pearle Bates   , on oath state that I am   22   years of age and a citizen by   blood   , of the   Chickasaw   Nation; that I am the lawful wife of   William A. Bates   , who is a citizen, by blood   of the   Chickasaw   Nation; that a male   child was born to me on   8   day of   Jan   , 1903; that said child has been named   Thomas Errol Bates   , and was living March 4, 1905.

M. Pearle Bates

Applications for Enrollment of Chickasaw Newborn
Act of 1905 Volume IV

Witnesses To Mark:
{ Dot Godfrey
  May Bates

Subscribed and sworn to before me this 8 day of April , 1905

F M Kizer
Notary Public.

AFFIDAVIT OF ATTENDING PHYSICIAN OR MID-WIFE.

UNITED STATES OF AMERICA, Indian Territory, }
Central DISTRICT. }

I, G.W. Greene , a Physician , on oath state that I attended on Mrs. M. Pearle Bates , wife of William A. Bates on the 8 day of Jan , 1903; that there was born to her on said date a male child; that said child was living March 4, 1905, and is said to have been named Thomas Errol Bates

G.W. Greene, M.D.

Witnesses To Mark:
{

Subscribed and sworn to before me this 10 day of April , 1905

F M Kizer
Notary Public.

BIRTH AFFIDAVIT.

DEPARTMENT OF THE INTERIOR.
COMMISSION TO THE FIVE CIVILIZED TRIBES.

IN RE APPLICATION FOR ENROLLMENT, as a citizen of the Chickasaw Nation, of Orman Leycester Bates , born on the 2nd day of December , 1904

Name of Father: William A Bates   a citizen of the Chickasaw Nation.
Name of Mother: M. Pearle Bates   a citizen of the Chickasaw Nation.

Postoffice   Robbers Roost, I.T.

Applications for Enrollment of Chickasaw Newborn
Act of 1905   Volume IV

AFFIDAVIT OF MOTHER.

UNITED STATES OF AMERICA, Indian Territory, }
    Central   DISTRICT.

I,   M. Pearle Bates   , on oath state that I am   22   years of age and a citizen by   Blood   , of the   Chickasaw   Nation; that I am the lawful wife of   William A. Bates   , who is a citizen, by Blood   of the   Chickasaw   Nation; that a   Male   child was born to me on   2nd day of   December   , 1904; that said child has been named   Orman Leycester Bates   , and was living March 4, 1905.

M. Pearle Bates

Witnesses To Mark:
{

Subscribed and sworn to before me this   25th day of   May   , 1905

C. T. Luttrell
Notary Public.

AFFIDAVIT OF ATTENDING PHYSICIAN OR MID-WIFE.

UNITED STATES OF AMERICA, Indian Territory, }
.... DISTRICT.

I,   Mrs Emma Bates   , a   midwife   , on oath state that I attended on Mrs.   M. Pearle Bates   , wife of   William A. Bates   on the   2nd day of December   , 1904; that there was born to her on said date a   Male   child; that said child was living March 4, 1905, and is said to have been named   Orman Leycester Bates

Emma Bates

Witnesses To Mark:
{

Subscribed and sworn to before me this   25th day of   May   , 1905

C. T. Luttrell
Notary Public.

Applications for Enrollment of Chickasaw Newborn
Act of 1905   Volume IV

9-1173

Muskogee, Indian Territory, March 6, 1905.

William A. Bates,
    Robbersroost, Indian Territory.

Dear Sir:

    Receipt is hereby acknowledged of the affidavits of M. Pearle Bates and Emma Bates to the birth of Orman Leycester Bates, infant son of William A. and M. Pearle Bates, December 2, 1904, which have been filed with our records as an application for the enrollment of said child.

    Respectfully,

    Commissioner in Charge.

9-1173

Muskogee, Indian Territory, April 4, 1905.

W. A. Bates,
    Robbersroost, Indian Territory.

Dear Sir:

    Receipt is hereby acknowledged of your letter of March 30, 1905, in which you state that you forwarded certificate for one of your children to the Enrolling Commission and one you sent to this Commission direct; you therefore ask if you will have to make out application for only one of your children or for both.

    In reply to your letter you are informed that the affidavits heretofore forwarded to the birth of Orman Leycester Bates, son of William A. Bates and Mary Pearle Godfrey have been filed with our records as an application for the enrollment of said child.

    It does not appear however, that affidavits have been forwarded to the birth of another child born to you since September 25, 1902, and for your convenience there is inclosed herewith blank for the enrollment of an infant child which you should have executed and returned to this office within sixty days from March 3, 1905

    Respectfully,

B.C.   Commissioner in Charge.

Applications for Enrollment of Chickasaw Newborn
Act of 1905   Volume IV

9-1173

Muskogee, Indian Territory, April 14, 1905.

William A. Bates,
    Robbersroost, Indian Territory.

Dear Sir:

    Receipt is hereby acknowledged of the affidavits of M. Pearle Bates and G. W. Greene to the birth of Thomas Errol Bates, son of William A. and M. Pearle Bates, January 8, 1903, and the same have been filed with our records as an application for the enrollment of said child.

                    Respectfully,

                                            Chairman.

Muskogee, Indian Territory, May 16, 1905.

William A. Bates,
    Robbers Roost, Indian Territory.

Dear Sir:

    There is enclosed you herewith for execution application for the enrollment of your infant child, Orman Leycester Bates, born December 2, 1904.

    The affidavits heretofore filed with the Commission show the child was living on February 23, 1905. It is necessary, for the child to be enrolled, that he was living on March 4, 1905.

    In having these affidavits executed care should be exercised to see that all names are written in full, as they appear in the body of the affidavit, and in the event that either of the persons signing the affidavit are unable to write, signatures by mark must be attested by two witnesses. Each affidavit must be executed before a Notary Public and the notarial seal and signature of the officer must be attached to each separate affidavit.

                    Respectfully,

                                            Chairman.

V 16/10.

Applications for Enrollment of Chickasaw Newborn
Act of 1905   Volume IV

9-N.B. 308.

Muskogee, Indian Territory, May 31, 1905.

William A. Bates,
  Robbers Roost, Indian Territory.

Dear Sir:

  Receipt is hereby acknowledged of the affidavits of M. Pearle Bates and Emma Bates to the birth of Orman Leycester Bates, son of William A. and M. Pearle Bates, December 2, 1904, and the same have been filed with our records as an application for the enrollment of said child.

      Respectfully,

           Chairman.

Chic. N.B. - 309
  (Edwin Johnston Patterson
  Born December 8, 1903)

BIRTH AFFIDAVIT.

DEPARTMENT OF THE INTERIOR.
COMMISSION TO THE FIVE CIVILIZED TRIBES.

  IN RE APPLICATION FOR ENROLLMENT, as a citizen of the   Chickasaw   Nation, of   Edwin Johnston Patterson   , born on the 8th day of December , 1903

Name of Father: James E Patterson   a citizen of the   Chickasaw Nation.
Name of Mother: Mollie J Patterson   a citizen of the   Chickasaw Nation.

      Postoffice Lindsay, I.T.

AFFIDAVIT OF MOTHER.

UNITED STATES OF AMERICA, Indian Territory, }
  Southern   DISTRICT. }

  I,   Mollie J Patterson   , on oath state that I am   28   years of age and a citizen by   marriage   , of the   Chickasaw   Nation; that I am the lawful wife of James E Patterson   , who is a citizen, by   blood   of the   Chickasaw

Applications for Enrollment of Chickasaw Newborn
Act of 1905   Volume IV

Nation; that a   male   child was born to me on   the 8th day of   December   , 1903; that said child has been named   Edwin Johnston Patterson   , and was living March 4, 1905.

Mollie J Patterson

Witnesses To Mark:
{

    Subscribed and sworn to before me this 18th day of   April   , 1905

Claire L McArthur
Notary Public.

AFFIDAVIT OF ATTENDING PHYSICIAN OR MID-WIFE.

UNITED STATES OF AMERICA, Indian Territory, }
   Southern   DISTRICT.

    I,   W T Haynes   , a   physician   , on oath state that I attended on Mrs.   Mollie J Patterson   , wife of   James E Patterson   on the   8th day of December   , 1903; that there was born to her on said date a   male   child; that said child was living March 4, 1905, and is said to have been named Edwin Johnston Patterson

W T Haynes

Witnesses To Mark:
{

    Subscribed and sworn to before me this 15th day of   April   , 1905

Claire L McArthur
Notary Public.

BIRTH AFFIDAVIT.

DEPARTMENT OF THE INTERIOR,
COMMISSION TO THE FIVE CIVILIZED TRIBES.

    IN RE Application for Enrollment, as a citizen of the   Chickasaw   Nation, of   Edwin Johnson[sic] Patterson , born on the   8   day of   December   , 1903

Name of Father: James E Patterson	a citizen of the Chickasaw Nation.
Name of Mother: Mollie J Patterson	a citizen of the Chickasaw Nation.

by marriage

Post-Office: Lindsay Ind. Ter.

Applications for Enrollment of Chickasaw Newborn
Act of 1905   Volume IV

AFFIDAVIT OF MOTHER.

UNITED STATES OF AMERICA,
INDIAN TERRITORY.
Southern District   District.

I,   Mollie J Patterson   , on oath state that I am   27   years of age and a citizen by   Marriage   , of the   Chickasaw   Nation; that I am the lawful wife of   James E Patterson   , who is a citizen, by   blood   of the   Chickasaw   Nation; that a male   child was born to me on   8   day of   December   , 1903 , that said child has been named   Edwin Johnson Patterson   , and is now living.

Mollie J Patterson

WITNESSES TO MARK:

{

Subscribed and sworn to before me this   15   day of   June   , 190 4

C.L. Grimes
NOTARY PUBLIC.

AFFIDAVIT OF ATTENDING PHYSICIAN OR MID-WIFE.

UNITED STATES OF AMERICA,
INDIAN TERRITORY.
Southern   District.

I,   W F Haynes   , a   Physician   , on oath state that I attended on Mrs.   Mollie J Patterson   , wife of   James E Patterson   on the   8   day of December   , 1903 ; that there was born to her on said date a   male   child; that said child is now living and is said to have been named   Edwin Johnson Patterson

W.F. Haynes M.D.

WITNESSES TO MARK:

{

Subscribed and sworn to before me this   15   day of   June   , 190 4

C.L. Grimes
NOTARY PUBLIC.

commission expires 3/25 '07

Applications for Enrollment of Chickasaw Newborn
Act of 1905 Volume IV

9-N B 309.

Muskogee, Indian Territory, April 27, 1905.

C. L. McArthur,
    Attorney at Law,
        Lindsay, Indian Territory.

Dear Sir:

    Receipt is hereby acknowledged of your letter of April 22, 1905 transmitting affidavits of Mollie J. Patterson and W. F. Haynes to the birth of Edwin Johnston Patterson, son of James E. and Mollie J. Patterson, December 8, 1903, and the same have been filed with our records in the matter of the enrollment of said child.

Respectfully,

Chairman.

(The Birth Affidavit below does not belong with the current applicant.)

BIRTH AFFIDAVIT.

DEPARTMENT OF THE INTERIOR,
COMMISSION TO THE FIVE CIVILIZED TRIBES.

    IN RE Application for Enrollment, as a citizen of the   Chickasaw   Nation, of   Bernice Hassell , born on the   26   day of   Oct   , 1901

Name of Father: W. T. Hassell   a citizen of the United States ~~Nation~~.
Name of Mother: Willie Hassell   a citizen of the   Chickasaw   Nation.

Post-Office: Byrne I. T.

AFFIDAVIT OF MOTHER.

UNITED STATES OF AMERICA, }
    INDIAN TERRITORY.
  Central   District.

    I,   Willie Hassell   , on oath state that I am   22   years of age and a citizen by   Blood , of the Chickasaw   Nation; that I am the lawful wife of   W. T. Hassell , who is a citizen, by .... of the .... Nation; that a   Female   child

Applications for Enrollment of Chickasaw Newborn
Act of 1905 Volume IV

was born to me on   26   day of   Oct   , 1901 , that said child has been named   Bernice Hassell   , and is now living.

Willie Hassell

WITNESSES TO MARK:

{

    Subscribed and sworn to before me this   24   day of   Mch   , 190 2

E.J. Ball
NOTARY PUBLIC.

AFFIDAVIT OF ATTENDING PHYSICIAN OR MID-WIFE.

UNITED STATES OF AMERICA,   }
   INDIAN TERRITORY.
  Central   District.

    I,   Mollie Ray   , a................., on oath state that I attended on Mrs.   Willie Hassell   , wife of   W. T. Hassell   on the   26   day of Oct   , 1901 ; that there was born to her on said date a   Female   child; that said child is now living and is said to have been named   Bernice Hassell

Mollie Ray

WITNESSES TO MARK:

{

    Subscribed and sworn to before me this   24   day of   Mch   , 190 2

E.J. Ball
NOTARY PUBLIC.

Chic. N.B. - 310
    (John Westley[sic] *Casey*
    Born March 21, 1903)

Applications for Enrollment of Chickasaw Newborn
Act of 1905   Volume IV

DEPARTMENT OF THE INTERIOR,
Commission to the Five Civilized Tribes.

---o-o---

IN RE APPLICATION FOR ENROLLMENT, as a citizen of the   Chickasaw Nation, of   John Westley Casey , born on the   21st day of   March   , 190 3.

Name of Father: Newt H. Casey   , a citizen of the   Chickasaw   Nation.

Name of Mother: Lula May Casey   , a citizen of the   Chickasaw   Nation. Postoffice   Purcell, I.T.

AFFIDAVIT OF MOTHER.
---o-o---

UNITED STATES OF AMERICA,)
   INDIAN TERRITORY,   )SS.
      SOUTHERN DISTRICT.)

I, Lula May Casey , on oath state that I am   24   years of age and a citizen by Blood   , of the   Chickasaw   Nation; that I am the lawful wife of   Newt H. Casey , who is a citizen, by   Intermarriage   of the   Chickasaw   Nation; that a   male   child was born to me on the   21st   day of   March   , 190 3; that said child has been named John Westley Casey   , and is now living.

    Signature   Lula May Casey

Witnesses to ~~Mark~~.
   MR Pugh
   BH Loomis

Subscribed and sworn to before me this   8th day of   March   , 190 5

                      OH Loomis
                      Notary Public.

AFFIDAVIT OF ATTENDING PHYSICIAN, OR MID-WIFE.

UNITED STATES OF AMERICA,)
   INDIAN TERRITORY,   )SS.
      SOUTHERN DISTRICT.)

I, Susan Goins   , a   Mid-Wife   , on oath state that I attended on Mrs.   Lula May Casey   , wife of   Newt H. Casey   , on the   21st day of   March   , 190 3; that

Applications for Enrollment of Chickasaw Newborn
Act of 1905 Volume IV

there was born to her on said date a   Male   child; that said child is now living and is said to have been named   John Westley Casey   .

Signature   Susan Goins

Witnesses to ~~Mark~~.
MR Pugh
BH Loomis

   Subscribed and sworn to before me this   8th   day of   March   , 190 5

                                                OH Loomis
                                                Notary Public.

BIRTH AFFIDAVIT.

DEPARTMENT OF THE INTERIOR.
COMMISSION TO THE FIVE CIVILIZED TRIBES.

   IN RE APPLICATION FOR ENROLLMENT, as a citizen of the   Chickasaw   Nation, of   John Wesley Casey   , born on the   21st   day of   March   , 1903.

Name of Father: Newt. H. Casey   a citizen of the   Chickasaw   Nation.
Name of Mother: Lula May Casey   a citizen of the   Chickasaw   Nation.

                    Postoffice   Purcell, Indian Territory.

AFFIDAVIT OF MOTHER.

UNITED STATES OF AMERICA, Indian Territory, }
       Southern   DISTRICT.   }

   I,   Lula May Casey   , on oath state that I am   25   years of age and a citizen by   blood   , of the   Chickasaw   Nation; that I am the lawful wife of   Newt H. Casey   , who is a citizen, by Marriage   of the   Chickasaw   Nation; that a male   child was born to me on   21st   day of   March   , 1903; that said child has been named   John Wesley Casey   , and was living March 4, 1905.

                                           Lula May Casey

Witnesses To Mark:
{

   Subscribed and sworn to before me this   28th day of   April   , 1905

                                        Joseph P. Smith
                                        Notary Public.

Applications for Enrollment of Chickasaw Newborn
Act of 1905 Volume IV

AFFIDAVIT OF ATTENDING PHYSICIAN OR MID-WIFE.

UNITED STATES OF AMERICA, Indian Territory, }
    Southern   DISTRICT.

    I, Susan Goins, a mid-wife, on oath state that I attended on Mrs. Lula May Casey, wife of Newt. H. Casey on the 21st day of March, 1903; that there was born to her on said date a male child; that said child was living March 4, 1905, and is said to have been named John Wesley Casey

                                                   Susan Goins

Witnesses To Mark:
{

    Subscribed and sworn to before me this 28th day of April, 1905.

                                              Joseph P. Smith
                                              Notary Public.

---

                                                   9 NB 310

                           Muskogee, Indian Territory, April 26, 1905.

Newton L[sic]. Casey,
    Purcell, Indian Territory.

Dear Sir:

    Receipt is hereby acknowledged of your letter of April 14, 1905, asking if the affidavits heretofore forwarded are sufficient for the enrollment of your child, or if it will be necessary for you to appear before the Commission.

    In reply to your letter you are informed that the affidavits heretofore forwarded in regard to your child, John Wesley Casey, have been filed as an application for the enrollment of said child, and in the event further evidence is needed to enable us to determine his right to enrollment you will be notified.

    The matter of land referred to in your letter will be made the subject of another communication.

                                     Respectfully,

                                                          Chairman.

Applications for Enrollment of Chickasaw Newborn
Act of 1905   Volume IV

9--N.B. 310

Muskogee, Indian Territory, May 9, 1905.

Newt H. Casey,
    Purcell, Indian Territory.

Dear Sir:

    Receipt is hereby acknowledged of your letter of April 28, enclosing the affidavits of Lula May Casey and Susan Goins to the birth of John Wesley Casey, son of Newt. H. Casey and Lula May Casey, March 21, 1903, and the same have been filed with our records in the matter of the application for the enrollment of said child.

Respectfully,

Commissioner in Charge.

Chic. N.B. - 311
    (William T. Jordan
    Born December 19, 1904)

DEPARTMENT OF THE INTERIOR,
COMMISSION TO THE FIVE CIVILIZED TRIBES.

Muskogee, Indian Territory, April 18, 1905.

    In the matter of the application for the enrollment of William T. Jordan as a citizen by blood of the Chickasaw Nation.

    George W. Jordan being first duly sworn on oath, testifies as follows:

Examination by the Commission:

Q What is your name? A George W. Jordan.
Q What is your Post-office address? A Bushyhead, Indian Territory.
Q An application has been filed with this Commission for the enrollment of William T. Jordan, born December 19, 1904, as a citizen by blood of the Chickasaw Nation, are you the father of that child? A Yes sir.
Q Who is the mother of that child? A Agnes Montressa Jordan.
Q What was the maiden name of the child's mother? A Agnes Montressa Landrum.
Q When were you married? A December 1st, 1903.

Applications for Enrollment of Chickasaw Newborn
Act of 1905 Volume IV

Q Where were you married? A At Prior Creek.
Q Is your wife a citizen by blood of the Chickasaw Nation? A Yes sir.
Q Did you get a marriage certificate at the time you were married? A Yes sir.
Q Have you that marriage certificate with you? A No sir. I have not.
Q Since your marriage to the mother of this child, you and she have lived together as husband and wife? A Yes sir.

The name of the mother of this child appears on the Chickasaw Field Card number 1682 as Agnes Montressa Landrum, and as number 4717 on the fianl[sic] roll of citizens by blood of the Chickasaw Nation and approved by the Secretary of the Interior September 12, 1903.
Q When was this child born? A December 19, 1904.
Q That child is now living, is it? A Yes sir.

In the matter of the application for the enrollment of this child, it will be necessary for you to forward to the Commission either the original or a certified copy of your marriage license and certificate.

Nina E. Coffey upon oath states that as stenographer to the Commission to the Five Civilized Tribes she correctly recorded the testimony in the above entitled cause and that the foregoing is an accurate transcript of her stenographic notes thereof.

Nina E Coffey

Subscribed and sworn to before me this April 18, 1905.

M Campbell
Notary Public.

CERTIFICATE OF RECORD.

United States of America,
INDIAN TERRITORY,   ss.
Northern District.

I, *CHARLES A. DAVIDSON*, Clerk of the United States Court in the Northern District, Indian Territory, do hereby certify that the instrument hereto attached was filed for record in my office the 1 day of JANUARY 190 3 at ....M., and duly recorded in Book B , Marriage Record, Page 346

WITNESS my hand and seal of said Court at Muscogee, in said Territory, this 1 day of JANUARY A. D. 190 3

Chas. A. Davidson   Clerk.
By...Deputy.

Applications for Enrollment of Chickasaw Newborn
Act of 1905 Volume IV

𝔐ARRIAGE 𝔏ICENSE.

𝔘nited 𝔖tates of 𝔄merica,
   INDIAN TERRITORY, } ss.   *No.* **105**
   Northern District.

To Any Person Authorized by Law to Solemnize Marriage---Greeting:

𝔜ou are 𝔥ereby 𝔠ommanded *to Solemnize the Rite and Publish the Banns of Matrimony between Mr.* George Jordan *of* Foyil IT *, in the Indian Territory, aged* 23 *years and M* iss Monnie Landrum *of* Foyil *in the Indian Territory aged* 18 *years according to law, and do you officially sign and return this License to the parties therein named.*

      WITNESS my hand and official seal at Muscogee Indian Territory this 1st *day of* Dec *A.D. 190* 3

                                          CHAS. A. DAVIDSON, Clerk.
                                                   Clerk of the U.S. Court

By   J C Burgess   *Deputy*

CERTIFICATE OF MARRIAGE.

𝔘nited 𝔖tates of 𝔄merica,
   INDIAN TERRITORY, } ss.
   Northern District.

      I,   J C Burgess Dpt Clerk   *, a Minister of the Gospel, DO HEREBY CERTIFY that on the* 1st *day of* Dec.. *A. D. 190* 3, *did duly and according to law as commanded in the foregoing License, solemnize the Rite and publish the Banns of Matrimony between the parties therein named.*

      WITNESS my hand this 1st *day of* Dec   *A. D. 1903*

      My credentials are recorded in the office of the Clerk of the United States Court, Indian Territory, Western District, Book ...., *Page* ....*.*

                                                   J C Burgess Deputy Clerk
                                                   A Minister of the Gospel

Note—This License and Certificate of Marriage must be returned to the Office of the Clerk of the United States Court in the Northern District, Indian Territory, from whence it was issued, within sixty days from the date thereof, or the party to whom the license was issued will be liable in the amount of the One Hundred Dollars ($100.00)

Applications for Enrollment of Chickasaw Newborn
Act of 1905   Volume IV

(The Birth Affidavit below typed as given.)

Birth affidavit.
                    DEPARTMENT OF THE INTERIOR.
                    Commission to the Five Civilized Tribes.

    IN RE APPLICATION for Enrollment, as a citizen of the Chickasaw Nation, of William T. Jordan born on the   19th   day of December   , 1904.

Name of Father: George W. Jordan   , a citizen of the U.S.

Name of Mother Agnes Mon Truss~~all~~ Jordan   , a citizen of the Chickasaw Nation.

                          Post office___Bushyhead, Ind. Ter.___

AFFIDAVIT OF MOTHER.

United States of America, |
Northern Judicial District, | SS.
Indian Territory. |

    I, Agnes Mon Tress~~all~~ Jordan on oath state that I am   18   yaers of age and a citizen, by blood , of the Chickasaw   Nation; that I am the lawful wife of George W. Jordan , who is a citizen, by adoption   , of the   Cherokee   Nation, that a   male   child was born to me on the 19th day of December   , 1904 ; that said child has been named William Thomas Jordan and is now living.

                                      Agness Monnie Tressa Jordan
Witnesses to Mark:
  (must be two)   _____
                          _____

Subscribed and sworn to before me this the   22   day of March   1905.

                                      John T Ezzard
                                          Notary Public.
My commission expires November 1st 1908.

AFFIDAVIT OF ATTENDING PHYSICIAN, OR MIDWIFE.

United States of America, |
Northern Judicial District, | SS.
Indian Territory. |

    I, Thomas B. Dixon   , a Physician   , on oath state that I attended on Mrs. Agnes Mon Tress*a* Jordan, wife of   George W. Jordan   on the   19th day of December 1904 ; that there was born to her on said date a   male   child; that said child is now living and is said to have been named William Thomas Jordan.

Applications for Enrollment of Chickasaw Newborn
Act of 1905   Volume IV

Thos. B. Dickson

Witness to Mark:
  (Must be Two) _____
  _____

Subscribed and sworn to before me this the 27 day of March 1905.

John T Ezzard
Notary Public.

My commission expires November 1 1908.

9-1682

Muskogee, Indian Territory, April 12, 1905.

George W. Jordan,
  Bushyhead, Indian Territory.

Dear Sir:

Receipt is hereby acknowledged of your letter of March 27, 1905, enclosing affidavits of Agnes Monnie Tressa Jordan and Thomas B. Dickson to the birth of William Thomas Jordan, December 19, 1904.

The information contained in this affidavit is insufficient to enable the Commission to identify Agnes Monnie Tressa Jordan as a citizen by blood of the Chickasaw Nation, but in conversation over the telephone with the post master at Bushyhead, it was ascertained that the maiden name of the mother was Landrum and this information enables the Commission to identify her as having been enrolled under the name of Agnes Montressa Landrum.

Respectfully,

Commissioner in Charge.

9-N.B. 311.

Muskogee, Indian Territory, May 25, 1905.

George W. Jordan,
  Foyil, Indian Territory.

Dear Sir:

Receipt is hereby acknowledged of your letter of April 19 and your letter of May 18, transmitting marriage license and certificate between yourself and Monnie Landrum,

Applications for Enrollment of Chickasaw Newborn
Act of 1905 Volume IV

which you offer in support of the application for the enrollment of your child, William Thomas Jordan, and the same have been filed with the records in this case.

You are advised that the name of your child has been placed upon a schedule of citizens by blood of the Chickasaw Nation prepared for forwarding to the Secretary of the Interior.

Respectfully,

Chairman.

Chic. N.B. - 312
    (Battiest Harris
    Born August 7, 1904)

BIRTH AFFIDAVIT.

DEPARTMENT OF THE INTERIOR.
COMMISSION TO THE FIVE CIVILIZED TRIBES.

IN RE APPLICATION FOR ENROLLMENT, as a citizen of the Chickasaw Nation, of Battiest Harris , born on the .... day of ...., 1 ....

Name of Father: Isaac Harris   a citizen of the Freedman Nation.
Name of Mother: Lila Harris   a citizen of the Chickasaw Nation.

Postoffice   Kinta I.T.

AFFIDAVIT OF MOTHER.

UNITED STATES OF AMERICA, Indian Territory,
    Western   DISTRICT.

I, Lila Harris , on oath state that I am 27 years of age and a citizen by blood , of the Chickasaw Nation; that I am the lawful wife of Isaac Harris , who is a ~~citizen~~ *Freedman*, by .... of the Choctaw Nation; that a Male child was born to me on 7th day of August , 1904; that said child has been named Battiest Harris , and was living March 4, 1905.

Lila Harris

Witnesses To Mark:
{

Applications for Enrollment of Chickasaw Newborn
Act of 1905 Volume IV

Subscribed and sworn to before me this 4 day of   April   , 1905

L D Allen
Notary Public.

AFFIDAVIT OF ATTENDING PHYSICIAN OR MID-WIFE.

UNITED STATES OF AMERICA, Indian Territory, }
Western   DISTRICT.   }

I,   Sarah Harris   , a mid wife   , on oath state that I attended on Mrs.   Mrs Lila Harris , wife of Isac[sic] Harris   on the 7 day of   Aug   , 1904; that there was born to her on said date a _____ child; that said child was living March 4, 1905, and is said to have been named Battiest Harris

                                     her
                              Sarah x Harris
Witnesses To Mark: mark
  { HM Moore
    CH Lewis

Subscribed and sworn to before me this 4 day of   April   , 1905

L D Allen
Notary Public.

Wm O.B.

COMMISSIONERS:
TAMS BIXBY,
THOMAS B. NEEDLES,
C.R. BRECKINBRIDGE.

DEPARTMENT OF THE INTERIOR,
COMMISSIONER TO THE FIVE CIVILIZED TRIBES.

REFER IN REPLY TO THE FOLLOWING:

9-1116

WM. O. BEALL
Secretary

ADDRESS ONLY THE
COMMISSION TO THE FIVE CIVILIZED TRIBES.

Muskogee, Indian Territory, April 12, 1905.

Isaac Harris,
    Kinta, Indian Territory.

Dear Sir:

    Receipt is hereby acknowledged of the affidavits of Lila Harris and Sarah Harris to the birth of Battiest Harris, son of Isaac and Lila Harris, August 7, 1904, and the same have been filed with our records as an application for the enrollment of said child.

                      Respectfully,
                      T.B. Needles
                      Commissioner in Charge.

Applications for Enrollment of Chickasaw Newborn
Act of 1905 Volume IV

Chic. N.B. - 313
(Levi McCoy
Born February 14, 1904)

BIRTH AFFIDAVIT.

DEPARTMENT OF THE INTERIOR.
COMMISSION TO THE FIVE CIVILIZED TRIBES.

IN RE APPLICATION FOR ENROLLMENT, as a citizen of the Chickasaw Nation, of Levi McCoy, born on the 14 day of February, 1904

Name of Father: Wesley McCoy   a ~~citizen~~ *Freedman* of the Choctaw Nation.
Name of Mother: Bethena McCoy   a citizen of the Chickasaw Nation.

Postoffice   Kinta I.T.

AFFIDAVIT OF MOTHER.

UNITED STATES OF AMERICA, Indian Territory,
Central   DISTRICT.

I, Bethena McCoy, on oath state that I am 28 years of age and a citizen by blood, of the Chickasaw Nation; that I am the lawful wife of Wesley McCoy, who is a citizen, by Freedman of the Choctaw Nation; that a male child was born to me on 14th day of February, 1904; that said child has been named Levi McCoy, and was living March 4, 1905.

                                              her
                              Bethena x McCoy
Witnesses To Mark: mark
   Chas T Difendafer
   OL Johnson

Subscribed and sworn to before me this 6 day of April, 1905

                                 OL Johnson
                                 Notary Public.

Applications for Enrollment of Chickasaw Newborn
Act of 1905 Volume IV

AFFIDAVIT OF ATTENDING PHYSICIAN OR MID-WIFE.

UNITED STATES OF AMERICA, Indian Territory, }
Central DISTRICT.

I, Belle Thompson , a midwife , on oath state that I attended on Mrs. Bethena McCoy , wife of Wesley McCoy on the 14 day of February , 1904; that there was born to her on said date a male child; that said child was living March 4, 1905, and is said to have been named Levi McCoy

Bell[sic] Thompson

Witnesses To Mark:
{

Subscribed and sworn to before me this 6 day of April , 1905

OL Johnson
Notary Public.

Chic. N.B. - 314
*(George Edward Richmond Love
Born June 26, 1904)*

BIRTH AFFIDAVIT.
DEPARTMENT OF THE INTERIOR.
COMMISSION TO THE FIVE CIVILIZED TRIBES.

IN RE APPLICATION FOR ENROLLMENT, as a citizen of the Chickasaw Nation, of George Edward Richmond Love , born on the 26 day of June , 1904

Name of Father: Sam N. Love a citizen of the Chickasaw Nation.
 an intermarried
Name of Mother: Nona Love a citizen of the Chickasaw Nation.

Postoffice White Bead, Ind. Ter.

Applications for Enrollment of Chickasaw Newborn
Act of 1905   Volume IV

AFFIDAVIT OF MOTHER.

UNITED STATES OF AMERICA, Indian Territory, }
  Southern   DISTRICT.

    I, Nona Love, on oath state that I am 26 years of age and a citizen by marriage, of the Chickasaw Nation; that I am the lawful wife of Sam N. Love, who is a citizen, by blood of the Chickasaw Nation; that a male child was born to me on 26 day of June, 1904; that said child has been named George Edward Richmond Love, and was living March 4, 1905.

                              Nona Love

Witnesses To Mark:
  { *(Name Illegible)*
    R McMillan

    Subscribed and sworn to before me this 6th day of April, 1905

                            Victor Griggs
                              Notary Public.

AFFIDAVIT OF ATTENDING PHYSICIAN OR MID-WIFE.

UNITED STATES OF AMERICA, Indian Territory, }
  Southern   DISTRICT.

    I, Susan Baker, a mid-wife, on oath state that I attended on Mrs. Nona Love, wife of Sam N Love on the 26th day of June, 1904; that there was born to her on said date a male child; that said child was living March 4, 1905, and is said to have been named George Edward Richmond Love

                            Susan Baker

Witnesses To Mark:
  { Nancy L Douglass
    Danie Baker

    Subscribed and sworn to before me this .... day of ...., 1905.

                            Notary Public.

Applications for Enrollment of Chickasaw Newborn
Act of 1905 Volume IV

BIRTH AFFIDAVIT.

DEPARTMENT OF THE INTERIOR.
COMMISSION TO THE FIVE CIVILIZED TRIBES.

IN RE APPLICATION FOR ENROLLMENT, as a citizen of the Chickasaw Nation, of George Edward Richmond Love, born on the 26th day of June, 1904

Name of Father: Sam N. Love a citizen of the Chickasaw Nation.
Name of Mother: Nona Love a citizen of the Chickasaw Nation.

Postoffice White Bead, I. T.

AFFIDAVIT OF MOTHER.

UNITED STATES OF AMERICA, Indian Territory,
Southern DISTRICT.

I, Nona Love, on oath state that I am 26 years of age and a citizen by Intermarriage, of the Chickasaw Nation; that I am the lawful wife of Sam N. Love, who is a citizen, by Blood of the Chickasaw Nation; that a Male child was born to me on 26th day of June, 1904; that said child has been named George Edward Richmond Love, and was living March 4, 1905.

Nona Love

Witnesses To Mark:
{ M C Grisham
{ G L Grisham

Subscribed and sworn to before me this 2$^{th[sic]}$ day of June, 1905.

G.L. Grisham
Notary Public.

my commission exp Dec 11 - 1907

AFFIDAVIT OF ATTENDING PHYSICIAN OR MID-WIFE.

UNITED STATES OF AMERICA, Indian Territory,
Southern DISTRICT.

I, Susan Baker, a midwife, on oath state that I attended on Mrs. Nona Love, wife of Sam Love on the 26th day of June, 1904; that there was born to her on said date a Male child; that said child was living March 4, 1905, and is said to have been named George Edward Richmond Love

Susan Baker

Applications for Enrollment of Chickasaw Newborn
Act of 1905   Volume IV

Witnesses To Mark:
 { M C Grisham
 { G L Grisham

    Subscribed and sworn to before me this 2^{st[sic]}   day of   June   , 1905

                                G.L. Grisham
                                Notary Public.
                        my commission exp Dec 11 - 1907

                                              9-460

              Muskogee, Indian Territory, April 12, 1905.

Carr & Roberts,
    Attorneys at Law,
        Pauls Valley, Indian Territory.

Gentlemen:

    Receipt is hereby acknowledged of your letter of April 6, 1905, enclosing the affidavits of Nona Love and Susan Baker to the birth of George Edward Richmond Love, son of Sam N. and Nona Love, June 26, 1904, and the same have been filed with our records as an application for the enrollment of said child.

                        Respectfully,

                                    Commissioner in Charge.

                                        9-NB-314.

              Muskogee, Indian Territory, May 16, 1905.

Sam N. Love,
    White Bead, Indian Territory.

Dear Sir:

    There is enclosed you herewith for execution application for the enrollment of your infant child, George Edward Richmond Love, born June 26, 1904.

    The application heretofore filed with the Commission was incorrect in that the notary public failed to attach his seal and signature to the attending mid-wife. It will, therefore, be necessary that the enclosed application be executed.

Applications for Enrollment of Chickasaw Newborn
Act of 1905   Volume IV

In having these affidavits executed care should be exercised to see that all names are written in full, as they appear in the body of the affidavit, and in the event that either of the persons signing the affidavit are unable to write, signatures by mark must be attested by two witnesses. Each affidavit must be executed before a Notary Public and the notarial seal and signature of the officer must be attached to each separate affidavit.

Respectfully,

Chairman.

V 16/9.

9-NB-314

Muskogee, Indian Territory, June 7, 1905.

Sam N. Love,
    Whitebead, Indian Territory.

Dear Sir:

Receipt is hereby acknowledged of the affidavits of Nona Love and Susan Baker to the birth of George Edward Richmond Love, son of Sam N. and Nona Love, June 26, 1904, and the same have been filed with our records as an application for the enrollment of said child.

Respectfully,

Chairman.

Chic. N.B. - 315
    (Christine Patricia King
    Born April 13, 1903)
    (Angela Gertrude King
    Born February 4, 1905)

Applications for Enrollment of Chickasaw Newborn
Act of 1905   Volume IV

BIRTH AFFIDAVIT.

DEPARTMENT OF THE INTERIOR.
COMMISSION TO THE FIVE CIVILIZED TRIBES.

IN RE APPLICATION FOR ENROLLMENT, as a citizen of the Chickasaw Nation, of Christine Patricia King , born on the 13 day of April , 1905

Name of Father: Felix J King   a citizen of the Chickasaw Nation.
Name of Mother: Callie Boyd King   a citizen of the Chickasaw Nation.

Postoffice   Ardmore I.T.

AFFIDAVIT OF MOTHER.

UNITED STATES OF AMERICA, Indian Territory, }
    Southern   DISTRICT.

I, Callie Boyd King , on oath state that I am Twenty Eight years of age and a citizen by blood , of the Chickasaw Nation; that I am the lawful wife of Felix J King , who is a citizen, by Intermarriage of the Chickasaw Nation; that a Female child was born to me on 13th day of April , 1903; that said child has been named Christine Patricia King , and was living March 4, 1905.

Callie Boyd King

Witnesses To Mark:
{

Subscribed and sworn to before me this 7th day of April , 1905

U.T. Rexroat
Notary Public.

AFFIDAVIT OF ATTENDING PHYSICIAN OR MID-WIFE.

UNITED STATES OF AMERICA, Indian Territory, }
    Southern Dist   DISTRICT.

I, Walter Hardy , a physician , on oath state that I attended on Mrs. Callie Boyd King , wife of Felix J King on the 13 day of April , 1903; that there was born to her on said date a female child; that said child was living March 4, 1905, and is said to have been named Christine Patricia King

Walter Hardy M.D.

Witnesses To Mark:
{

Applications for Enrollment of Chickasaw Newborn
Act of 1905   Volume IV

Subscribed and sworn to before me this 7 day of   April   , 1905

                                        U. T. Rexroat
                                        Notary Public.

BIRTH AFFIDAVIT.

DEPARTMENT OF THE INTERIOR.
COMMISSION TO THE FIVE CIVILIZED TRIBES.

    IN RE APPLICATION FOR ENROLLMENT, as a citizen of the   Chickasaw   Nation, of   Angela Gertrude King   , born on the 4th day of Feb , 1905

Name of Father: Felix J King   a citizen of the   Chickasaw Nation.
Name of Mother: Callie Boyd King   a citizen of the   Chickasaw Nation.

                          Postoffice   Ardmore I.T.

AFFIDAVIT OF MOTHER.

UNITED STATES OF AMERICA, Indian Territory, }
   Southern   DISTRICT. }

    I,   Callie Boyd King   , on oath state that I am Twenty Eight   years of age and a citizen by   blood   , of the   Chickasaw   Nation; that I am the lawful wife of Felix J King   , who is a citizen, by Intermarriage   of the   Chickasaw Nation; that a   female   child was born to me on 4th day of Feb   , 1905; that said child has been named   Angela Gertrude King   , and was living March 4, 1905.

                                Callie Boyd King

Witnesses To Mark:
{

    Subscribed and sworn to before me this 7th day of   April   , 1905

                                  U.T. Rexroat
                                  Notary Public.

AFFIDAVIT OF ATTENDING PHYSICIAN OR MID-WIFE.

UNITED STATES OF AMERICA, Indian Territory, }
   Southern Dist   DISTRICT. }

    I,   Walter Hardy   , a physician   , on oath state that I attended on Mrs. Callie Boyd King , wife of   Felix J King   on the 4th day of February   ,

Applications for Enrollment of Chickasaw Newborn
Act of 1905   Volume IV

1905; that there was born to her on said date a   female   child; that said child was living March 4, 1905, and is said to have been named Angela Gertrude King

           Walter Hardy M.D.

Witnesses To Mark:

 { Subscribed and sworn to before me this   7 day of   April   , 1905

            U. T. Rexroat
             Notary Public.

                 &[sic] 9 N.B. 315.

        Muskogee, Indian Territory, May 15, 1905.

Felix King,
   Ardmore, Indian Territory.

Dear Sir:

   Receipt is hereby acknowledged of your letter of May 8, asking if the applications forwarded for the enrollment of your children have been received.

   In reply to your letter you are advised that the affidavits to the birth of Christine Patricia and Angela Gertrude King, have been filed with our records as applications for the enrollment of said children.

         Respectfully,

                Chairman.

Chic. N.B. - 316
   (Vinnie Ream
   Born September 9, 1903)

Applications for Enrollment of Chickasaw Newborn
Act of 1905   Volume IV

BIRTH AFFIDAVIT.

DEPARTMENT OF THE INTERIOR.
COMMISSION TO THE FIVE CIVILIZED TRIBES.

IN RE APPLICATION FOR ENROLLMENT, as a citizen of the   Chickasaw   Nation, of   Vinnie Ream   , born on the   9   day of   Sept.   , 1903

Roll #2564

Name of Father: Boudinot Ream   a citizen of the   Chickasaw   Nation.
Name of Mother: Mattie Ream   a citizen of the   "   Nation.

Postoffice   Wapanucka, I. T.

AFFIDAVIT OF MOTHER.

UNITED STATES OF AMERICA, Indian Territory, }
   Central   DISTRICT. }

I,   Mattie Ream   , on oath state that I am   27   years of age and a citizen by marriage   , of the   Chickasaw   Nation; that I am the lawful wife of   Boudinot Ream   , who is a citizen, by blood   of the   Chickasaw   Nation; that a female   child was born to me on   9   day of   Sept   , 1903; that said child has been named   Vinnie   , and was living March 4, 1905.

Mattie Ream

Witnesses To Mark:
{

Subscribed and sworn to before me this   6th   day of   April   , 1905

E. J. Ball
Notary Public.

AFFIDAVIT OF ATTENDING PHYSICIAN OR MID-WIFE.

UNITED STATES OF AMERICA, Indian Territory, }
   Southern   DISTRICT. }

I,   J. T. Looney   , a physician   , on oath state that I attended on Mrs.   Mattie Ream   , wife of   Boudinot Ream   on the   9   day of   Sept   , 1903; that there was born to her on said date a   female   child; that said child was living March 4, 1905, and is said to have been named   Vinnie

J. T. Looney M.D.

Witnesses To Mark:
{ *(Name Illegible)*

Applications for Enrollment of Chickasaw Newborn
Act of 1905   Volume IV

Subscribed and sworn to before me this 8 day of   April   , 1905

(Name Illegible)
Notary Public.

Chickasaw 867.

Muskogee, Indian Territory, April 12, 1905.

Boudinot Ream,
    Wapanucka, Indian Territory.

Dear Sir:

    Receipt is hereby acknowledged of the affidavits of Mattie Ream and J. T. Looney to the birth of Vinnie Ream, daughter of Boudinot and Mattie Ream, September 9th, 1903, and the same have been filed with our records as an application for the enrollment of said child.

Respectfully,

Commissioner in Charge.

Chic. N.B. - 317
    (Allinton Guy Ream
    February 13, 1903)

BIRTH AFFIDAVIT.

DEPARTMENT OF THE INTERIOR.
COMMISSION TO THE FIVE CIVILIZED TRIBES.

    IN RE APPLICATION FOR ENROLLMENT, as a citizen of the   Chickasaw   Nation, of   Alinton[sic] Guy Ream   , born on the   13th   day of   February   , 1903

Name of Father: Robert Lee Ream   a citizen of the   Chickasaw   Nation.
Name of Mother: Ona O'Neal Ream   a citizen of the   Chickasaw   Nation.

    Postoffice   Wapanucka I.T.

Applications for Enrollment of Chickasaw Newborn
Act of 1905   Volume IV

AFFIDAVIT OF MOTHER.

UNITED STATES OF AMERICA, Indian Territory,
    Central   DISTRICT.

I, Ona Oneal[sic] Ream, on oath state that I am 26 years of age and a citizen by intermarriage, of the Chickasaw Nation; that I am the lawful wife of Robert Lee Ream, who is a citizen, by blood of the Chickasaw Nation; that a male child was born to me on 13th day of February, 1903; that said child has been named Allinton Guy Ream, and was living March 4, 1905.

                      Ona O'Neal Ream

Witnesses To Mark:

    Subscribed and sworn to before me this 3d day of April, 1905

                      W Richard
                      Notary Public.

AFFIDAVIT OF ATTENDING PHYSICIAN OR MID-WIFE.

UNITED STATES OF AMERICA, Indian Territory,
    Central   DISTRICT.

I, M.P. Skeen, a Physician, on oath state that I attended on Mrs. Ona Oneal Ream, wife of Robert Lee Ream on the 13th day of February, 1903; that there was born to her on said date a male child; that said child was living March 4, 1905, and is said to have been named Allinton Guy Ream

                      M. P. Skeen

Witnesses To Mark:

    Subscribed and sworn to before me this 3d day of April, 1905

                      W Richard
                      Notary Public.

Applications for Enrollment of Chickasaw Newborn
Act of 1905   Volume IV

9-868

Muskogee, Indian Territory, April 12, 1905.

R. L. Ream,
    Wapanucka, Indian Territory.

Dear Sir:

    Receipt is hereby acknowledged of your letter of April 4, 1905, enclosing affidavits of One O'Neal Ream and M. P. Skeen to the birth of Alinton[sic] Guy Ream, son of Robert Lee and Ona O'Neal Ream, February 13, 1903, and the same have been filed with our records as an application for the enrollment of said child.

                  Respectfully,

                                  Commissioner in Charge.

---

9 NB 317

Muskogee, Indian Territory, April 19, 1905.

R. L. Ream,
    Wapanucka, Indian Territory.

Dear Sir:

    Receipt is hereby acknowledged of your letter of April 13, 1905, asking if the application for the enrollment of your child Alinton Guy Ream has been received.

    In reply to your letter you are informed that the affidavits heretofore forwarded to the birth of your child Allinton Guy Ream have been filed with our records as an application for the enrollment of said child.

                  Respectfully,

                                  Chairman.

Applications for Enrollment of Chickasaw Newborn
Act of 1905   Volume IV

Chic. N.B. - 318
    (Thomas Jefferson Hughes
    Born September 1, 1903)

BIRTH AFFIDAVIT.

DEPARTMENT OF THE INTERIOR.
COMMISSION TO THE FIVE CIVILIZED TRIBES.

IN RE APPLICATION FOR ENROLLMENT, as a citizen of the Chickasaw Nation, of Thomas Jefferson, born on the 1st day of Sept, 1903

Name of Father: A. B. Hughes   a citizen of the Chickasaw Nation.
Name of Mother: Mamie Hughes   a citizen of the Chickasaw Nation.

Postoffice   Belton Ind. T.

AFFIDAVIT OF MOTHER.

UNITED STATES OF AMERICA, Indian Territory,
    22nd DISTRICT.

I, Mamie Hughes, on oath state that I am 27 years of age and a citizen by blood, of the Chickasaw Nation; that I am the lawful wife of A. B. Hughes, who is a citizen, by intermarriage of the Chickasaw Nation; that a Male child was born to me on 1st day of September, 1903; that said child has been named Thomas Jefferson Hughes, and was living March 4, 1905.

                         Mamie Hughes

Witnesses To Mark:

Subscribed and sworn to before me this 6th day of April, 1905

                         C.F. Ebisch
                         Notary Public.

AFFIDAVIT OF ATTENDING PHYSICIAN OR MID-WIFE.

UNITED STATES OF AMERICA, Indian Territory,
    22nd DISTRICT.

I, Ada Hearrell, a Mid Wife, on oath state that I attended on Mrs. Mamie Hughes, wife of A. B. Hughes on the 1st day of Sept.,

Applications for Enrollment of Chickasaw Newborn
Act of 1905   Volume IV

1903; that there was born to her on said date a   Male   child; that said child was living March 4, 1905, and is said to have been named   Thomas Jefferson Hughes

Ada Hearrell

Witnesses To Mark:

{

Subscribed and sworn to before me this 6th day of April   , 1905

C.F. Ebisch
Notary Public.

Chickasaw 236.

Muskogee, Indian Territory, April 13, 1905.

A. B. Hughes,
   Belton, Indian Territory.

Dear Sir:

Receipt is hereby acknowledged of the affidavit of Mamie Hughes and Ada Hearrell to the birth of Thomas Jefferson Hughes, son of A. B. and Mamie Hughes, September 1, 1903, and the same have been filed with our records as an application for the enrollment of said child.

Respectfully,

Commissioner in Charge.

Chic. N.B. - 319
   (Bernice Lee Love
   Born January 24, 1904)

Applications for Enrollment of Chickasaw Newborn
Act of 1905 Volume IV

BIRTH AFFIDAVIT.   #121

DEPARTMENT OF THE INTERIOR.
COMMISSION TO THE FIVE CIVILIZED TRIBES.

IN RE APPLICATION FOR ENROLLMENT, as a citizen of the Chickasaw Nation, of Bernice Lee Love, born on the 24 day of January, 1904

Name of Father: Mart Love   a citizen of the Chickasaw Nation.
Name of Mother: Minnie Love   a citizen of the Chickasaw Nation.

Postoffice Sterett[sic]

AFFIDAVIT OF MOTHER.

UNITED STATES OF AMERICA, Indian Territory,
Central DISTRICT.

I, Minnie Love, on oath state that I am 23 years of age and a citizen by Intermarriage, of the Chickasaw Nation; that I am the lawful wife of Mart Love, who is a citizen, by blood of the Chickasaw Nation; that a female child was born to me on 24 day of January, 1904, that said child has been named Bernice Lee, and is now living.

Minnie Love

Witnesses To Mark:
{ J.H. Mashburn
{ Laura A Mashburn

Subscribed and sworn to before me this 23 day of February, 1905.

S M Mead
Notary Public.

AFFIDAVIT OF ATTENDING PHYSICIAN OR MID-WIFE.

UNITED STATES OF AMERICA, Indian Territory,
Central DISTRICT.

I, C C Yeiser, a M D, on oath state that I attended on Mrs. Minnie Love, wife of Mart Love on the 24 day of January, 1904; that there was born to her on said date a male child; that said child is now living and is said to have been named Bernice Lee

C.C. Yeiser M.D.

Applications for Enrollment of Chickasaw Newborn
Act of 1905 Volume IV

Witnesses To Mark:
- J.H. Mashburn
- Laura A Mashburn

Subscribed and sworn to before me this 23 day of February , 1905.

S M Mead
Notary Public.

BIRTH AFFIDAVIT.

DEPARTMENT OF THE INTERIOR.
COMMISSION TO THE FIVE CIVILIZED TRIBES.

IN RE APPLICATION FOR ENROLLMENT, as a citizen of the Chickasaw Nation, of Bernice Lee Love , born on the 24 day of Jan , 1904

Name of Father: Mart Love   a citizen of the Chickasaw Nation.
Name of Mother: Minnie Love   a citizen of the Chickasaw Nation.

Postoffice   Sterrett IT

AFFIDAVIT OF MOTHER.

UNITED STATES OF AMERICA, Indian Territory,
Central   DISTRICT.

I, Minnie Love , on oath state that I am 23 years of age and a citizen by Marriage , of the Chickasaw Nation; that I am the lawful wife of Mart Love , who is a citizen, by Blood of the Chickasaw Nation; that a Female child was born to me on 24 day of Jan , 1904; that said child has been named Bernice Lee Love , and was living March 4, 1905.

Minnie Love

Witnesses To Mark:

Subscribed and sworn to before me this 8 day of April , 1905

Chas E Bacon
Notary Public.

Applications for Enrollment of Chickasaw Newborn
Act of 1905   Volume IV

AFFIDAVIT OF ATTENDING PHYSICIAN OR MID-WIFE.

UNITED STATES OF AMERICA, Indian Territory, }
    Central   DISTRICT. }

    I,   C C Yeiser   , a   M.D.   , on oath state that I attended on Mrs.   Minnie Love , wife of Mart Love on the 24 day of Jan , 1904; that there was born to her on said date a Female child; that said child was living March 4, 1905, and is said to have been named Bernice Lee Love

                                      C.C. Yeiser M.D.

Witnesses To Mark:
{

    Subscribed and sworn to before me this 8 day of April   , 1905

                                      Chas E Bacon
                                      Notary Public.

                                      Chickasaw 1132.

                Muskogee, Indian Territory, April 13, 1905.

Mart Love,
    Sterrett, Indian Territory.

Dear Sir:

    Receipt is hereby acknowledged of the affidavits of Minnie Love and C. C. Yeiser to the birth of Bernice Lee Love, daughter of Mart and Minnie Love, January 24, 1904, and the same have been filed with our records as an application for the enrollment of said child.

                        Respectfully,

                                  Commissioner in Charge.

Chic. N.B. - 320
    (Lena Noeutubby OR Anoatubby
    Born March 13, 1904)

Applications for Enrollment of Chickasaw Newborn
Act of 1905   Volume IV

BIRTH AFFIDAVIT.

DEPARTMENT OF THE INTERIOR.
COMMISSION TO THE FIVE CIVILIZED TRIBES.

IN RE APPLICATION FOR ENROLLMENT, as a citizen of the   Chickasaw   Nation, of   Lena Noeutubby   , born on the 13th   day of March   , 1904

Name of Father: Lankford Noeutubby   a citizen of the   Chickasaw   Nation.
Name of Mother: Laticia Noeutubby   a citizen of the   Chickasaw   Nation.

Postoffice   Isom I.T.

AFFIDAVIT OF MOTHER.

UNITED STATES OF AMERICA, Indian Territory,
Southern   DISTRICT.

I,   Laticia Noeutubby   , on oath state that I am   22   years of age and a citizen by   blood   , of the   Chickasaw   Nation; that I am the lawful wife of Lankford Noeutubby   , who is a citizen, by   blood   of the   Chickasaw   Nation; that a   female   child was born to me on   13th   day of March   , 1904; that said child has been named   Lena Noeutubby   , and was living March 4, 1905.

                            her
                    Laticia x Noeutubby
Witnesses To Mark: mark
 { Andrew Beam
 { J.H. Burris

Subscribed and sworn to before me this   21st   day of   March   , 1905

                    DR Johnston
                    Notary Public.

AFFIDAVIT OF ATTENDING PHYSICIAN OR MID-WIFE.

UNITED STATES OF AMERICA, Indian Territory,
.... DISTRICT.

I,   Sina Beam   , a Midwife   , on oath state that I attended on Mrs. Laticia Noeutubby   , wife of   Lankford Noeutubby   on the 13th   day of March   , 1904; that there was born to her on said date a   female   child; that said child was living March 4, 1905, and is said to have been named   Lena Noeutubby

                            her
                    Sina x Beam
                        mark

Applications for Enrollment of Chickasaw Newborn
Act of 1905   Volume IV

Witnesses To Mark:
{ Andrew Beam
{ J.H. Burris

Subscribed and sworn to before me this 21ˢᵗ day of   March   , 1905

DR Johnston
Notary Public.

BIRTH AFFIDAVIT.

DEPARTMENT OF THE INTERIOR.
COMMISSION TO THE FIVE CIVILIZED TRIBES.

IN RE APPLICATION FOR ENROLLMENT, as a citizen of the   Chickasaw   Nation, of   Lena Anoatubby   , born on the 13ᵗʰ   day of March   , 1904

Name of Father: Lankford Anoatubby   a citizen of the   Chickasaw Nation.
Name of Mother: Laticia Anoatubby   a citizen of the   Chickasaw Nation.

Postoffice   Isom I.T.

AFFIDAVIT OF MOTHER.

UNITED STATES OF AMERICA, Indian Territory, }
  Southern   DISTRICT.   }

I,   Laticia Anoatubby   , on oath state that I am   22   years of age and a citizen by   blood   , of the   Chickasaw   Nation; that I am the lawful wife of Lankford Anoatubby   , who is a citizen, by blood   of the   Chickasaw   Nation; that a   female   child was born to me on 13ᵗʰ   day of March   , 1904; that said child has been named   Lena Anoatubby   , and was living March 4, 1905.

Sinnie Beam

Witnesses To Mark:
{
{

Subscribed and sworn to before me this 6ᵗʰ   day of   April   , 1905

DR Johnston
Notary Public.

245

Applications for Enrollment of Chickasaw Newborn
Act of 1905   Volume IV

AFFIDAVIT OF ATTENDING PHYSICIAN OR MID-WIFE.

UNITED STATES OF AMERICA, Indian Territory,
Southern   DISTRICT.

I, Sinnie Beam   , a Midwife   , on oath state that I attended on Mrs. Laticia Anoatubby   , wife of Lankford Anoatubby   on the 13th day of March , 1904; that there was born to her on said date a   female   child; that said child was living March 4, 1905, and is said to have been named Lena Anoatubby

Latice[sic] Anoatubby

Witnesses To Mark:

{

Subscribed and sworn to before me this   6th day of   April   , 1905

DR Johnston
Notary Public.

BIRTH AFFIDAVIT.

DEPARTMENT OF THE INTERIOR,
COMMISSIONER TO THE FIVE CIVILIZED TRIBES.

ENROLLMENT OF MINORS. ACT OF CONGRESS, APPROVED APRIL 26, 1906.

IN RE APPLICATION FOR ENROLLMENT, as a citizen of the   Chickasaw   Nation, of   Lena Anoatubby   , born on the   13   day of March   , 1904

Name of Father: no father   a citizen of the   Chickasaw   Nation.
Name of Mother: Letica Apalla   a citizen of the   Chickasaw   Nation.

Tribal enrollment of father .... Tribal enrollment of mother Chickasaw

Postoffice   Isom Springs I.T.

AFFIDAVIT OF MOTHER.

UNITED STATES OF AMERICA, Indian Territory,
Southern   District.

I,   Letica Apalla   , on oath state that I am   23   years of age and a citizen by   birth   , of the   Chickasaw   Nation; that I am the lawful wife of   no husband   , who is a citizen, by................. of the .... Nation; that a   female   child was born to me on   13   day of

246

Applications for Enrollment of Chickasaw Newborn
Act of 1905 Volume IV

March   , 1904 , that said child has been named   Lena Anoatubby   , and was living March 4, 1906.

Letica Apalla

WITNESSES TO MARK:
{ Johnnie Wolf
{ Jessie Belt

Subscribed and sworn to before me this   17   day of   May , 1906.

M.D. Belt
Notary Public.

AFFIDAVIT OF ATTENDING PHYSICIAN OR MID-WIFE.

UNITED STATES OF AMERICA, Indian Territory, }
Southern   District. }

I,   Sinie Beams   , a   midwife   , on oath state that I attended on   Letica Apala[sic] , wife of   no husband   on the 13 day of March , 1904 ; that there was born to her on said date a   female   child; that said child was living March 4, 1906, and is said to have been named Lena Anoatubby

Sinie Beams

WITNESSES TO MARK:
{ Johnnie Wolf
{ Jessie Belt

Subscribed and sworn to before me this   17   day of   May , 1906.

M.D. Belt
Notary Public.

BIRTH AFFIDAVIT.

DEPARTMENT OF THE INTERIOR.
COMMISSION TO THE FIVE CIVILIZED TRIBES.

IN RE APPLICATION FOR ENROLLMENT, as a citizen of the   Chickasaw   Nation, of   Lena Anoatubby   , born on the 13th day of March , 1904

Name of Father: Lankford Anoatubby   a citizen of the   Chickasaw   Nation.
Name of Mother: Leticia[sic] Apala   a citizen of the   Chickasaw   Nation.

Postoffice   Isom Springs, I.T.

Applications for Enrollment of Chickasaw Newborn
Act of 1905   Volume IV

AFFIDAVIT OF MOTHER.

UNITED STATES OF AMERICA, Indian Territory, }
   Southern   DISTRICT.

I, Leticia Apala, on oath state that I am 22 years of age and a citizen by blood, of the Chickasaw Nation; that I am *not* the lawful wife of Lankford Anoatubby, who is a citizen, by blood of the Chickasaw Nation; that a female child was born to me on 13th day of March, 1904; that said child has been named Lena Anoatubby, and was living March 4, 1905.

Laticia Apala

Witnesses To Mark:
{

Subscribed and sworn to before me this 11 day of Oct, 1905

M.D. Belt
Notary Public.

my commission exp 1/19 1909

AFFIDAVIT OF ATTENDING PHYSICIAN OR MID-WIFE.

UNITED STATES OF AMERICA, Indian Territory, }
   Southern   DISTRICT.

I, Sinie Beam, a mid-wife, on oath state that I attended on Mrs. Leticia Apala, wife of Lankford Anoatubby on the 13th day of March, 1904; that there was born to her on said date a female child; that said child was living March 4, 1905, and is said to have been named Lena Anoatubby

Sinnie Beam

Witnesses To Mark:
{

Subscribed and sworn to before me this 11 day of Oct, 1905

M.D. Belt
Notary Public.

Applications for Enrollment of Chickasaw Newborn
Act of 1905   Volume IV

Chickasaw 958.

Muskogee, Indian Territory, April 13, 1905.

Lankford Anoatubby,
    Isom, Indian Territory.

Dear Sir:

    Receipt is hereby acknowledged of the affidavits of Sinie Beam and Latice Anatuby[sic] to the birth of Lena Anoatubby, daughter of Lankford and Laticia Anoatubby, March 13, 1904, and the same have been filed with our records as an application for the enrollment of said child.

        Respectfully,

        Commissioner in Charge.

Sub   9-NB-320.

Muskogee, Indian Territory, May 17, 1905.

Lankford Anoatubby,
    Isom Springs, Indian Territory.

Dear Sir:

    Referring to the application for the enrollment of your infant child, Lena Anoatubby, born March 13, 1904, it is noted that your wife, Laticia Anoatubby, claims to be a Chickasaw citizen by blood.

    If this is correct you are requested to state when, where and under what name she was listed for enrollment, the names of her parents and other members of her family for whom application was made at the same time, and if she has selected an allotment, give her roll number as the same appears on her allotment certificate.

        Respectfully,

        Chairman.

Applications for Enrollment of Chickasaw Newborn
Act of 1905   Volume IV

9-NB-320

Muskogee, Indian Territory, May 26, 1906.

M. D. Belt,
    Isom Springs, Indian Territory.

Dear Sir:

    Receipt is hereby acknowledged of your letter of May 17, 1906, inclosing affidavits to the birth of Lena Anoatubby and asking that this child be enrolled if possible.

    In reply to your letter you are advised that the name of Lena Anoatubby has been placed upon a schedule of new born citizens of the Chickasaw Nation which has been forwarded to the Secretary of the Interior and you will be notified when her enrollment is approved by the Department.

                        Respectfully,

                                    Acting Commissioner.

(The letter below typed as given.)

                        Isom Springs, I.T.

                        July 18/1905.

Commissioner to the Five Civilized Tribes.

Sir:-   Muskogee, I.T.

I have received a letter from the Department and which it was asking whether my wife is a citizen by blood. Yes sir- my wife is a Chickasaw citizen by Blood and her name is Jane Anoatubby and she is still living. I have no other woman except her-so I havnt nothing to do with those others. I have no childrens at all Letice Arpela who she claims to you to be my wife is mistake.

                        Verry Respectfully.

                        Lankford Anoatubby.

Applications for Enrollment of Chickasaw Newborn
Act of 1905 Volume IV

9-NB-320

Muskogee, Indian Territory, August 4, 1905.

Leticia Anoatubby,
    Isom Springs, Indian Territory.

Dear Madam:

    Referring to the application for the enrollment of your infant child, Lena Anoatubby, born March 13, 1904, it is noted in your affidavit of March 21, 1905, and April 6, 1905, you allege that you are a citizen by blood of the Chickasaw Nation, and the lawful wife of Lankford Anoatubby.

    You are advised that this office is unable to identify you as a citizen by blood of the Chickasaw Nation. You will please state when, where and under what name application was made for your enrollment, the names of your father and mother, and if you have selected an allotment, give your roll number as it appears upon your certificate.

    You should give this matter your immediate attention as no further action can be taken relative to the enrollment of your said child, until the evidence requested is supplied.

    Respectfully,

    Commissioner.

Kingston, I.T., August 14th 1905

Commissioners to the Five Civilized Tribes,
    Muskogee, Ind. Ter.,

Dear Sirs-- Referring to yours of August 4, 1905, 9-NB-320, concerning the infant child of Latice Anoatubby,

    I filed at Tishomingo and do not remember the date. The certificates were sent to me here at this office on March 6th and the post office here was burned up on March 7th 1904 and was then burned up. I filed under the name of Latice Appler and my father's name was Daniel Colbert and my mother was named Delpha Wolfe. Yes I have selected an allotment but have no certificate for the reason above states.

    Please give this matter your immediate attention. this your attention and call on me for any information needed and if possible I will furnish it.

    Respectfully,
    (Signed)   Latice Appler

Applications for Enrollment of Chickasaw Newborn
Act of 1905 Volume IV

9-NB-320

Muskogee, Indian Territory, August 18, 1905.

Lattice Apala,
    Kingston, Indian Territory.

Dear Madam:

    Receipt is hereby acknowledged of your letter of August 14, 1905, giving the names of your parents in the matter of the enrollment of your infant child, Lena Anoatubby. The information has enabled this office to identify you as an enrolled citizen by blood of the Chickasaw Nation, and has been made a part of the record in the matter of the application of Lena Anoatubby as a citizen by blood of the Chickasaw Nation.

    Respectfully,

    Acting Commissioner.

9-NB-320.

Muskogee, Indian Territory, September 26, 1905.

Leticia Apala,
    Isom Springs, Indian Territory.

Dear Madam:

    In the matter of the application for the enrollment of your minor daughter Lena Anoatubby as a citizen by blood of the Chickasaw Nation it will be necessary for you to furnish this office with proper proof of the birth of said child and a blank for that purpose, which has been filled out, is inclosed herewith.

    In your affidavits, as to the birth of said child, heretofore filed with this office you stated that you were the lawful wife of Lankford Anoatubby. On July 18, 1905, Lankford Anoatubby addressed a letter to this office stating that his wife, Jane Anoatubby was still living and that she was the only wife he had and that if you claimed to be his wife it was a mistake. A blank for proof of birth which is inclosed has been made to conform to the above facts.

    Be careful to sign your name to the affidavit a to the birth of your said daughter as the same appears in the body of the affidavit and to see that the notary public, before whom the affidavits are sworn to attached his name and seal to each affidavit. In case any signature is by mark the same must be attested by two disinterested witnesses.

Applications for Enrollment of Chickasaw Newborn
Act of 1905   Volume IV

Respectfully,

Commissioner.

CTD-1
Env.

9-320

Muskogee, Indian Territory, October 19, 1905.

Leticia Apala,
    Iron[sic] Springs, Indian Territory.

Dear Madam:

    Receipt is hereby acknowledged of your affidavit and the affidavit of Simie[sic] Beam to the birth of Lena Anoatubby, March 13, 1904, and the same have been filed with the records of this office in the matter of the enrollment of said child.

Respectfully,

Commissioner.

9-NB-320

Muskogee, Indian Territory, November 24, 1905.

Leticia Apela[sic],
    Isom Springs, Indian Territory.

Dear Madam:

    Receipt is hereby acknowledged of your letter of November 20, 1905, asking if you can file for your child Lena Anoatubby.

    In reply to your letter you are advised that the name of your child Lena Anoatubby has not yet been placed upon a schedule of citizens by blood of the Chickasaw Nation prepared for forwarding to the Secretary of the Interior and pending her enrollment and the approval thereof by the Department no selection of allotment can be made in her behalf.

Respectfully,

Acting Commissioner.

Applications for Enrollment of Chickasaw Newborn
Act of 1905   Volume IV

Chic. N.B. - 321
    (Dave Hardwicke
    Born February 20, 1904)

BIRTH AFFIDAVIT.

DEPARTMENT OF THE INTERIOR.
COMMISSION TO THE FIVE CIVILIZED TRIBES.

IN RE APPLICATION FOR ENROLLMENT, as a citizen of the   Chickasaw   Nation, of   Dave Hardicke[sic]   , born on the   20th day of   Feb   , 1904

Name of Father: Brit Hardwicke   a citizen of the   Chickasaw   Nation.
Name of Mother: Minnie Hardwicke   a citizen of the   ———   Nation.

Postoffice   Kingston I.T.

AFFIDAVIT OF MOTHER.

UNITED STATES OF AMERICA, Indian Territory, }
    Southern   DISTRICT.

I,   Minnie Hardwicke   , on oath state that I am   22   years of age and a citizen by   intermarriage   , of the   Chickasaw   Nation; that I am the lawful wife of   Brit Hardwicke   , who is a citizen, by   blood   of the   Chickasaw   Nation; that a   male   child was born to me on   20th day of   Feb   , 1904; that said child has been named   Dave Hardwicke   , and was living March 4, 1905.

                            Minnie Hardwicke

Witnesses To Mark:
{

Subscribed and sworn to before me this   4th day of   April   , 1905

                            DR Johnston
                            Notary Public.

AFFIDAVIT OF ATTENDING PHYSICIAN OR MID-WIFE.

UNITED STATES OF AMERICA, Indian Territory, }
    Southern   DISTRICT.

I,   Crecie Merriman   , a   midwife   , on oath state that I attended on Mrs.   Minnie Hardwicke   , wife of   Brit Hardwicke   on the   20th day of   Feb   ,

Applications for Enrollment of Chickasaw Newborn
Act of 1905 Volume IV

1904; that there was born to her on said date a   male   child; that said child was living March 4, 1905, and is said to have been named Dave Hardwicke

Crecie Merriman

Witnesses To Mark:

{

Subscribed and sworn to before me this 4th   day of   April   , 1905

DR Johnston
Notary Public.

Chickasaw 1020

Muskogee, Indian Territory, April 13, 1905.

Brit Hardwicke,
    Kingston, Indian Territory.

Dear Sir:

Receipt is hereby acknowledged of the affidavits of Minnie Hardwicke and Crecie Merriman to the birth of Dave Hardwicke, son of Brit and Minnie Hardwicke, February 20, 1904, and the same have been filed with our records as an application for the enrollment of said child.

Respectfully,

Commissioner in Charge.

Chic. N.B. - 322
    (Lula Brown
    Born October 21, 1903)

Applications for Enrollment of Chickasaw Newborn
Act of 1905 Volume IV

BIRTH AFFIDAVIT.

DEPARTMENT OF THE INTERIOR.
COMMISSION TO THE FIVE CIVILIZED TRIBES.

IN RE APPLICATION FOR ENROLLMENT, as a citizen of the Chickasaw Nation, of Lula Brown, born on the 21st day of Oct, 1903

Name of Father: Chiggling Brown   a citizen of the Chickasaw Nation.
Name of Mother: Linda Brown   a citizen of the Chickasaw Nation.

Postoffice   Powell, I.T.

AFFIDAVIT OF MOTHER.

UNITED STATES OF AMERICA, Indian Territory, }
    Southern   DISTRICT. }

I, Linda Brown, on oath state that I am 39 years of age and a citizen by blood, of the Chickasaw Nation; that I am the lawful wife of Chiggling Brown, who is a citizen, by blood of the Chickasaw Nation; that a female child was born to me on 21st day of Oct, 1903; that said child has been named Lula Brown, and was living March 4, 1905.

                                       her
                                Linda x Brown
Witnesses To Mark: mark
    { L E Gregory
    { W.E. Parker

Subscribed and sworn to before me this 4th day of April, 1905

                            DR Johnston
                            Notary Public.

AFFIDAVIT OF ATTENDING PHYSICIAN OR MID-WIFE.

UNITED STATES OF AMERICA, Indian Territory, }
    Southern   DISTRICT. }

I, Polly Lewis, a midwife, on oath state that I attended on Mrs. Linda Brown, wife of Chiggling Brown on the 21st day of Oct., 1903; that there was born to her on said date a female child; that said child was living March 4, 1905, and is said to have been named Lula Brown

                                      her
                              Polly x Lewis
                                 mark

Applications for Enrollment of Chickasaw Newborn
Act of 1905 Volume IV

Witnesses To Mark:
{ L E Gregory
{ W.E. Parker

Subscribed and sworn to before me this 7th day of   April   , 1905

DR Johnston
Notary Public.

Chickasaw 871.

Muskogee, Indian Territory, April 13, 1905.

Chiggling Brown,
    Powell, Indian Territory.

Dear Sir:

    Receipt is hereby acknowledged of the affidavits of Linda Brown and Polly Lewis to the birth of Lula Brown, daughter of Chiggling and Linda Brown, October 21, 1903, and the same have been filed with our records as an application for the enrollment of said child.

Respectfully,

Commissioner in Charge.

Chic. N.B. - 323
    (Ora Nichols
    Born July 28, 1903)

BIRTH AFFIDAVIT.

Department of the Interior,
COMMISSION TO THE FIVE CIVILIZED TRIBES.

    IN RE APPLICATION FOR ENROLLMENT, as a citizen of the   Chickasaw   Nation, of   Ora Nichols   , born on the   28   day of   July   , 190 3

Name of Father: Louis Nichols   a citizen of the Chickasaw Nation.
Name of Mother: Hannah Nichols   a citizen of the Chickasaw Nation.

Post-Office: Byars Ind Ter

Applications for Enrollment of Chickasaw Newborn
Act of 1905   Volume IV

AFFIDAVIT OF MOTHER.

UNITED STATES OF AMERICA,
   INDIAN TERRITORY,
  Southern   District.

    I,   Hannah Nichols   , on oath state that I am   25   years of age and a citizen by   Blood , of the   Chickasaw   Nation; that I am the lawful wife of Louis Nichols , who is a citizen, by marriage   of the   Chickasaw   Nation; that a   Female   child was born to me on 28 day of   July   , 190 3, that said child has been named   Ora Nichols   , and is now living.

                                Hannah Nichols

WITNESSES TO MARK:
  { W A Arnote
    (Name Illegible)

    Subscribed and sworn to before me this   25   day of   March   , 190

                                WW Smith
                                Notary Public.

AFFIDAVIT OF ATTENDING PHYSICIAN OR MID-WIFE.

UNITED STATES OF AMERICA,
   INDIAN TERRITORY,
  Southern   District.

    I,   Dr. C. E. Logan   , a Physician   , on oath state that I attended on Mrs.   Hannah Nichols , wife of   Louis Nichols   on the 28th day of   July , 190 3; that there was born to her on said date a   female   child; that said child is now living and is said to have been named   Ora Nichols

                              Dr C.E. Logan

WITNESSES TO MARK:
  { W.T. Brady
    Oral C Busby

    Subscribed and sworn to before me this   3^{d} day of   April   , 190 5

                              (Name Illegible)
                              Notary Public.

Applications for Enrollment of Chickasaw Newborn
Act of 1905 Volume IV

Chickasaw 1386

Muskogee, Indian Territory, April 13, 1905.

Louis Nichols,
    Byars, Indian Territory.

Dear Sir:

    Receipt is hereby acknowledged of the affidavits of Hannah Nichols and Dr. C. E. Logan to the birth of Ora Nichols, daughter of Louis and Hannah Nichols, July 28, 1903, and the same have been filed with our records as an application for the enrollment of said child.

                  Respectfully,

                  Commissioner in Charge.

Chic. N.B. - 324
    (Roy Hudgeons
    Born February 23, 1905)

BIRTH AFFIDAVIT.
DEPARTMENT OF THE INTERIOR.
COMMISSION TO THE FIVE CIVILIZED TRIBES.

    IN RE APPLICATION FOR ENROLLMENT, as a citizen of the Chickasaw Nation, of Roy Hudgeons, born on the 23 day of February, 1905

Name of Father: A.R. Hudgeons   a citizen of the United States Nation.
Name of Mother: Josie Leader (Hudgeons)   a citizen of the Chickasaw Nation.

                Postoffice   Stonewall I.T.

AFFIDAVIT OF MOTHER.

UNITED STATES OF AMERICA, Indian Territory,
    Southern   **DISTRICT.**

    I, Josie Leader, on oath state that I am 19 years of age and a citizen by Blood, of the Chickasaw Nation; that I am the lawful wife of A.R. Hudgeons, who is a citizen, by .... of the United States ~~Nation~~; that a Male

Applications for Enrollment of Chickasaw Newborn
Act of 1905   Volume IV

child was born to me on   23 day of February   , 1905; that said child has been named   Roy Hudgeons   , and was living March 4, 1905.

                                        Josie Leader
Witnesses To Mark:
{

   Subscribed and sworn to before me this 6th day of   April   , 1905

                                        W.F. Harrison
                                        Notary Public.

AFFIDAVIT OF ATTENDING PHYSICIAN OR MID-WIFE.

UNITED STATES OF AMERICA, Indian Territory, }
   Southern   DISTRICT.

   I,   Dr. Geo H Truax   , a Physician   , on oath state that I attended on Mrs. Josie Leader   , wife of A.R. Hudgeons   on the 23 day of February , 1905; that there was born to her on said date a   Male   child; that said child was living March 4, 1905, and is said to have been named Roy Hudgeons

                                        Geo. H. Truax, M.D.
Witnesses To Mark:
{

   Subscribed and sworn to before me this 8th day of   April   , 1905

                                        W.F. Harrison
                                        Notary Public.

BIRTH AFFIDAVIT.
                        DEPARTMENT OF THE INTERIOR.
                  COMMISSION TO THE FIVE CIVILIZED TRIBES.

   IN RE APPLICATION FOR ENROLLMENT, as a citizen of the   Chickasaw   Nation, of Roy Hudgeons   , born on the 23 day of February , 1905

Name of Father: A.R. Hudgeons   a citizen of the   U S   Nation.
Name of Mother: Josie Leader Hudgeons   a citizen of the   Chickasaw Nation.

                     Postoffice   ~~Stonewall~~ Ind. Ter.
                                   Jesse

Applications for Enrollment of Chickasaw Newborn
Act of 1905   Volume IV

AFFIDAVIT OF MOTHER.

UNITED STATES OF AMERICA, Indian Territory,
.... DISTRICT.

I,   Josie Leader Hudgeons   , on oath state that I am   19   years of age and a citizen by   Blood , of the   Chickasaw   Nation; that I am the lawful wife of   A.R. Hudgeons , who is a citizen, by   ———   of the   United States   ~~Nation~~; that a Male   child was born to me on   23   day of   February   , 1905; that said child has been named   Roy Hudgeons   , and was living March 4, 1905.

Josie Leader Hudgeons

Witnesses To Mark:

{

Subscribed and sworn to before me this   5th   day of   July   , 1905

Price Statler
Notary Public.

AFFIDAVIT OF ATTENDING PHYSICIAN OR MID-WIFE.

UNITED STATES OF AMERICA, Indian Territory,
Southern   DISTRICT.

We,   *Mattie Sparks & S. Hudgeons*   , on oath state that I attended on Mrs.   Josie Leader Hudgeons   , wife of   A.R. Hudgeons   on the   23   day of   February , 1905; that there was born to her on said date a   Male   child; that said child was living March 4, 1905, and is said to have been named   Roy Hudgeons

Mattie Sparks
S Hudgeons

Witnesses To Mark:

{

Subscribed and sworn to before me this   5th   day of   July   , 1905

Price Statler
Notary Public.

Applications for Enrollment of Chickasaw Newborn
Act of 1905   Volume IV

Chickasaw 294.

Muskogee, Indian Territory, April 13, 1905.

A. R. Hudgeons,
    Stonewall, Indian Territory.

Dear Sir:

    Receipt is hereby acknowledged of the affidavits of Josie Leader and Geo. H. Truax to the birth of Roy Hudgeons, son of A. R. and Josie Leader Hudgeons, February 23, 1905, and the same have been filed with our records as an application for the enrollment of said child.

Respectfully,

Commissioner in Charge.

9-NB-324.

Muskogee, Indian Territory, May 22, 1905.

A. R. Hudgeons,
    Stonewall, Indian Territory.

Dear Sir:

    There is enclosed you herewith for execution application for the enrollment of your infant child, Roy Hudgeons, born February 23, 1905.

    In the affidavits heretofore filed with the Commission, your wife signs her name as Josie Leader, which appears from the records of the commission to be her maiden name, but at the same time she states that she is your lawful wife. If she is your wife please have her to execute the enclosed affidavits, signing her name as Josie Leader Hudgeons.

    In having these affidavits executed care should be exercised to see that all names are written in full, as they appear in the body of the affidavit, and in the event that either of the persons signing the affidavit are unable to write, signatures by mark must be attested by two witnesses. Each affidavit must be executed before a Notary Public and the notarial seal and signature of the officer must be attached to each separate affidavit.

Respectfully,

VH 22-13.   Chairman.

Applications for Enrollment of Chickasaw Newborn
Act of 1905   Volume IV

9-NB-324

Muskogee, Indian Territory, July 8, 1905.

A. R. Hudgeons,
    Jesse, Indian Territory.

Dear Sir:

    Receipt is hereby acknowledged of the affidavits of Josie Leader Hudgeons, Mattie Sparks and S. Hudgeons to the birth of Roy Hudgeons and the same have been filed with the records of this office in the matter of the enrollment of said child.

        Respectfully,

            Commissioner.

Chic. N.B. - 325
    (Roy Thomas Downing
    Born March 9, 1904)

BIRTH AFFIDAVIT.

DEPARTMENT OF THE INTERIOR.
COMMISSION TO THE FIVE CIVILIZED TRIBES.

IN RE APPLICATION FOR ENROLLMENT, as a citizen of the Chickasaw Nation, of Roy Thomas Downing, born on the 9th day of Mch, 1904

Name of Father: Mose Downing   a citizen of the Chickasaw Nation.
Name of Mother: Mattie Downing   a citizen of the Chickasaw Nation.

        Postoffice   Caddo I T

AFFIDAVIT OF MOTHER.

UNITED STATES OF AMERICA, Indian Territory,
    Central   DISTRICT.

    I, Mattie Downing, on oath state that I am 23 years of age and a citizen by intermarriage, of the Chickasaw Nation; that I am the lawful wife of Mose Downing, who is a citizen, by blood of the Chickasaw Nation;

Applications for Enrollment of Chickasaw Newborn
Act of 1905   Volume IV

that a   male   child was born to me on   9th   day of   Mch   , 1904; that said child has been named   Roy Thomas Downing   , and was living March 4, 1905.

Mrs Mattie Downing

Witnesses To Mark:
{

Subscribed and sworn to before me this 5th   day of   April   , 1905

AT West
Notary Public.

AFFIDAVIT OF ATTENDING PHYSICIAN OR MID-WIFE.

UNITED STATES OF AMERICA, Indian Territory, }
Central   DISTRICT. }

I,   H G Goben   , a   Physician   , on oath state that I attended on Mrs.   Mattie Downing   , wife of   Mose Downing   on the 9th day of   Mch   , 1904; that there was born to her on said date a   male   child; that said child was living March 4, 1905, and is said to have been named   Roy Thomas Downing

H.G. Goben M.D.

Witnesses To Mark:
{

Subscribed and sworn to before me this 8th   day of   April   , 1905

AT West
Notary Public.

Chickasaw 1714.

Muskogee, Indian Territory, April 13, 1905.

Mose Downing,
   Caddo, Indian Territory.

Dear Sir:

   Receipt is hereby acknowledged of the affidavits of Mrs. Mattie Downing and H. G. Goben to the birth of Roy Thomas Downing, son of Mose and Mattie Downing, March 9, 1904, and the same have been filed with our records as an application for the enrollment of said child.

Respectfully,
Commissioner in Charge.

Applications for Enrollment of Chickasaw Newborn
Act of 1905 Volume IV

Chic. N.B. - 326
*(Retia P. Carter
Born March 17, 1904)*

BIRTH AFFIDAVIT.

DEPARTMENT OF THE INTERIOR.
COMMISSION TO THE FIVE CIVILIZED TRIBES.

IN RE APPLICATION FOR ENROLLMENT, as a citizen of the Chickasaw Nation, of Retia P Carter , born on the 17 day of March , 1904

Name of Father: Colbert Carter   a citizen of the Chickasaw Nation.
Name of Mother: Minnie Carter   a citizen of the Chickasaw Nation.

Postoffice   Yuba IT

AFFIDAVIT OF MOTHER.

UNITED STATES OF AMERICA, Indian Territory,
Central   DISTRICT.

I, Minnie Carter , on oath state that I am 25 years of age and a citizen by Marriage , of the Chickasaw Nation; that I am the lawful wife of Colbert Carter , who is a citizen, by Blood of the Chickasaw Nation; that a Girl child was born to me on 17 day of March , 1904; that said child has been named Retia P Carter , and was living March 4, 1905.

Minnie Carter

Witnesses To Mark:

Subscribed and sworn to before me this 5 day of April , 1905

Chas P Walker
Notary Public.

Applications for Enrollment of Chickasaw Newborn
Act of 1905   Volume IV

AFFIDAVIT OF ATTENDING PHYSICIAN OR MID-WIFE.

UNITED STATES OF AMERICA, Indian Territory, }
    Central   DISTRICT.

I, Era Lyles, a midwife, on oath state that I attended on Mrs. Minnie Carter, wife of Colbert Carter on the 17 day of March, 1904; that there was born to her on said date a Girl child; that said child was living March 4, 1905, and is said to have been named Retia P Carter

                                     Era Lyles

Witnesses To Mark:
{

     Subscribed and sworn to before me this 5 day of April, 1905

                                Chas P Walker
                                  Notary Public.

                                          Chickasaw 1178.

                   Muskogee, Indian Territory, April 13, 1905.

Colbert Carter,
     Yuba, Indian Territory.

Dear Sir:

     Receipt is hereby acknowledged of the affidavits of Minnie Carter and Era Lyles, to the birth of Katie[sic] P Carter, daughter of Colbert and Minnie Carter, March 17, 1904, and the same have been filed with our records as an application for the enrollment of said child.

                             Respectfully,

                                     Commissioner in Charge.

Chic. N.B. - 327
     (Earnest Leonard Thaxton
     Born April 3, 1903)

Applications for Enrollment of Chickasaw Newborn
Act of 1905   Volume IV

BIRTH AFFIDAVIT.   #144
DEPARTMENT OF THE INTERIOR.
COMMISSION TO THE FIVE CIVILIZED TRIBES.

IN RE APPLICATION FOR ENROLLMENT, as a citizen of the   Chickasaw   Nation, of   Ernest Lenord Thaxton   , born on the   3   day of   April   , 1903

Name of Father: Tullas Thaxton   a citizen of the   Chickasaw   Nation.
Name of Mother: Rose E Thaxton   a citizen of the   Chickasaw   Nation.

Postoffice   Yarnabby[sic]

AFFIDAVIT OF MOTHER.

UNITED STATES OF AMERICA, Indian Territory, }
   Central   DISTRICT.   }

I,   Rosa E Thaxton   , on oath state that I am   21   years of age and a citizen by   blood   , of the   Chickasaw   Nation; that I am the lawful wife of   Tullas Thaxton , who is a citizen, by   intermarriage   of the   Chickasaw   Nation; that a   male   child was born to me on   3   day of   April   , 1903, that said child has been named   Ernest Lenord   , and is now living.

Rose E Thaxton

Witnesses To Mark:
 { C.T. Cravens
 { Willie Cravens

Subscribed and sworn to before me this 20 day of February , 1905.

S M Mead
Notary Public.

AFFIDAVIT OF ATTENDING PHYSICIAN OR MID-WIFE.

UNITED STATES OF AMERICA, Indian Territory, }
   Central   DISTRICT.   }

I,   Mary Cravens   , a   midwife   , on oath state that I attended on Mrs.   Rosa E Thaxton , wife of   Tullas Thaxton   on the   3   day of April , 1903; that there was born to her on said date a   male   child; that said child is now living and is said to have been named   Ernest Lenord

Mary Cravens

Applications for Enrollment of Chickasaw Newborn
Act of 1905   Volume IV

Witnesses To Mark:
- C.T. Cravens
- Willie Cravens

Subscribed and sworn to before me this 20 day of February , 1905.

S M Mead
Notary Public.

BIRTH AFFIDAVIT.

DEPARTMENT OF THE INTERIOR.
COMMISSION TO THE FIVE CIVILIZED TRIBES.

IN RE APPLICATION FOR ENROLLMENT, as a citizen of the Chickasaw Nation, of Earnest Leonard Thaxton , born on the 3 day of April , 1903

Name of Father: Tullas Thaxton   a citizen of the Chickasaw Nation.
Name of Mother: Rosa E Thaxton   a citizen of the Chickasaw Nation.

Postoffice   Yarnaby IT

AFFIDAVIT OF MOTHER.

UNITED STATES OF AMERICA, Indian Territory,
Central   DISTRICT.

I, Rosa E Thaxton , on oath state that I am 22 years of age and a citizen by Blood , of the Chickasaw Nation; that I am the lawful wife of Tullas Thaxton , who is a citizen, by Intermarriage of the Chickasaw Nation; that a male child was born to me on third day of April , 1903; that said child has been named Earnest Leonard Thaxton , and was living March 4, 1905.

Rosa E Thaxton

Witnesses To Mark:

Subscribed and sworn to before me this 1 day of April , 1905

Chas P Walker
Notary Public.

268

Applications for Enrollment of Chickasaw Newborn
Act of 1905 Volume IV

AFFIDAVIT OF ATTENDING PHYSICIAN OR MID-WIFE.

UNITED STATES OF AMERICA, Indian Territory, } Central DISTRICT.

I, Mary Cravens, a midwife, on oath state that I attended on Mrs. Rosa E Thaxton, wife of Tullas Thaxton on the third day of April, 1903; that there was born to her on said date a male child; that said child was living March 4, 1905, and is said to have been named Earnest Leonard Thaxton

                                             her
                                 Mary x Cravens

Witnesses To Mark: mark
    { Lida Thaxton
      O J Vandiver

Subscribed and sworn to before me this 1 day of April, 1905

                                   Chas P Walker
                                     Notary Public.

                                                                 Chickasaw 1116.

Muskogee, Indian Territory, April 13, 1905.

Tullas Thaxton,
    Yarnaby, Indian Territory.

Dear Sir:

    Receipt is hereby acknowledged of the affidavits of Rosa E. Thaxton and Mary Cravens to the birth of Earnest Leonard Thaxton, son of Rosa E. and Tullas Thaxton, April 3, 1903, and the same have been filed with our records as an application for the enrollment of said child.

                                           Respectfully,

                                                         Commissioner in Charge.

Chic. N.B. - 328
    (Rena Jones
    Born December 16, 1903)

Applications for Enrollment of Chickasaw Newborn
Act of 1905 Volume IV

United States of America
Indian Territory

This is to certify that Mrs. Susan J. Matubby who was the mid wife who attended on Mrs Ellen Jones wife of Wesley Jones on the 16th Dec 1903 and the said Mrs Susan J. Matubby died on the 26th day of March 1905

Given under my hand and seal this the 8th day of April 1905

Hannah J. Matubby

Subscribed and sworn to before me this the 8th day of April 1905.

W. J. O'Donby
Notary Public

BIRTH AFFIDAVIT.

DEPARTMENT OF THE INTERIOR.
COMMISSION TO THE FIVE CIVILIZED TRIBES.

IN RE APPLICATION FOR ENROLLMENT, as a citizen of the Chickasaw Nation, of Rena Jones, born on the 16th day of Dec, 1903

Name of Father: Wesley Jones   a citizen of the Chickasaw Nation.
Name of Mother: Ellen Jones   a citizen of the Chickasaw Nation.

Postoffice   Albany I.T.

AFFIDAVIT OF MOTHER.

UNITED STATES OF AMERICA, Indian Territory,
Central   DISTRICT.

I, Ellen Jones, on oath state that I am 20 years of age and a citizen by blood, of the Chickasaw Nation; that I am the lawful wife of Wesley Jones, who is a citizen, by Blood of the Chickasaw Nation; that a Female child was born to me on 16th day of December, 1903; that said child has been named Rena Jones, and was living March 4, 1905.

Ellen Jones

Witnesses To Mark:

Applications for Enrollment of Chickasaw Newborn
Act of 1905   Volume IV

Subscribed and sworn to before me this 8th day of   April   , 1905

W.J. O'Donby
Notary Public.

AFFIDAVIT OF ATTENDING PHYSICIAN OR MID-WIFE.

UNITED STATES OF AMERICA, Indian Territory, }
   Central   DISTRICT. }

I, ..., a ...., on oath state that I attended on Mrs. ...., wife of ...., on the .... day of ...., 1.......; that there was born to her on said date a .... child; that said child was living March 4, 1905, and is said to have been named ....

Witnesses To Mark:
{ ....
  .... }

Subscribed and sworn to before me this .... day of ...., 1905.

....
Notary Public.

United States of America,)
Indian Territory,   ) SS:
Central District.   )

    John West deposes and says: That he is 31 years of age, and is a member of the Choctaw Tribe of Indians, having been identified as a Mississippi Choctaw, and received his allotment as such.

    That on the 16th day of December, A. D. 1903, he was residing and living at the home of Wesley Jones whose wife's name is Ellen Jones, and that on said date there was born to said Ellen Jones, wife of the said Wesley Jones, a girl child, who was afterwards named Rena, and is now called Rena Jones, and that said child called Rena Jones was living on the 4th day of March, A.D. 1905. That he did not see said child when it was born, but that he saw it within a very few hours, on the same day it was born, and that he continued to live at the home of Wesley and Ellen Jones for several months after the birth of said child, and it is the same identical child, and he swears that said child is the child of Ellen Jones and that it was born on the 16th day of December, A.D. 1903. That he is disinterested in this matter, and is not related in any way to either Ellen Jones or Wesley Jones. *Attest*

   A. J. Bradley
   A. B. McDonald

his
John x West
mark

Applications for Enrollment of Chickasaw Newborn
Act of 1905 Volume IV

Subscribed and sworn to before me this   15   day of July, A.D. 1905.

J.M. Reasor

My commission expires May 5 1908

United States of America,   )
Indian Territory,   ) SS:
Central District.   )

    Albert McDonald deposes and says: That he is   30   years of age, and a member of the Chickasaw tribe of Indians.

    That on the 17th day of December, A. D. 1903 he was at the home of Wesley and Ellen Jones, and an infant girl child had been born to said Ellen Jones that seemed to be only a few hours old; that afterwards this child was named Rena, and is now called Rena Jones; that she is a girl and was living on the 4th day of March, A. D. 1905; that at the time he saw said child on the 17th day of December, A. D. 1903, it did not appear to be over twenty-four hours old; that its said mother, Ellen Jones was in bed and seemed to be sick, and the said child was in bed with her and showed that it was just a few hours old; and that he has known said child ever since then, and the said Ellen Jones has continued to nurse and attend to said child as the mother of the child, and it is known in the community where Ellen Jones and Wesley Jones live as their child; that he is disinterested in this matter, and is not related in any way to either Wesley Jones or Ellen Jones.

Albert S. McDonald

Subscribed and sworn to before me this   15   day of July, A.D. 1905.

J.M. Reasor

My commission expires May 5 1908

Chickasaw 289.

Muskogee, Indian Territory, April 13, 1905.

Wesley Jones,
    Albany, Indian Territory.

Dear Sir:

    Receipt is hereby acknowledged of the affidavits of Ellen Jones and Hannah Imatubby to the birth of Rena Jones, daughter of Wesley and Ellen Jones, December 16, 1903, and the same have been filed with our records as an application for the enrollment of said child.

Applications for Enrollment of Chickasaw Newborn
Act of 1905   Volume IV

Respectfully,

Commissioner in Charge.

9-NB-328

Muskogee, Indian Territory, July 21, 1905.

Wesley Jones,
    Albany, Indian Territory.

Dear Sir:

    Receipt is hereby acknowledged of the affidavits of Albert S. McDonald and John West to the birth of Rena Jones, daughter of Wesley and Ellen Jones, December 16, 1903, and the same have been filed with the record in this case.

Respectfully,

Commissioner.

9-NB-*328*.

Muskogee, Indian Territory, May 16, 1905.

Wesley Jones,
    Albany, Indian Territory.

Dear Sir:

    Referring to the application for the enrollment of your infant child, Rena Jones, born December 16, 1903, it is noted from the affidavits of Hannah Imatubby, heretofore filed with the Commission, that the mid-wife, Mrs. Susan I. Matubby, who attended upon your wife at the birth of the applicant is dead.

    If this is correct it will be necessary for you to file with the Commission the affidavits of two disinterested persons who have actual knowledge of the facts that the child was born, the date of its birth; that it was living on March 4, 1905, and that Ellen Jones was her mother.

    In having these affidavits executed care should be exercised to see that all names are written in full, as they appear in the body of the affidavit, and in the event that either of the persons signing the affidavit are unable to write, signatures by mark must be

Applications for Enrollment of Chickasaw Newborn
Act of 1905 Volume IV

attested by two witnesses. Each affidavit must be executed before a Notary Public and the notarial seal and signature of the officer must be attached to each separate affidavit.

Respectfully,

Chairman.

Chic. N.B. - 329
    (Kutman Walton
    Born June 23, 1904)

(The Birth Affidavit below typed as given.)

Birth Affidivat.

Department of the Interior.
COMMISSION TO THE FIVE CIVILIZED TRIBES.

IN RE APPLICATION FOR ENROLLMENT, as a citizen of the Chickasaw Nation, of   Kutman Walton   born on the   23   day of   June , 190 4

Name of father: Simon Walton   a citizen of the   Chickasaw   Nation.
                                      Walton
Name of mother: Minnie Stick *nee*   a citizen of the   Chickasaw   Nation.

Postoffice   Conway I.T.

####################
Affidivat of mother.

United States of america,
  Southern Judicial District
of the Indian Territory.

      I,   Minnie Stick   , on oath state that I am   20 - Twenty   years of age and a citizen by   Blood , of the   Chickasaw   Nation; that I am the lawful wife of   Simon Walton   who is a citizen , by   Blood   of the   Chickasaw   Nation; that a   male   child was born to me on   23   day of   June   , 1904 ; that said child has been named   Kutman Walton , and was living March 4, 1905.

Minnie Walton

Applications for Enrollment of Chickasaw Newborn
Act of 1905   Volume IV

Witnesses to mark:

_____

_____

Subscribed and sworn to before me this   6   day of   April   , 190 5

My Commission expires,   Aug 19-1908   Joseph Anderson
                                              Notary Public in and for the
Post-office: Roff I.T.   Southern District of the
                                              Indian Territory.

####################
Affidavit of attending physician or midwife.

United States of america,
Southern Judicial District
of the Indian Territory.

    I,   Alice Stick   a mid-wife, on oath state that I attended on Mrs.   Minnie Walton , wife of   Simon Walton   on the   23   day of   June , 1904 ; that there was born to her on said date a   male   child; that said child was living March 4, 1905, and is said to have been named   Kutman Walton

                          Alice Stick

Witnesses to mark:

_____

_____

Subscribed and sworn to before me this   6   day of   April   , 190 5

My Commission expires,   Aug 19-1908   Joseph Anderson
                                              Notary Public in and for the
Post-office: Roff I.T.   Southern District of the
                                              Indian Territory.

_____

                                Chickasaw 165.

Muskogee, Indian Territory, April 13, 1905.

Simon Walton,
    Conway, Indian Territory.

Dear Sir:

    Receipt is hereby acknowledged of the affidavits of Minnie Walton and Alice Stick to the birth of Kutman Walton, son of Simon and Minnie Walton, June 23, 1904, and the same have been filed with our records as an application for the enrollment of said child.

Applications for Enrollment of Chickasaw Newborn
Act of 1905   Volume IV

Respectfully,

Commissioner in Charge.

9-NB-329

Muskogee, Indian Territory, January 8, 1906.

James B. Vandiver,
Roff, Indian Territory.

Dear Sir:

Receipt is hereby acknowledged of your letter of January 3, 1906, asking the status of the application for the enrollment of Kutman Walton, son of Simon and Minnie Walton; you inclose a letter acknowledging receipt of the application and ask why no further action can be taken relative to the enrollment of said child until the has been taken in this matter.

In reply to your letter you are advised that Kutman Walton has been enrolled as a new born citizen of the Chickasaw Nation and his name placed upon said roll opposite No. 298, his enrollment having been approved by the Secretary of the Interior, June 1, 1905.

The communication of the Commission to the Five Civilized Tribes of April 13, 1905, inclosed with your letter is herewith returned.

Respectfully,

Commissioner.

EB 1-8.

9-NB-329.

Muskogee, Indian Territory, January 27, 1906.

James B. Vandiver,
Roff, Indian Territory.

Dear Sir:

Receipt is hereby acknowledged of your letter of January 17, 1906, in which you state that it appears that Kutman Walton has been enrolled and approved and you ask if there is not a certificate of enrollment for him to present when he goes to file; you also state that sometime ago you wrote in regard to the enrollment of Lillie Kinner and asked

Applications for Enrollment of Chickasaw Newborn
Act of 1905 Volume IV

if Thomas Stick, deceased, could be enrolled; you also request blank application for the enrollment of adults and infants and regulations governing same.

In reply to your letter you are advised that it will not be necessary that a certificate of the enrollment of Kutman Walton be forwarded in order that selection of allotment may be made in his behalf as the office have been advised of the approval of his enrollment by the Secretary of the Interior.

You are further advised that the information contained in your letter is not sufficient to enable this office to identify Lillie Kinner and Thomas Stick upon its records as applicants for enrollment as citizens of the Choctaw or Chickasaw Nations[sic].

You are also advised that this office has no blanks for the purpose of making application for the enrollment of adults, and as there is now no provisions for the enrollment of infant children, it is inpracticable[sic] to furnish you blanks of this character.

Respectfully,

Acting Commissioner.

Circular.

9-NB-329

Muskogee, Indian Territory, January 26, 1906.

James B. Vandiver,
Roff, Indian Territory.

Dear Sir:

Receipt is hereby acknowledged of your letter of January 17, 1906, in which you state that it appears that Kutman Walton has been enrolled and approved and you ask if there is not a certificate of enrollment for him to present when he goes to file; you also state that sometime ago you wrote in regard to the enrollment of Lillie Kinner and ask if Thomas Stick deceased can be enrolled; you also request blank application for the enrollment of adults and infants and regulations governing same.

In reply to your letter you are advised that it will not be necessary that a certificate of the enrollment of Kutman Walton be forwarded in order that selection of allotment may be made in his behalf as the land offices have been advised of the approval of his enrollment by the Secretary of the Interior.

You are further advised that the information contained in your letter is not sufficient to enable this office to identify Lillie Kinner and Thomas Stick upon its records for enrollment as citizens of the Choctaw or Chickasaw Nations.

Applications for Enrollment of Chickasaw Newborn
Act of 1905   Volume IV

Respectfully,

Acting Commissioner.

19-106
9-NB-329

Muskogee, Indian Territory, February 16, 1906.

James B. Vandiver,
    Roff, Indian Territory.

Dear Sir:

    Receipt is hereby acknowledged of your letter of February 12, 1906, in which you ask the status of the application of Elijah Harland a freedman for transfer to the Chickasaw roll; you also ask what was the time limit in which application for the transfer of freedman to the roll of citizens should be made; you also ask the time limit in which application for enrollment of infants and adult Chickasaws should be made and the time within which application for the enrollment of children of intermarried citizens should have been made; you further ask if Kutman Walton for whose enrollment application was made prior to the per capita payment of August 1904 is not entitled to that and subsequent payments, although he was not enrolled until 1905. You also ask if an intermarried citizen forfeits his right to enrollment by his marriage to a white woman after the death of his Indian wife.

    In reply to your letter you are advised that it does not appear from the records of this office that application has been made by or in behalf of Elijah Harland for the transfer of his name from the roll of Chickasaw freedmen to the roll of citizens by blood of the Chickasaw Nation.

    You are further advised that under the act of Congress approved July 1, 1902, the Commission to the Five Civilized Tribes was authorized for a period of ninety days from September 25, 1902, the date of the ratification of said act, to receive applications for enrollment in the Choctaw and Chickasaw Nations, and subsequent to that time the application of no person whomsoever for enrollment on the Choctaw and Chickasaw Nation should be received.

    This act was modified by the act of Congress approved March 3, 1905, which authorized the reception, for a period of ninety days from that date, of applications for the enrollment of children born prior to March 4, 1905, to citizens by blood of the Choctaw and Chickasaw Nations whose enrollment has been approved by the Secretary of the Interior prior to March 4, 1905.

    Relative to the per capita payment to Kutman Walton you are advised that the payment of moneys to citizens of the Choctaw and Chickasaw Nations is a matter which

Applications for Enrollment of Chickasaw Newborn
Act of 1905   Volume IV

is within the jurisdiction of the United States Indian Agent and for information upon that subject you should address him at Muskogee, Indian Territory.

Replying to that portion of your letter in which you ask relative to the right to enrollment of an intermarried citizen who subsequent to the death of his citizen wife marries a white woman, you are advised that you do not state the name of the person to whom you refer and this office does not render opinions upon hypothetical questions of citizenship and enrollment.

Respectfully,

Acting Commissioner.

Chic. N.B. - 330
    (Mary Alice Kemp
    Born September 30, 1904)

BIRTH AFFIDAVIT.

DEPARTMENT OF THE INTERIOR.
COMMISSION TO THE FIVE CIVILIZED TRIBES.

IN RE APPLICATION FOR ENROLLMENT, as a citizen of the Chickasaw Nation, of Mary Alice Kemp, born on the 30th day of September, 1904

Name of Father: Frank Kemp   a citizen of the Chickasaw Nation.
Name of Mother: Annie Kemp   a citizen of the Chickasaw Nation.

Postoffice   Mill Creek I. T.

AFFIDAVIT OF MOTHER.

UNITED STATES OF AMERICA, Indian Territory,
.... DISTRICT.

I, Annie Kemp, on oath state that I am 31 years of age and a citizen by Blood, of the Chickasaw Nation; that I am the lawful wife of Frank Kemp, who is a citizen, by Blood of the Chickasaw Nation; that a Female child was born to me on 30th day of September, 1904; that said child has been named Mary Alice Kemp, and was living March 4, 1905.

Annie Kemp

Applications for Enrollment of Chickasaw Newborn
Act of 1905   Volume IV

Witnesses To Mark:
{

Subscribed and sworn to before me this 29 day of May , 1905

S.W. Frost
Notary Public.

AFFIDAVIT OF ATTENDING PHYSICIAN OR MID-WIFE.

UNITED STATES OF AMERICA, Indian Territory,
.... DISTRICT.

physician
I, Thos M. Berry , a practicing , on oath state that I attended on Mrs. Annie Kemp , wife of Frank Kemp on the 30th day of September , 1904; that there was born to her on said date a female child; that said child was living March 4, 1905, and is said to have been named Mary Alice Kemp

Thos. M. Berry M.D.

Witnesses To Mark:
{

Subscribed and sworn to before me this 26th day of May , 1905

J.H. Hannigan
Notary Public.

BIRTH AFFIDAVIT.

DEPARTMENT OF THE INTERIOR.
COMMISSION TO THE FIVE CIVILIZED TRIBES.

IN RE APPLICATION FOR ENROLLMENT, as a citizen of the Chickasaw Nation, of Mary Allice[sic] Kemp , born on the 30 day of September , 1904

Name of Father: Frank Kemp   a citizen of the Chickasaw Nation.
Name of Mother: Annie Kemp   a citizen of the Chickasaw Nation.

Postoffice   Mill Creek I. T.

Applications for Enrollment of Chickasaw Newborn
Act of 1905   Volume IV

AFFIDAVIT OF MOTHER.

UNITED STATES OF AMERICA, Indian Territory, }
    Southern   DISTRICT.

I, Annie Kemp, on oath state that I am 31 years of age and a citizen by Blood, of the Chickasaw Nation; that I am the lawful wife of Frank Kemp, who is a citizen, by Blood of the Chickasaw Nation; that a Female child was born to me on 30 day of September, 1904; that said child has been named Mary Allice Kemp, and was living March 4, 1905.

                                Annie Kemp

Witnesses To Mark:

Subscribed and sworn to before me this 8 day of April, 1905

                                S.W. Frost
                                    Notary Public.

UNITED STATES OF AMER...

I, ...
Mrs. .... state that I attended on .... day of ...., 1........;
that there was born .... d child was living March 4, 1905, and is said ....

Witnesses To Mark:

Subscribed ...., 1905.
                                    ry Public.

[Handwritten insert:]

This is to certify that I T. M. Berry, a Practising [sic] Physician of the Indian Territory, attended Anne Kemp, Indian Territory wife of Frank Kemp and a baby girl was born on the 30th day of September 1904

Name of baby Mary Alice Kemp

United States of America Indian Territory Southern District

On this 20 day of Feb - 1905 Personally appeared before me a Notary Public of the above named District - T M Berry Physi-

Applications for Enrollment of Chickasaw Newborn
Act of 1905   Volume IV

BIRTH AFFIDAVIT.

DEPARTMENT OF THE INTERIOR.
COMMISSION TO THE FIVE CIVILIZED TRIBES.

IN RE APPLICATION FOR ENROLLMENT, as a citizen of the   Chickasaw   Nation,
of   Mary Allice[sic] Kemp   , born on the   30   day of September   , 1904

Name of Father: Frank Kemp   a citizen of the   Chickasaw   Nation.
Name of Mother: Annie Kemp   a citizen of the   Chickasaw   Nation.

Postoffice   Mill Creek I. T.

AFFIDAVIT OF MOTHER.

UNITED STATES OF AMERICA, Indian Territory,
Southern   DISTRICT.

I,   Annie Kemp   , on oath state that I am   31   years of age and a citizen by Blood   , of the   Chickasaw   Nation; that I am the lawful wife of Frank Kemp   , who is a citizen, by   Blood   of the   Chickasaw   Nation; that a   Female   child was born to me on   30   day of   September   , 1904; that said child has been named   Mary Allice Kemp   , and was living March 4, 1905.

Annie Kemp

Witnesses To Mark:

Subscribed and sworn to before me this   8   day of   April   , 1905

S.W. Frost
_____ Notary Public.

UNITED STATES OF AMER[ICA]

I, _____
Mrs. _____
that there was born
4, 1905, and is said

This is to certify that I T. M. Berry, a Practising[sic] Physician of the Indian Territory, attended Anne Kemp, Indian Territory wife of Frank Kemp and a baby girl was born on the 30th day of September 1904
Name of baby Mary Alice Kemp

h state that I attended on
. day of _____, 1____;
d child was living March

282

Applications for Enrollment of Chickasaw Newborn
Act of 1905   Volume IV

Witnesses To Mark:

Subscribed and

> United States of America Indian Territory
> Southern District
> On this 20 day of Feb - 1905 Personally appeared before me a Notary Public of the above named District - T M Berry Physician to me personally well known as the person named in the foregoing instrument and had acknowledge and sworned to before me this 20 of Feb - 1905
>
> J.H.Clark
> Notary Public

..., 1905.

y Public.

Chickasaw 1261.

Muskogee, Indian Territory, April 13, 1905.

Frank Kemp,
    Mill Creek, Indian Territory.

Dear Sir:

    Receipt is hereby acknowledged of the affidavits of Annie Kemp and T. M. Berry to the birth of Mary Alice Kemp, daughter of Frank and Annie Kemp, September 30, 1904, and the same have been filed with our records as an application for the enrollment of said child.

                Respectfully,

                              Commissioner in Charge.

9-NB-330.

Muskogee, Indian Territory, May 17, 1905.

Frank Kemp,
    Mill Creek, Indian Territory.

Dear Sir:

    Referring to the application for the enrollment of your infant child, Mary Alice Kemp, born September 30, 1904, it is noted that the physician in his affidavit fails to state that the above mentioned applicant was living on March 4, 1905.

Applications for Enrollment of Chickasaw Newborn
Act of 1905 Volume IV

In order that the child may be enrolled it is necessary that the affidavit of the physician show that he[sic] was living on March 4, 1905. So you will please secure his affidavit to that effect, using the enclosed blank.

Respectfully,

Chairman.

17/1.

9-N.B. 330.

Muskogee, Indian Territory, June 2, 1905.

Frank Kemp,
    Millcreek, Indian Territory.

Dear Sir:

Receipt is hereby acknowledged of the affidavits of Annie Kemp and Thos. M. Berry, M. D., to the birth of Mary Alice Kemp, daughter of Frank and Annie Kemp, September 30, 1904, and the same have been filed with our records in the matter of the application for the enrollment of said child.

Respectfully,

Commissioner in Charge.

Chic. N.B. - 331
    (Iva Lois Colbert
    Born January 7, 1904)

Applications for Enrollment of Chickasaw Newborn
Act of 1905   Volume IV

Certificate of Record of Marriage

UNITED STATES OF AMERICA,
INDIAN TERRITORY,   } sct.
Southern District.

DEPARTMENT OF THE INTERIOR,
COMMISSION TO THE FIVE CIVILIZED TRIBES.
FILED
JUL 11 1905
Tams Bixby CHAIRMAN.

I, C. M. CAMPBELL, Clerk of the United States Court, in the Territory and District aforesaid, DO HEREBY CERTIFY, that the License for and Certificate of Marriage of

Mr   Ode Colbert   and

M   Lillie Stubblefield

were filed in my office in said Territory and District the 15 day of July A.D., 190 1 and duly recorded in Book   E   of Marriage Record Page 477

WITNESS my hand and seal of said Court, at Ardmore, this 15" day of July   A.D. 190 1

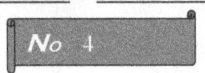

C. M. CAMPBELL, Clerk.
Southern Dist. Ind. Ter.
C. M. Campbell
CLERK.

Marriage License

No 4

United States of America,
INDIAN TERRITORY,   } ss:
SOUTHERN DISTRICT.

To Any Person Authorized by Law
to Solemnize Marriage, Greeting:

You Are Hereby Commanded To solemnize the Rite and publish the Banns of Matrimony between Mr.   Ode. Colbert,
of   Duncan   in the Indian Territory, aged   22   years, and
M   Lillie Stubblefield,   of   Duncan
in the Indian Territory, aged   20   years, according to law; and do you officially sign and return this License to the parties therein named.

285

Applications for Enrollment of Chickasaw Newborn
Act of 1905   Volume IV

Witness My hand and official Seal, this   29"   day
of   June   A. D. 190 1

By
J.H. Worton   Deputy.
C.M. Campbell
Clerk of the United States Court.

Certificate of Marriage.

United States of America, }
INDIAN TERRITORY,   } ss:
SOUTHERN DISTRICT.   }
I,   C. Stubblefield
a   Minister of the gospel

do hereby certify that on the   2   day of   July   A. D. 190 1 , I did duly and according to law, as commanded in the foregoing License, solemnize the Rite and publish the Banns of Matrimony between the parties therein named.

WITNESS my hand, this   2   day of   July   A. D. 190 1

My credentials are recorded in the office of the Clerk of the United States Court, Indian Territory, Southern District, at Ardmore, Book   A   , Page   15

(NOTE.--The person officiating should fill in the spaces
for book and page and sign here.)
C. Stubblefield
a   Durant I.T.

NOTE. (a) - This License and Certificate of Marriages must be returned to the office of the Clerk of the United States Court in   the   Indian Territory, at Ardmore, within sixty days from the date thereof, or the party to whom the License was issued will be liable in the amount of ONE HUNDRED DOLLARS ($100).
NOTE. (b) - No person is authorized to perform the Marriage Ceremony in the Southern District unless the proper credentials have first been recorded in the Clerk's office.

BIRTH AFFIDAVIT.   No 92

IN RE-APPLICATION FOR ENROLLMENT, as a citizen of the   Chickasaw   Nation, of   Iva Lois Culbert[sic]   , born on the   7th day of   January   , 190 4

Name of Father: Thomas R. Culbert   a citizen of the   Chickasaw   Nation.
Name of Mother: Lillie Colbert   a citizen of the   ———   Nation.

Postoffice   Hope, Indian Territory

Applications for Enrollment of Chickasaw Newborn
Act of 1905   Volume IV

AFFIDAVIT OF MOTHER.

UNITED STATES OF AMERICA, INDIAN TERRITORY, }
Southern   District.

I, Lillie Colbert, on oath state that I am 24 years of age ~~and a citizen by~~ , ~~of the~~ ~~Nation~~; that I am the lawful wife of Thomas R Colbert, who is a citizen, by blood of the Chickasaw Nation; that a female child was born to me on 7th day of January, 1904, that said child has been named Iva Lois Colbert, and is now living.

Lillie Colbert

Witnesses To Mark:

Subscribed and sworn to before me this 15 day of February, 1905.

E.H. Bond
Notary Public.

AFFIDAVIT OF ATTENDING PHYSICIAN OR MID-WIFE.

UNITED STATES OF AMERICA, INDIAN TERRITORY, }
District.

I, J.T. Wharton, a Practicing Physician, on oath state that I attended on Mrs. Lillie Colbart[sic], wife of Thos R. Colbart on the 7th day of Jany, 190 4; that there was born to her on said date a female child; that said child is now living and is said to have been named Iva Louis[sic].

Dr. J.T. Wharton

Witnesses To Mark:

Subscribed and sworn to before me this 15 day of February, 1905.

E.H. Bond
Notary Public.

Applications for Enrollment of Chickasaw Newborn
Act of 1905 Volume IV

BIRTH AFFIDAVIT.

DEPARTMENT OF THE INTERIOR.
COMMISSION TO THE FIVE CIVILIZED TRIBES.

IN RE APPLICATION FOR ENROLLMENT, as a citizen of the Chickasaw Nation, of Iva Lois Colbert , born on the 7 day of Jany , 1904

Name of Father: Thomas R Colbert   a citizen of the Chickasaw Nation.
Name of Mother: Lillie Colbert   a citizen of the United States Nation.

Postoffice   Hope, Ind. Ter

AFFIDAVIT OF MOTHER.

UNITED STATES OF AMERICA, Indian Territory,
    Southern   DISTRICT.

I, Lillie Colbert , on oath state that I am 24 years of age and a citizen by ...., of the United States ~~Nation~~; that I am the lawful wife of Thomas R Colbert , who is a citizen, by blood of the Chickasaw Nation; that a female child was born to me on 7th day of January , 1904; that said child has been named Iva Lois Colbert , and was living March 4, 1905.

                                       Lillie Colbert

Witnesses To Mark:
{

Subscribed and sworn to before me this 5 day of April , 1905

                                       E.H. Bond
                                            Notary Public.

AFFIDAVIT OF ATTENDING PHYSICIAN OR MID-WIFE.

UNITED STATES OF AMERICA, Indian Territory,
    Southern   DISTRICT.

I, J. T. Wharton , a physician , on oath state that I attended on Mrs. Lillie Colbert , wife of Thomas R Colbert on the 7 day of January, 1904; that there was born to her on said date a female child; that said child was living March 4, 1905, and is said to have been named Iva Lois Colbert

                                       J.T. Wharton M.D.

Witnesses To Mark:
{

Applications for Enrollment of Chickasaw Newborn
Act of 1905   Volume IV

Subscribed and sworn to before me this 5 day of   April   , 1905

E.H. Bond
Notary Public.

(The affidavit below typed as given.)

Indian Territory,
              SS.
Southern District,

    Before me, the undersigned authority, on this the 1 0th day of July, 1905, personally appeared Frank *W* Jones, and J.R.Prentice, who on oath say that there postoffice address is Duncan, Indian Territory; their ages respectively are _45_ and _28_; occupation, Vice President and Cashier of the First National Bank of Duncan,I.T; that they have known Thomas R. (ode) Colbert _20_ and _12_ years; and that Thomas R. Colbert and Ode Colbert is one and the same person; that Ode is a nickname and he has always been known by that; and that Thomas R.Colbert is the same and identical person as mentioned in marriage license 769, issued 29th day of June, 1902 hereto attached, in the name of Ode Colbert.

Frank W Jones
J R Prentice

Subscribed and sworn to before me on this the 10th day of July, 1905.

(Name Illegible)
Notary Public.

9-1284

Muskogee, Indian Territory, April 10, 1905.

Thomas R. Colbert,
    Hope, Indian Territory.

Dear Sir:

    Receipt is hereby acknowledged of the affidavits of Lillie Colbert and J. F[sic]. Wharton to the birth of Ira[sic] Lois Colbert, daughter of Thomas R. and Lillie Colbert, January 7, 1904, and the same have been filed with our records as an application for the enrollment of said child.

Respectfully,

Commissioner in Charge.

Applications for Enrollment of Chickasaw Newborn
Act of 1905   Volume IV

9-NB-331

Muskogee, Indian Territory, July 18, 1905.

Thomas R. Colbert,
    Duncan, Indian Territory.

Dear Sir:

    Receipt is hereby acknowledged of your letter of July 10, 1905, enclosing marriage license and certificate between Ode Colbert and Lillie Stubblefield and joint affidavit of Frank W. Jones and J. R. Prentice to the effect that Thomas r. and Ode Colbert are the same person and the same have been filed with the record in the matter of the enrollment of your child Iva Lois Colbert as a citizen by blood of the Chickasaw Nation.

                  Respectfully,

                                  Commissioner.

Chic. N.B. - 332
    (Garland Wardlow Collins
    Born October 7, 1903)

BIRTH AFFIDAVIT.
#113

DEPARTMENT OF THE INTERIOR.
COMMISSION TO THE FIVE CIVILIZED TRIBES.

    IN RE APPLICATION FOR ENROLLMENT, as a citizen of the Chickasaw Nation, of Garland W Collins, born on the 7 day of October, 1903

Name of Father: Danni[sic] Collins   a citizen of the Chickasaw Nation.
Name of Mother: Nancie[sic] Collins   a citizen of the Chickasaw Nation.

                    Postoffice   Colbert

Applications for Enrollment of Chickasaw Newborn
Act of 1905   Volume IV

AFFIDAVIT OF MOTHER.

UNITED STATES OF AMERICA, Indian Territory, }
    Central   DISTRICT.

I, Nancie Collins , on oath state that I am 20 years of age and a citizen by blood , of the Chickasaw Nation; that I am the lawful wife of Danni Collins , who is a citizen, by blood of the Chickasaw Nation; that a male child was born to me on 7 day of October , 1903, that said child has been named Garland Wardlow , and is now living.

Nancy Collins

Witnesses To Mark:
{ J.H. Mashburn
{ Laura A Mashburn

Subscribed and sworn to before me this 23 day of February , 1905.

S M Mead
Notary Public.

BIRTH AFFIDAVIT.

DEPARTMENT OF THE INTERIOR.
COMMISSION TO THE FIVE CIVILIZED TRIBES.

IN RE APPLICATION FOR ENROLLMENT, as a citizen of the Chickasaw Nation, of Garland Wardlow Collins , born on the 7 day of Oct , 1903

Name of Father: Dannie Collins   a citizen of the Chickasaw Nation.
Name of Mother: Nancy Collins   a citizen of the Chickasaw Nation.

Postoffice   Colbert I.T.

AFFIDAVIT OF MOTHER.

UNITED STATES OF AMERICA, Indian Territory, }
    Central   DISTRICT.

I, Nancy Collins , on oath state that I am 20 years of age and a citizen by blood , of the Chickasaw Nation; that I am the lawful wife of Dannie Collins , who is a citizen, by blood of the Chickasaw Nation; that a male child was born to me on 7 day of Oct. , 1903, that said child has been named Garland Wardlow Collins , and is now living.

Nancy Collins

Applications for Enrollment of Chickasaw Newborn
Act of 1905 Volume IV

Witnesses To Mark:
{

Subscribed and sworn to before me this 30 day of March , 1905.

EK Smith
Notary Public.

AFFIDAVIT OF ATTENDING PHYSICIAN OR MID-WIFE.

UNITED STATES OF AMERICA, Indian Territory, }
   Central   DISTRICT.

I, WH McCarley M.D. , a Physician , on oath state that I attended on Mrs. Nancy Collins , wife of Dannie Collins on the 7 day of Oct , 1903; that there was born to her on said date a male child; that said child is now living and is said to have been named Garland Wardlow Collins

W.H. McCarley M.D.

Witnesses To Mark:
{

Subscribed and sworn to before me this 30 day of March , 1905.

EK Smith
Notary Public.

This is to certify that I am a regular practicing Physician, located at Colbert Ind Ty.

On Oct 7th 1903 I attended Mrs. Nancy Collins, wife of Dan Collins, in confinement and there was borned[sic] a male child and child is still living.

Very Resp.
W. H. Mc Carley M. D.

This Jan 1th 1905.

Colbert I.T. Feb 11th 1905 sworn and subscribed to before me EK Smith a Notary Public in and for the Central district of the Indian Territory

EK Smith
Notary Public

Applications for Enrollment of Chickasaw Newborn
Act of 1905 Volume IV

Chic. N.B. - 333
(Sarah Arinda Self
Born March 20, 1903)
(Joseph W. Self
Born September 3, 1904)

W.F.

9-NB-333.

DEPARTMENT OF THE INTERIOR,
COMMISSIONER TO THE FIVE CIVILIZED TRIBES.

In the matter of the application for the enrollment of Sarah Arinda Self and Joseph W. Self as citizens by blood of the Chickasaw Nation.

--: D E C I S I O N :--

It appears from the record herein that on April 18, 1905 there was filed with the Commission application for the enrollment of Sarah Arinda Self and Joseph W. Self as citizens by blood of the Chickasaw Nation.

It further appears from the record in this case and the records of the Commission that the applicants, Sarah Arinda Self and Joseph W. Self, were born on March 20, 1903 and September 3, 1904, respectively, and are the children of Fannie Self, a recognized and enrolled citizen of the Chickasaw Nation whose name (as Fannie Garsides) appears as number 4652 upon the final roll of citizens of the Chickasaw Nation, approved by the Secretary of the Interior April 11, 1903, and James Self, a recognized and enrolled citizen by intermarriage of the Chickasaw Nation.

From a copy of a letter of the Commission to the Honorable Secretary of the Interior dated March 23, 1903 transmitting partial roll of citizens of the Chickasaw Nation, numbers 4564 to 4659, inclusive, upon which partial roll the name of the said Fannie Self (as Fannie Garsides) is found, it appears that it was stated in said letter that the rights of the said Fannie Self (as Fannie Garsides), and other specifically mentioned therein, to enrollment as citizens of the Chickasaw Nation "are established by tribal recognition and by their descent from Polly McKinney, who was adopted by the Chickasaw tribe of Indians in the State of Mississippi prior to the year 1834, and who obtained a patent to land in that state under the treaty of 1834, between the United States and the Chickasaw Nation, in which patent the said Polly McKinney was characterized as 'a Chickasaw Indian'." However, on February 21, 1903 the Commission rendered a decision enrolling the said Fannie Self (as Fannie Garsides), and others, as citizens by blood of the Chickasaw Nation, thereby establishing the status of the said Fannie Self as a citizen by blood of said nation. A copy of said decision is filed herewith and made a part of the record in this case.

It further appears from the record herein that both of the applicants were living on March 4, 1905.

The Act of Congress approved March 3, 1905 (Public No. 212) among other things provides:

Applications for Enrollment of Chickasaw Newborn
Act of 1905   Volume IV

"That the Commission to the Five Civilized Tribes is authorized for sixty days after the date of the approval of this act to receive and consider applications for enrollment of children born subsequent to September twenty-fifth, nineteen hundred and two, and prior to March fourth, nineteen hundred and five, and who were living on said latter date, to citizens by blood of the Choctaw and Chickasaw tribes of Indians whose enrollment has been approved by the Secretary of the Interior prior to the date of the approval of this act; and to enroll and make allotments to such children."

It is the opinion of this Commission that Sarah Arinda Self and Joseph W. Self are children of a citizen by blood of the Chickasaw tribe of Indians, within the meaning of the provision of the law above quoted and that, therefore, the application for their enrollment as citizens by blood of the Chickasaw Nation should be granted and it is so ordered.   COMMISSION TO THE FIVE CIVILIZED TRIBES,

                                        Tams Bixby
                                            Chairman.

                                        T. B. Needles
                                          Commissioner.

                                        C.R. Breckinridge
                                          Commissioner.

Muskogee, Indian Territory.
JUN 22 1905

T.W.L.
G.D.R.   DEPARTMENT OF THE INTERIOR,
                COMMISSION TO THE FIVE CIVILIZED TRIBES.

In the matter of the application of Harris McKinney, et al., for enrollment as citizensxby[sic] blood of the Chickasaw Nation, consolidating the applications of --

Harris McKinney, et al.,	9 D 176
Oyd McKinney,	9 D 339
Fannie Garsides, et al.,	9 D 292

COPY

--- D E C I S I O N ---

It appears from the census cards in the possession of the Commission and the other records in this case that at Colbert, Indian Territory, on October 14, 1898, application was made for the enrollment of Harris McKinney and his minor child, Laura

Applications for Enrollment of Chickasaw Newborn
Act of 1905   Volume IV

Etta McKinney, as citizens by blood of the Chickasaw Nation, since which time birth affidavits have been filed in the matter of the application for the enrollment of his infant children, Cecial Berthal and Maude Lee McKinney, as citizens by blood of the Chickasaw Nation; that at the same place and on the same date application was made for the enrollment of Charley Hayes as a citizen by intermarriage of the Chickasaw Nation, and for the enrollment of his minor children, Daniel, Minnie, Maggie and Edward Hayes, as citizens by blood of the Chickasaw Nation, that also at the same place and on the same date application was made for the enrollment of Martha McKinney as a citizen by intermarriage of the Chickasaw Nation; that at Ardmore, Indian Territory, on November 25, 1898, application was made for the enrollment of Oyd McKinney as a citizen by blood of the Chickasaw Nation; that at Atoka, Indian Territory, on December 5, 1899, application was made for the enrollment of Joseph Garsides as a citizen by intermarriage of the Chickasaw Nation, and for the enrollment of his seven minor children, Fannie, Ben, Alex, Jim, Nellie, Mattie and Joe Garsides Jr., as citizens by blood of the Chickasaw Nation.

Further proceedings in the matter of said applications were had at Durant, Indian Territory, at the session of the Commission commencing August 14, and ending August 18, 1899, and at Atoka, Indian Territory, on December 3, and December 8, 1900.

The applicants, Martha McKinney, Charley Hayes and his minor children, Daniel, Minnie, Maggie and Edward Hayes, and Joseph Garsides, are differently classified and are not embraced in this decision.

It appears from the evidence submitted and the records in the possession of the Commission that the applicants, Harris McKinney, and his three minor children, Laura Etta, Cecial Berthal and Maude Lee McKinney, and Oyd McKinney, Fannie Garsides, Ben Garsides, Alex Garsides, Jim Garsides, Nellie Garsides, Mattie Garsides and Joe Garsides Jr., claim rights to enrollment as citizens by blood of the Chickasaw Nation, by reason of being descendants of Polly McKinney (or McKinnie), who obtained a patent to land in Mississippi under the treaty of 1834 between the United States and the Chickasaw Nation, in which patent the said Polly McKinney (or McKinnie) was characterized as "a Chickasaw Indian;" that the principal applicants herein are, and have been for may[sic] years past, actual and bona fide residents of the Chickasaw country in Indian Territory, and are duly recognized as citizens of the Chickasaw Nation; that Harris McKinney's name is identified on the 1893 Chickasaw pay roll, book 2, page 8, No. 226; that Oyd McKinney's name is identified on the 1893 Chickasaw pay roll, No. 1, at page 140; that the applicants, Fannie Garsides, Ben Garsides, Ale Garsides, Jim Garsides, Nellie Garsides, Mattie Garsides and Joe Garsides Jr., are identified on the Maytubby 1893 Chickasaw pay roll, No. 2, duly enrolled with their father, Joseph Garsides; that Laura Etta McKinney, Cecial Berthal McKinney and Maude Lee McKinney, the minor children of the principal applicant, Harris McKinney, having been born subsequent to the tribal enrollment of their father, are identified from proper birth affidavits filed herein and made a part of the record in this case.

It is the contention of counsel for the Choctaw and Chickasaw Nations that the said Polly McKinney (or McKinnie) was a Cherokee Indian by blood, and that notwithstanding the recognition given the principal applicants herein as citizens of the Chickasaw Nation, they are not entitled to said citizenship as they are Cherokee Indians by blood and are not citizens by adoption of the Chickasaw Nation by an act of the Chickasaw legislature.

Applications for Enrollment of Chickasaw Newborn
Act of 1905   Volume IV

The contention that the said Polly McKinney (or McKinnie) was a Cherokee Indian and had no Chickasaw blood is not established by the evidence. She was recognized by the government of the United States as a Chickasaw Indian when the patent referred to was given to her, and was also recognized by the Chickasaws themselves, both in Mississippi and Indian Territory, as a member of said tribe of Indians; and it further appears from the testimony submitted, and the records in the possession of the Commission, that her descendants have been recognized and enrolled as citizens of the Chickasaw tribe of Indians.

The records in the possession of the Commission further show that none of the applicants herein has ever been recognized or enrolled by the Cherokee tribal authorities as a citizen of said Nation, nor has any of them ever been listed for enrollment as a citizen of the Cherokee Nation by the Commission to the Five Civilized Tribes.

It further appears that all of the applicants considered herein, except Cecial Berthal McKinney, who was born February 17, 1901, were residents in good faith of Indian Territory on June 28, 1898.

It is therefore the opinion of the Commission that the applications for the enrollment of Harris McKinney, Laura Etta McKinney, Cecial Berthal McKinney, Maude Lee McKinney, Oyd McKinney, Fannie Garsides, Ben Garsides, Alex Garsides, Jim Garsides, Nellie Garsides, Mattie Garsides and Joe Garsides Jr., as citizens by blood of the Chickasaw Nation should be granted under the provisions of section twenty-one of the Act of Congress approved June 28, 1898 (30 Stats., 495), and it is so ordered.

COMMISSION TO THE FIVE CIVILIZED TRIBES,

SIGNED   *Tams Bixby*
Chairman.

SIGNED   *T. B. Needles.*
Commissioner.

SIGNED   *C.R. Breckinridge.*
Commissioner.

Muskogee, Indian Territory.
FEB 2 1 1903

BIRTH AFFIDAVIT.

DEPARTMENT OF THE INTERIOR.
COMMISSION TO THE FIVE CIVILIZED TRIBES.

IN RE APPLICATION FOR ENROLLMENT, as a citizen of the   Chickasaw   Nation, of   Sarah Arinda Self   , born on the 20   day of March   , 1903

Name of Father: James W. Self   a citizen of the   Chickasaw   Nation.
Name of Mother: Fannie Self   a citizen of the   Chickasaw   Nation.
(nee Fannie Garside)

Applications for Enrollment of Chickasaw Newborn
Act of 1905 Volume IV

Postoffice ....

AFFIDAVIT OF MOTHER.

UNITED STATES OF AMERICA, Indian Territory, }
   Central   DISTRICT.

I, Fannie Self (nee Fannie Garside)   , on oath state that I am 22   years of age and a citizen by   blood   , of the   Chickasaw   Nation; that I am the lawful wife of   James W. Self   , who is a citizen, by Marriage   of the   Chickasaw Nation; that a   female   child was born to me on 20   day of   March   , 1903; that said child has been named   Sarah Arinda Self   , and was living March 4, 1905.

Fannie Self

Witnesses To Mark:
{

Subscribed and sworn to before me this 25th   day of   Mch   , 1905

D.S. Kennedy
Notary Public.

AFFIDAVIT OF ATTENDING PHYSICIAN OR MID-WIFE.

UNITED STATES OF AMERICA, Indian Territory, }
   Central   DISTRICT.

I,   J.S. Fulton   , a Physician   , on oath state that I attended on Mrs. Fannie Self   , wife of   James W. Self   on the 20 day of   March   , 1903; that there was born to her on said date a   female   child; that said child was living March 4, 1905, and is said to have been named Sarah Arinda Self

J.S. Fulton

Witnesses To Mark:
{

Subscribed and sworn to before me this 24 day of   March   , 1905

D.N. Linebaugh
Notary Public.

Applications for Enrollment of Chickasaw Newborn
Act of 1905   Volume IV

BIRTH AFFIDAVIT.

DEPARTMENT OF THE INTERIOR.
COMMISSION TO THE FIVE CIVILIZED TRIBES.

IN RE APPLICATION FOR ENROLLMENT, as a citizen of the   Chickasaw   Nation, of   Joseph W. Self   , born on the 3^d day of Sept   , 1904

Name of Father: James W. Self   a citizen of the   Chickasaw Nation.
Name of Mother: Fannie Self   a citizen of the   Chickasaw Nation.
(nee Fannie Garside)
Postoffice   Stringtown I.T.

AFFIDAVIT OF MOTHER.

UNITED STATES OF AMERICA, Indian Territory,
Central Judicial   DISTRICT.

I,   Fannie Self nee Fannie Garside   , on oath state that I am   22   years of age and a citizen by   blood   , of the   Chickasaw   Nation; that I am the lawful wife of   James W. Self   , who is a citizen, by marriage   of the   Chickasaw Nation; that a   Male   child was born to me on 3^d day of Sept   , 1904; that said child has been named   Joseph W. Self   , and was living March 4, 1905.

Fannie Self

Witnesses To Mark:
{

Subscribed and sworn to before me this 25th day of   Mch   , 1905

D.S. Kennedy
Notary Public.

AFFIDAVIT OF ATTENDING PHYSICIAN OR MID-WIFE.

UNITED STATES OF AMERICA, Indian Territory,
Central Judicial   DISTRICT.

I,   J.A. Dabney   , a Physician   , on oath state that I attended on Mrs.   Fannie Self   , wife of   James W. Self   on the 3^d day of Sept   , 1904; that there was born to her on said date a   male   child; that said child was living March 4, 1905, and is said to have been named   Joseph W.Self

J.A. Dabney M.D.

Witnesses To Mark:
{

Applications for Enrollment of Chickasaw Newborn
Act of 1905 Volume IV

Subscribed and sworn to before me this 25th day of Mch , 1905

D.S. Kennedy
Notary Public.

9 N B 333

Muskogee, Indian Territory, October 4, 1905.

James Self,
    Stringtown, Indian Territory.

Dear Sir:

    Receipt is hereby acknowledged of your letter of October 2, asking that your children, Sarah Arinda and Joseph W. Self be enrolled as soon as practicable, in order that you may make selection of allotments in their behalf.

    In reply to your letter you are advised that the names of your children, Sarah Arinda and Joseph W. Self will probably be placed upon the next schedule of new born citizens of the Chickasaw Nation prepared for forwarding to the Secretary of the Interior and you will be notified of the approval of their enrollment.

                Respectfully,

                            Commissioner.

Chic. N.B. - 334
    (James Gardner Mays
    Born October 20, 1902)

BIRTH AFFIDAVIT.

DEPARTMENT OF THE INTERIOR.
COMMISSION TO THE FIVE CIVILIZED TRIBES.

IN RE APPLICATION FOR ENROLLMENT, as a citizen of the Chickasaw Nation, of Thomas Gardner Mays , born on the 20 day of Oct , 1902

Name of Father: Thomas Gardner Mays   a citizen of the Chickasaw Nation.
Name of Mother: Birdy Mays   a citizen of the Chocktaw[sic] Nation.

Applications for Enrollment of Chickasaw Newborn
Act of 1905 Volume IV

Postoffice   Maysville I.T.

AFFIDAVIT OF MOTHER.

UNITED STATES OF AMERICA, Indian Territory, }
Southern   DISTRICT.

I, Birdy Mays, on oath state that I am 24 years of age and a citizen by blood, of the Chocktaw Nation; that I am the lawful wife of Thomas Gardner Mays, who is a citizen, by blood of the Chickasaw Nation; that a Male child was born to me on 20th day of Oct, 1902, that said child has been named Thomas Gardner Mays, and is now living.

Birdy Mays

Witnesses To Mark:
{

Subscribed and sworn to before me this 18th day of March, 1905.

My commission   F.C. Cook
Expires Nov 21st 1906   Notary Public.

AFFIDAVIT OF ATTENDING PHYSICIAN OR MID-WIFE.

UNITED STATES OF AMERICA, Indian Territory, }
Southern   DISTRICT.

I, P.P. Ham, a midwife, on oath state that I attended on Mrs. Birdy Mays, wife of T.G. Mays on the 20th day of Oct, 1902; that there was born to her on said date a male child; that said child is now living and is said to have been named Thomas Gardner Mayo

P.P. Ham

Witnesses To Mark:
{

Subscribed and sworn to before me this 18th day of March, 1905.

My commission   F.C. Cook
Expires Nov 21st 1906   Notary Public.

Applications for Enrollment of Chickasaw Newborn
Act of 1905   Volume IV

Indian Territory,)
)
Southern District.)

I, T. G. Mays, being duly sworn, on oath state that I am a citizen of the Chickasaw Nation, and that my wife, Birdy Mays, is a citizen of the Choctaw Nation; that I have a child named Thomas Gardner Mays, Jr., and that it is my desire that he be enrolled as a citizen of the Chickasaw Nation.

TG Mays

Subscribed and sworn to before me this April 13, 1905.   C - 4441

JE Williams
Notary Public.

7-122
N. B.

Muskogee, Indian Territory, April 10, 1905.

T. G. Mays,
Maysville, Indian Territory.

Dear Sir:

Referring to the application for the enrollment of your infant child, Thomas Gardner Mays Jr., it appears that you are a citizen by blood of the Chickasaw Nation, while your wife is a citizen by blood of the Choctaw Nation.

Your attention is called to the provisions of the Act of Congress approved June 28, 1898, as follows:

"The several tribes may, by agreement, determine the right of persons who for any reason may claim citizenship in two or more tribes, and to allotment of lands and distribution of moneys belonging to each tribe; but if no such agreement be made, then such claimant shall be entitled to such rights in one tribe only, and may elect in which tribe he will take such right; but if he fail or refuse to make such selection in due time, he shall be enrolled in the tribe with whom he has resided, and there be given such allotment and distributions, and not elsewhere."

It will therefore be necessary for you to appear before a Notary Public or other officer authorized to administer oaths, and by affidavit elect in which nation you desire to have said child enrolled, forwarding same, when properly executed, to the Commission.

Applications for Enrollment of Chickasaw Newborn
Act of 1905   Volume IV

Respectfully,

LM   Commissioner in Charge.

Choctaw 122.

Muskogee, Indian Territory, April 18, 1905.

T. G. Mayes[sic],
   Mayesville[sic], Indian Territory.

Dear Sir:

Receipt is hereby acknowledged of your letter of April 13, transmitting your affidavit electing to have your son, Thomas Gardner Mayes, enrolled as a citizen of the Chickasaw Nation and this affidavit has been filed with our records in the matter of the enrollment of said child.

Respectfully,

Chairman.

Chic. N.B. - 335
   (Sam Potts Statons
   Born October 1, 1904)

BIRTH AFFIDAVIT.

DEPARTMENT OF THE INTERIOR.
COMMISSION TO THE FIVE CIVILIZED TRIBES.

IN RE APPLICATION FOR ENROLLMENT, as a citizen of the   Chickasaw   Nation, of   Sam Potts Statons   , born on the 1 day of October , 1904

Name of Father: H.A. Statons *(noncitizen)*   a citizen of the .... Nation.
Name of Mother: Marina B. Statons   a citizen of the   Chickasaw   Nation.

Postoffice   Mead I.T.

Applications for Enrollment of Chickasaw Newborn
Act of 1905   Volume IV

AFFIDAVIT OF MOTHER.

UNITED STATES OF AMERICA, Indian Territory,　}
　　Central　　　　　　　　DISTRICT.

　　I,　Marina B. Statons　, on oath state that I am　25　years of age and a citizen by　Blood　, of the　Chickasaw　Nation; that I am the lawful wife of H. A. Statons (non-citizen)　, who is a citizen, by .... of the .... Nation; that a　male　child was born to me on　1　day of　October　, 1904; that said child has been named　Sam Potts Statons　, and was living March 4, 1905.

　　　　　　　　　　　　　　　　Marina B. Statons

Witnesses To Mark:
{

　　Subscribed and sworn to before me this　25　day of　April　, 1905

　　　　　　　　　　　　　　　Claude C. *(Illegible)*
　　　　　　　　　　　　　　　Notary Public.

AFFIDAVIT OF ATTENDING PHYSICIAN OR MID-WIFE.

UNITED STATES OF AMERICA, Indian Territory,　}
　　Central　　　　　　　　DISTRICT.

　　I,　E.W. Morrison　, a physician　, on oath state that I attended on Mrs.　Marina B Statons　, wife of　H.A. Statons　on the　1st　day of October, 1904; that there was born to her on said date a　male　child; that said child was living March 4, 1905, and is said to have been named　Sam Potts Statons

　　　　　　　　　　　　　　　　E W Morrison MD

Witnesses To Mark:
{

　　Subscribed and sworn to before me this　25　day of　April　, 1905

　　　　　　　　　　　　　　　Claude C. *(Illegible)*
　　　　　　　　　　　　　　　Notary Public.

Applications for Enrollment of Chickasaw Newborn
Act of 1905 Volume IV

H. A. Statons,
    Mead, Indian Territory.

Dear Sir:

    Receipt is hereby acknowledged of the affidavits of Marina B. Statons and E. W. Morrison to the birth of Sam Potts Statons, son of H. A. and Marina B. Statons, October 1, 1904, and the same have been filed with our records as an application for the enrollment of said child.

                    Respectfully,

                                    Chairman.

Chic. N.B. - 336
    (Cecil Rayford Burkett
    Born July 4, 1904)

BIRTH AFFIDAVIT.

DEPARTMENT OF THE INTERIOR.
COMMISSION TO THE FIVE CIVILIZED TRIBES.

    IN RE APPLICATION FOR ENROLLMENT, as a citizen of the   Chickasaw   Nation, of   Cecil Rayford Burkett   , born on the   4 day of   July , 1904

Name of Father: George Burkett   a citizen of the   Chickasaw Nation.
Name of Mother: Mary B. Burkett   a citizen of the   Chickasaw Nation.

                      Postoffice   Newcastle Chickasaw Nation

AFFIDAVIT OF MOTHER.

UNITED STATES OF AMERICA, Indian Territory, }
    Southern   DISTRICT.

    I, Mary B. Burkett , on oath state that I am Twenty years of age and^ a citizen by   Chickasaw , of the .... Nation; that I am the lawful wife of George Burkett   , who is a citizen, by   Blood of the Chickasaw Nation; that a   Male child was born to me on   4th day of   July , 1904, that said child has been named   Cecil Rayford Burkett , and is now living.

Applications for Enrollment of Chickasaw Newborn
Act of 1905 Volume IV

Mary B. Burkett

Witnesses To Mark:
- JH Hartley
- Myrtie E Harned

Subscribed and sworn to before me this 7th day of January , 1905.

My commission
expires May 8 1906

JH Hartley
Notary Public.

AFFIDAVIT OF ATTENDING PHYSICIAN OR MID-WIFE.

UNITED STATES OF AMERICA, Indian Territory,
Southern DISTRICT.

I, Myrtie E Harned , a midwife , on oath state that I attended on Mrs. Mary B Burkett , wife of George Burkett on the 4 day of July , 1904; that there was born to her on said date a male child; that said child is now living and is said to have been named Cecil Rayford Burkett

Myrtie E Harned

Witnesses To Mark:
- JH Hartley
- Oda Womack

Subscribed and sworn to before me this 5 day of January , 1905.

My commission
expires May 8 1906

JH Hartley
Notary Public.

BIRTH AFFIDAVIT.

DEPARTMENT OF THE INTERIOR.
COMMISSION TO THE FIVE CIVILIZED TRIBES.

IN RE APPLICATION FOR ENROLLMENT, as a citizen of the Chickasaw Nation, of Cecil Rayford Burkett , born on the 4th day of July , 1904

Name of Father: George Burkett   a citizen of the Chickasaw Nation.

Name of Mother: Mary B Burkett   a citizen of the ~~Chickasaw~~ *United States* Nation.

Postoffice Newcastle, I.T.

Applications for Enrollment of Chickasaw Newborn
Act of 1905   Volume IV

AFFIDAVIT OF MOTHER.

UNITED STATES OF AMERICA, Indian Territory, ⎫
  Southern   DISTRICT. ⎭

I, Mary B Burkett , on oath state that I am 20 years of age and a citizen by blood , of the United States Nation; that I am the lawful wife of George Burkett , who is a citizen, by blood of the Chickasaw Nation; that a male child was born to me on 4th day of July , 1904; that said child has been named Cecil Rayford Burkett , and was living March 4, 1905.

Mary B Burkett

Witnesses To Mark:
{

Subscribed and sworn to before me this 4th day of April , 1905

JE Williams
Notary Public.

AFFIDAVIT OF ATTENDING PHYSICIAN OR MID-WIFE.

UNITED STATES OF AMERICA, Indian Territory, ⎫
  Southern   DISTRICT. ⎭

I, Myrtie E Harned , a Mid-wife , on oath state that I attended on Mrs. Mary B Burkett , wife of George Burkett on the 4th day of July , 1904; that there was born to her on said date a male child; that said child was living March 4, 1905, and is said to have been named Cecil Rayford Burkett

Myrtie E Harned

Witnesses To Mark:
{

Subscribed and sworn to before me this 4th day of April , 1905

JE Williams
Notary Public.

Applications for Enrollment of Chickasaw Newborn
Act of 1905   Volume IV

Muskogee, Indian Territory, January 13, 1905

George Burkett,
    Newcastle, Indian Territory.

Dear Sir:

    Receipt is hereby acknowledged of the affidavits of Mary B. Burkett and Myrtie E. Harned relative to the birth of Cecil Rayford Burkett infant son of George and Mary B Burkett, July 4, 1904.

    It is stated in the affidavits of the mother that George Burkett the father of this child is a citizen by blood of the Chickasaw Nation. If this is correct you are requested to state when, where and under what name application was made for the enrollment of George Burkett, his age, the names of his parents, and other members of his family who have been enrolled and such other information as you may possess which will enable the Commission to identify you upon its records.

Respectfully,

Chairman.

Muskogee, Indian Territory, March 7, 1905.

George Burkett,
    Newcastle, Indian Territory.

Dear Sir:

    On January 13, 1905, receipt was acknowledged of the affidavits of Mary B. Burkett, and Myrtie E. Harned to the birth of Cecil Rayford Burkett infant son of George and Mary B. Burkett, July 4, 1904. As it was stated in the affidavit of the mother that you were a citizen by blood of the Chickasaw Nation you were requested to state when, where and under what name application was made for your enrollment, the names of your parents and other members of your family who were enrolled with you and such other information as will enable the Commission to identify you upon its records as an applicant for enrollment as a citizen of the Chickasaw Nation but up to this time no reply has been received to this request.

    You are again requested to furnish the above information as early as practicable in order that disposition may be made of the enrollment of the above named child.

Respectfully,

Commissioner in Charge.

Applications for Enrollment of Chickasaw Newborn
Act of 1905   Volume IV

9-NB-336.

Muskogee, Indian Territory, May 16, 1905.

George Burkett,
    Newcastle, Indian Territory.

Dear Sir:

    Referring to the application for the enrollment of your infant child, Cecil Rayford Burkett, born July 4, 1904, it is noted that the applicant claims through you.

    Before this matter can be finally determined it will be necessary for you to file in this office either the original or a certified copy of the license and certificate of your marriage to the applicant's mother, Mary B. Burkett.

Respectfully,

Chairman.

C   O   P   Y.

MARRIAGE LICENSE.

TERRITORY OF OKLAHOMA
                       SS   IN THE PROBATE COURT,
ROGER MILLS COUNTY,

TO ANY PERSON AUTHORIZED TO PERFORM THE MARRIAGE CEREMONY, GREETING:

    You are hereby authorized to join in marriage Mr. George Burkett and Miss Mary Lyng of the County aforesaid, whose ages, residence, etc, are as follows:

NAMES OF PARTIES		AGE	COLOR	PLACE OF BIRTH	RESIDENCE
George Burkett	Groom	20	White	Indian Territory	New Castle Ind. Ter.
Mary Lyng	Bride	19	"	Texas	Elk City, Roger Mills Co O.T.

    And of this license you will make due return of my office within thirty days from this date.
    In Testimony Whereof, I have hereunto set my hand and affixed the seal of said Court at my office in Cheyenne in said County, this 12 day of September 1903.

Applications for Enrollment of Chickasaw Newborn
Act of 1905 Volume IV

(Seal) R. K. Houston
Judge of the Probate Court.

CERTIFICATE OF MARRIAGE.

TERRITORY OF OKLAHOMA, SS.

I, R. K. Houston, Probate Judge, Probate Court of Cheyenne, in Roger Mills County, Oklahoma Territory, do hereby certify that I joined in marriage the persons named in and authorized by this Court to be married on the 12 day of September A.D. 1903, at Cheynne[sic] in Roger Mills County, O.T., in the presence of Miss Volina Miller of Cheyenne O.T. and E. F. Cornells of Cheynne O.T.

Volina Miller
        WITNESSES.   R. K. Houston.
E. F. Cornells.

Territory of Oklahoma.
        SS.
County of Roger Mills.
ENDORSED AS FOLLOWS:
    I, C. S. Gilkerson, Judge of the Probate Court in and for the above named County and territory hereby certify that the within is a true and correct copy of the Marriage License and Marriage Certificate now on Record in my office in Book 2, Page 84 Marriage Record.
    Witness my hand and seal this the 18th day of April 1905.

C. S. Gilkerson,
(Seal) Probate Judge.

I, Helen C. Miller, Stenographer for the Commission to the Five Civilized Tribes hereby certify the above is a correct copy of the marriage license and certificate of marriage of George Burkett and Mary Lyng.

Helen C. Miller

Subscribed and sworn to before me this 22nd day of May, 1905.

JE Williams
Notary Public.

Chic. N.B. - 337
    (Lavader Jewel James
    Born September 29, 1904)

Applications for Enrollment of Chickasaw Newborn
Act of 1905 Volume IV

BIRTH AFFIDAVIT.

DEPARTMENT OF THE INTERIOR.
COMMISSION TO THE FIVE CIVILIZED TRIBES.

IN RE APPLICATION FOR ENROLLMENT, as a citizen of the Chickasaw Nation, of Levada Jewel James , born on the 29 day of September , 1904

Name of Father: Emerson James   a citizen of the Chickasaw Nation.
Name of Mother: Annie James   a citizen of the Chickasaw Nation.

Postoffice Mead

AFFIDAVIT OF MOTHER.

UNITED STATES OF AMERICA, Indian Territory, }
   Central   DISTRICT. }

   I, Annie James , on oath state that I am 23 years of age and a citizen by Intermarriage , of the Chickasaw Nation; that I am the lawful wife of Emerson James , who is a citizen, by blood of the Chickasaw Nation; that a female child was born to me on 29 day of September , 1904, that said child has been named Levada Jewel , and is now living.

                                Annie James

Witnesses To Mark:
{

   Subscribed and sworn to before me this 27 day of February , 1905.

                                S M Mead
                                    Notary Public.

BIRTH AFFIDAVIT.

DEPARTMENT OF THE INTERIOR.
COMMISSION TO THE FIVE CIVILIZED TRIBES.

IN RE APPLICATION FOR ENROLLMENT, as a citizen of the Chickasaw Nation, of Lavader Jewel James , born on the 29 day of September , 1904

Name of Father: Emerson James   a citizen of the Chickasaw Nation.
Name of Mother: Annie James   a citizen of the United States Nation.

Postoffice Mead Ind Ter

Applications for Enrollment of Chickasaw Newborn
Act of 1905 Volume IV

AFFIDAVIT OF MOTHER.

UNITED STATES OF AMERICA, Indian Territory, }
   Central   DISTRICT.

    I, Annie James , on oath state that I am 23 years of age and a citizen by Birth , of the United States of America; that I am the lawful wife of Emerson James , who is a citizen, by Blood of the Chickasaw Nation; that a Female child was born to me on 29 day of September , 1904; that said child has been named Lavader Jewel James , and was living March 4, 1905.

                                  Annie James

Witnesses To Mark:
{

    Subscribed and sworn to before me this 3 day of April , 1905

                                  E O Franklin
                                      Notary Public.

AFFIDAVIT OF ATTENDING PHYSICIAN OR MID-WIFE.

UNITED STATES OF AMERICA, ~~Indian Territory~~, }
   Memphis, Tenn.   DISTRICT.

    I, William Walter Beach , a Physician , on oath state that I attended on Mrs. Annie James , wife of Emerson James on the 29 day of September , 1904; that there was born to her on said date a Female child; that said child was living March 4, 1905, and is said to have been named Lavader Jewel

                              William Walter Beach

Witnesses To Mark:
{

    Subscribed and sworn to before me this 5 day of April , 1905

                                  J C McDavitt
                                  Notary Public.
                                  in Shelby County, Tennessee

Applications for Enrollment of Chickasaw Newborn
Act of 1905   Volume IV

State of Tennessee }
Shelby County } W.W. Beach, duly sworn, states that he is a medical student of the Memphis Hospital Medical College, and that on or about the 29th day of September 1904, five miles west of Mead, Indian Territory, he attended professionally and delivered Anna James, wife of Emerson James, of a female child; and he further states that said child is or was lately still living.

This 24th February, 1905.

W.W. Beach

Subscribed and sworn to before me this sworn to before me, a Notary Public in and for said County and state, yes Feby 24, 1906.

J C McDavitt
Notary Public

9-1217

Muskogee, Indian Territory, April 14, 1905.

Emerson James,
    Mead, Indian Territory.

Dear Sir:

Receipt is hereby acknowledged of your letter of April 6, 1905, enclosing affidavits of Annie James and William Walter Beach to the birth of Lavader Jewel James, daughter of Emerson and Annie James, September 29, 1904, and the same have been filed with our records as an application for the enrollment of said child.

Respectfully,

Commissioner in Charge.

Chic. N.B. - 338
    (Alice Greenwood
    Born September 6, 1904)

Applications for Enrollment of Chickasaw Newborn
Act of 1905 Volume IV

BIRTH AFFIDAVIT.

DEPARTMENT OF THE INTERIOR,
COMMISSION TO THE FIVE CIVILIZED TRIBES.

IN RE Application for Enrollment, as a citizen of the Chickasaw Nation, of Alice , born on the 6th day of September , 1904

Name of Father: Simeon Greenwood a citizen of the Chickasaw Nation.
Name of Mother: [sic] Moore a citizen of the Chickasaw Nation.

Post-Office: Reagan I.T.

AFFIDAVIT OF MOTHER.

UNITED STATES OF AMERICA,
    INDIAN TERRITORY.
.... District.

I, Nancy Moore , on oath state that I am about 30 years of age and a citizen by Blood , of the Chickasaw Nation; that I am the ~~lawful~~ *Cohort* wife of Simeon Greenwood , who is a citizen, by Blood of the Chickasaw Nation; that a female child was born to me on 6th day of September , 1904 , that said child has been named Alice Greenwood , and is now living.

                            her
                       Nancy x Moore
WITNESSES TO MARK: mark
  { A.A. Chapman
    (Name Illegible)

Subscribed and sworn to before me this 28th day of March , 1905.

                     A A Chapman
                       NOTARY PUBLIC.

AFFIDAVIT OF ATTENDING PHYSICIAN OR MID-WIFE.

UNITED STATES OF AMERICA,
    INDIAN TERRITORY.
  Southern District.

I, Sarah Jane Saunders , a midwife , on oath state that I attended on Mrs. Nancy Moore , ~~wife~~ *Cohort* of Simeon Greenwood on the 6th

Applications for Enrollment of Chickasaw Newborn
Act of 1905 Volume IV

day of September , 190 4; that there was born to her on said date a   female   child; that said child is now living and is said to have been named   Alice Greenwood

her
Sarah Jane x Saunders
mark

WITNESSES TO MARK:
{ A.A. Chapman
{ *(Name Illegible)*

Subscribed and sworn to before me this 28th   day of   March   , 1905.

A A Chapman
<small>NOTARY PUBLIC.</small>

BIRTH AFFIDAVIT.

DEPARTMENT OF THE INTERIOR,
COMMISSION TO THE FIVE CIVILIZED TRIBES.

   IN RE Application for Enrollment, as a citizen of the   Chickasaw   Nation, of   Alice Greenwood   , born on the   6   day of   September , 1905[sic]

Name of Father: Sim Greenwood   a citizen of the Chickasaw   Nation.
Name of Mother: Nancy Moore   a citizen of the Chickasaw   Nation.

Post-Office: Reagan I.T.

AFFIDAVIT OF MOTHER.

UNITED STATES OF AMERICA, }
   INDIAN TERRITORY.
   Southern   District. }

   I, Nancy Moore   , on oath state that I am   29   years of age and a citizen by   Blood   , of the Chickasaw   Nation; that I am the lawful wife of _____ , who is a citizen, by _____ of the _____ Nation; that a   Female   child was born to me on   6   day of September , 1905[sic] , that said child has been named   Alice   , and is now living.

Nancy Moore

WITNESSES TO MARK:
{
{

314

Applications for Enrollment of Chickasaw Newborn
Act of 1905   Volume IV

Subscribed and sworn to before me this   12   day of   April   , 1905.

J.R. Vinyard

NOTARY PUBLIC.

AFFIDAVIT OF ATTENDING PHYSICIAN OR MID-WIFE.

UNITED STATES OF AMERICA,
    INDIAN TERRITORY.
.... District.

I,   A G Cranfill   , a   Physician   , on oath state that I attended on Mrs.   Nancy Moore   wife of *the child was born before I arrived* on the   6   day of   September   , 1905[sic]; that there was born to her on said date a   Female   child; that said child is now living and is said to have been named   Alice

A G Cranfill

WITNESSES TO MARK:

Subscribed and sworn to before me this   12   day of   April   , 1905.

J.R. Vinyard

NOTARY PUBLIC.

Nancy Moore is a Chickasaw Indian her husband is dead died 6 or 7 years Since she claims the child for Sim Greenwood a Chickasaw Indian I arrived just after the child was born and (illegible) her of the (illegible) and am (illegible) certain she is the mother and that Sim Greenwood is the father

A G Cranfill MD

Applications for Enrollment of Chickasaw Newborn
Act of 1905 Volume IV

9-723

Muskogee, Indian Territory, April 14, 1905.

A. A. Chapman,
    Ravia, Indian Territory.

Dear Sir:

    Receipt is hereby acknowledged of your letter of April 6, 1905, enclosing affidavits of Nancy Moore and Sarah Jane Saunders to the birth of Alice Greenwood, daughter of Simon Greenwood and Nancy Moore, September 6, 1904, and the same have been filed with our records as an application for the enrollment of said child.

    Replying to that part of your letter in which you ask when lands can be reserved for children for whom application is now being made, you are advised that no reservation of land can be made or allotment selected for children enrolled under the provisions of the act of Congress approved March 3, 1905, until their enrollment has been approved by the Secretary of the Interior.

                    Respectfully,

                                     Commissioner in Charge.

9-723

Muskogee, Indian Territory, April 25, 1905.

Nancy Moore,
    Reagan, Indian Territory.

Dear Madam:

    Receipt is hereby acknowledged of the affidavits of Nancy Moore and A. G. Cranfill to the birth of Alice Greenwood, daughter of Sim Greenwood and Nancy Moore, and the same have been filed with our records as an application for the enrollment of said child.

                    Respectfully,

                                     Chairman.

Applications for Enrollment of Chickasaw Newborn
Act of 1905   Volume IV

Chic. N.B. - 339
    (Robert Blake McKeel
    Born July 9, 1904)

BIRTH AFFIDAVIT.   100

IN RE-APPLICATION FOR ENROLLMENT, as a citizen of the   Chickasaw   Nation, of   Robert Blake McKeel   , born on the   9th   day of   July   , 190 4

Name of Father: John F. McKeel   a citizen of the   Chickasaw   Nation.
Name of Mother: Cora C. McKeel   a citizen of the   Chickasaw   Nation.

                    Postoffice   Ada, I.T.

AFFIDAVIT OF MOTHER.

UNITED STATES OF AMERICA, INDIAN TERRITORY, }
    Southern   District.

    I,   Cora C. McKeel, on oath state that I am   32   years of age and a citizen by Blood   , of the   Chickasaw   Nation; that I am the lawful wife of   John F. McKeel   , who is a citizen, by   Intermarriage   of the   Chickasaw   Nation; that a   Male   child was born to me on   9th   day of   July   , 1904   , that said child has been named   Robert Blake McKeel   , and is now living.

                                Cora C McKeel
Witnesses To Mark:

    Subscribed and sworn to before me this   18   day of   Febr   , 1905.

                                W.S. Kern
                                  Notary Public.

AFFIDAVIT OF ATTENDING PHYSICIAN OR MID-WIFE.

UNITED STATES OF AMERICA, INDIAN TERRITORY, }
    Southern   District.

    I,   W.W. Carson   , a   Physician   , on oath state that I attended on Mrs.   Cora C. McKeel   , wife of   John F. McKeel   on the   9th   day of   July   , 190 4; that there was born to her on said date a   male   child; that said child is now living and is said to have been named   Robert Blake McKeel

                                W.W. Carson M.D.

Applications for Enrollment of Chickasaw Newborn
Act of 1905 Volume IV

Witnesses To Mark:
{

Subscribed and sworn to before me this 18 day of Febr , 1905.

W.S. Kern
Notary Public.

BIRTH AFFIDAVIT.

DEPARTMENT OF THE INTERIOR.
COMMISSION TO THE FIVE CIVILIZED TRIBES.

IN RE APPLICATION FOR ENROLLMENT, as a citizen of the Chickasaw Nation, of Robert Blake McKeel , born on the 9th day of July , 1904

Name of Father: John F. McKeel   a citizen of the Chickasaw Nation.
Name of Mother: Cora C. McKeel   a citizen of the Chickasaw Nation.

Postoffice   Ada I.T.

AFFIDAVIT OF MOTHER.

UNITED STATES OF AMERICA, Indian Territory,}
    Southern   DISTRICT.

    I, Cora C. McKeel , on oath state that I am 32 years of age and a citizen by Blood , of the Chickasaw Nation; that I am the lawful wife of John F. McKeel , who is a citizen, by Marriage of the Chickasaw Nation; that a male child was born to me on 9th day of July , 1904; that said child has been named Robert Blake McKeel , and was living March 4, 1905.

Cora C. McKeel

Witnesses To Mark:
{

Subscribed and sworn to before me this 3rd day of April , 1905

W.S. Kern
Notary Public.

Applications for Enrollment of Chickasaw Newborn
Act of 1905   Volume IV

AFFIDAVIT OF ATTENDING PHYSICIAN OR MID-WIFE.

UNITED STATES OF AMERICA, Indian Territory, }
    Southern   DISTRICT. }

    I, Mrs. C. J. Norman, a Midwife, on oath state that I attended on Mrs. Cora C. McKeel, wife of John F. McKeel on the 9th day of July, 1904; that there was born to her on said date a male child; that said child was living March 4, 1905, and is said to have been named Robert Blake McKeel

                                              her
                                    C. J. x Norman
Witnesses To Mark: mark
    { Sherwood W. Hill
    { Joe Lovette

    Subscribed and sworn to before me this 3rd day of April, 1905

                                       W.S. Kern
                                       Notary Public.

                                                9-1369

                        Muskogee, Indian Territory, April 14, 1905.

J. F. McKeel,
    Ada, Indian Territory.

Dear Sir:

    Receipt is hereby acknowledged of your letter of April 8, 1905, enclosing affidavits of Cora C. McKeel and C. J. Norman to the birth of Robert Blake McKeel, son of John F. and Cora C. McKeel, July 9, 1904, and the same have been filed with our records as an application for the enrollment of said child.

                                       Respectfully,

                                       Commissioner in Charge.

Chic. N.B. - 340
    (Edna Bradley
    Born February 17, 1905)

Applications for Enrollment of Chickasaw Newborn
Act of 1905   Volume IV

BIRTH AFFIDAVIT.

DEPARTMENT OF THE INTERIOR.
COMMISSION TO THE FIVE CIVILIZED TRIBES.

IN RE APPLICATION FOR ENROLLMENT, as a citizen of the   Chickasaw   Nation, of   Edna Bradley   , born on the 17th day of Feb. , 1905

Name of Father: Frank Colbert Bradley   a citizen of the   Chickasaw   Nation.
Name of Mother: Dora Bradley   a citizen of the .... Nation.

Postoffice   Bradley, I.T.

AFFIDAVIT OF ATTENDING PHYSICIAN OR MID-WIFE.

UNITED STATES OF AMERICA, Indian Territory, }
.... DISTRICT. }

I,   Mrs. Mattie E. White   , a Mid-wife   , on oath state that I attended on Mrs. Dora Bradley   , wife of   Frank Colbert Bradley   on the 17th day of February , 1905; that there was born to her on said date a   Female   child; that said child was living March 4, 1905, and is said to have been named   Edna Bradley

Mrs. Mattie E. White

Witnesses To Mark:
{

Subscribed and sworn to before me this   21st day of   March   , 1905

J.D. Armstrong
Notary Public.
My commission expires Feb 25 - 1909

MARRIAGE LICENSE

No. 1041.

UNITED STATES OF AMERICA) TO ANY PERSON AUTHORIZED BY LAW TO
   INDIAN TERRITORY,   )
   SOUTHERN DISTRICT.   ) SOLEMNIZE MARRIAGE, GREETING:

YOU ARE HEREBY COMMANDED, to solemnize the Rite and publish the Banns of Matrimony between Mr. Frank C. Bradley of Bradley, in the Indian Territory, aged 22 years, and Miss Dora White, of Bradley, in the Indian Territory, aged 19 years,

Applications for Enrollment of Chickasaw Newborn
Act of 1905   Volume IV

according to law; and do you officially sign and return this license to the parties therein named.
    Witness my hand and official Seal, this 9th day of January, A. D. 1904.

                                                          C. M. Campbell,
                                        Clerk of the United States Court.
By J. W. Speake Deputy.
      (SEAL)

                              CERTIFICATE OF MARRIAGE
UNITED STATES OF AMERICA,   )
    INDIAN TERRITORY,   )ss.
SOUTHERN DISTRICT.   )   I, W. T. Cantrell, a Minister of the Gospel, do hereby certify that on the 10th day of January, A. D. 1904, I did duly and according to law, as commanded in the foregoing license, solemnize the Rite and publish the Banns of Matrimony between the parties therein named:
    Witness my hand this 11th day of January, A. D. 1904.
    My credentials are recorded in the office of the Clerk of the United States Court, Indian Territory, Central District, at S. McAlester, Book B, Page 227

                                            (Signed) W. T. Cantrell.
                                            A minister of the Gospel.
The foregoing is endorsed as follows: CERTIFICATE OF RECORD OF MARRIAGE. United States of America, Indian Territory, Southern District, Sct. I, C. M. Campbell, Clerk of the United States Court, in the Territory and District aforesaid, do hereby certify that the License for and certificate of marriage of Mr. Frank C. Bradley and Miss Dora Bradley were filed in my office in said Territory and District the 11 day of January, A. D. 1904, and duly recorded in Book H of Marriage Record, Page 36. Witness my hand and Seal of said court at Ardmore this 11 day of January, A. D. 1904, C. M. Campbell Clerk, (SEAL) Filed at Ardmore Jan. 13, 1904 8 AM C. M. Campbell, Clerk and Exofficio Recorder District No. 21 Ind. Ter.

                                      ---------oOo---------

    I, J. E. Williams, do hereby certify that the above and foregoing is a true and correct copy of the Marriage License and Certificate of Marriage of Frank C. Bradley and Dora White filed with the Commission in re application for enrollment of Edna Bradley as a citizen of the Chickasaw Nation. Dated this April 10, 1905.

                                                  JE Williams

Applications for Enrollment of Chickasaw Newborn
Act of 1905   Volume IV

Affidavit.

KNOW ALL MEN BY THESE PRESENTS. That I,   Winter P. Bradley , do state on oath, that on the 17th day of Feb. 1905 there was born a female child, to Dora Bradley, the lawful and legal wife of Frank Colbert Bradley, a citizen of the Chickasaw Nation by birth. That the child has been named Edna Bradley, that the aforesaid Dora Bradley died on the 28th day of Feb. 1905 and that the said Edna Bradley is still living. Given under my hand and seal this 28th day of March 1905.

Winter P. Bradley

Subscribed and sworn to before me this 28th day of March 1905.

J.R. Armstrong
Notary Public.

My commission expires   Feb. 25-1909

AFFIDAVIT.

KNOW ALL MEN BY THESE PRESENTS. That I, Frank Colbert Bradley a citizen by blood of the Chickasaw Nation, do state on oath, that on the 17th day of Feb. 1905 there was born to to[sic] my wife, Dora Bradley a female child, that has been named Edna Bradley. That my wife Dora Bradley died on the 28th day of Feb. 1905 and that the aforesaid child Edna Bradley is still living. Given under my hand and seal this 29th day of March 1905.

Frank Colbert Bradley

Subscribed and sworn to before me this 28th day of March 1905.

J.R. Armstrong
Notary Public.

My commission expires   Feb. 25-1909

AFFIDAVIT.

KNOW ALL MEN BY THESE PRESENTS. That I,   E White , do state on oath, that on the 17th day of Feb. 1905 there was born a female child, to Dora Bradley, the lawful and legal wife of Frank Colbert Bradley, a citizen of the Chickasaw Nation by birth. That the child has been named Edna Bradley, that the aforesaid Dora Bradley died on the 28th day of Feb. 1905 and that the said Edna Bradley is still living. Given under my hand and seal this 28th day of March 1905.

E White

Applications for Enrollment of Chickasaw Newborn
Act of 1905   Volume IV

Subscribed and sworn to before me this 28th day of March 1905.

J.R. Armstrong
Notary Public.

My commission expires   Feb. 25-1909

UNITED STATES OF AMERICA,   )
    Southern District.   )

On this 3rd day of June A.D. 1905 personally appeared before me, a Notary Public, within and for the Southern District of the Indian Territory
    J.H. Easley   to me well known to be the person subscribed hereto, and being duly sworn according to law, testifies as follows.
That Dora Bradley was the legal and lawful wife of Frank Colbert Bradley. who is a Citizen of the Chickasaw Nation by blood, that said Dora Bradley on the 17th day of February 1905 did give birth to a female child, that said Dora Bradley died from complications arising from said birth. That said child was living March 4th 1905 and was said to have been named Edna Bradley. Affiant further states that he is of no relation to any of the parties interested, and has no personal interest in this claim.

(Signed)   J.H. Easley

Subscribed and sworn to before me, this 3rd of June   1905.

J.R. Armstrong
Notary Public.
My commission expires   Feb 25 - 1909

Seal.

UNITED STATES OF AMERICA,   )
    Southern District.   )

On this 3rd day of June A.D. 1905 personally appeared before me, a Notary Public, within and for the Southern District of the Indian Territory
    Etta Easley   to me well known to be the person subscribed hereto, and being duly sworn according to law, testifies as follows.
That Dora Bradley was the legal and lawful wife of Frank Colbert Bradley. who is a Citizen of the Chickasaw Nation by blood, that said Dora Bradley on the 17th day of February 1905 did give birth to a female child, that said Dora Bradley died from complications arising from said birth. That said child was living March 4th 1905 and was said to have been named Edna Bradley. Affiant further states that she is of no relation to any of the parties interested, and has no personal interest in this claim.

(Signed)   Mrs Etta Easley

Applications for Enrollment of Chickasaw Newborn
Act of 1905   Volume IV

Subscribed and sworn to before me, this 3rd of June   1905.

J.R. Armstrong
Notary Public.
My commission expires   Feb 25 - 1909

Seal.

9-NB-340.

Muskogee, Indian Territory, May 17, 1905.

Frank Colbert Bradley,
   Bradley, Indian Territory.

Dear Sir:

    Referring to the application for the enrollment of your infant child, Edna Bradley, born February 17, 1905, it is noted from the affidavits heretofore filed in this office that the mother of the applicant, Dora Bradley, is dead. In place of her affidavit you have filed the affidavit of Winter P. Bradley, the applicant's grandfather, and Frank Colbert Bradley, her father.

    Before this matter can be finally disposed of it will be necessary for you to file with the Commission the affidavits of two persons, who are disinterested and not related to the applicant, who have actual knowledge of the facts that the child was born, the date of her birth; that she was living on March 4, 1905, and that Dora Bradley was her mother.

    In having these affidavits executed care should be exercised to see that all names are written in full, as they appear in the body of the affidavit, and in the event that either of the persons signing the affidavit are unable to write, signatures by mark must be attested by two witnesses. Each affidavit must be executed before a Notary Public and the notarial seal and signature of the officer must be attached to each separate affidavit.

Respectfully,

Chairman.

Applications for Enrollment of Chickasaw Newborn
Act of 1905 Volume IV

9 NB 340

Muskogee, Indian Territory, June 8, 1905.

Frank Colbert Bradley,
    Bradley, Indian Territory.

Dear Sir:

    Receipt is hereby acknowledged of the affidavits of J. H. Easley and Mrs. Etta Easley to the birth of Edna Bradley, daughter of Colbert and Dora Bradley, February 17, 1905, and the same have been filed in the matter of the enrollment of said child.

                    Respectfully,

                            Chairman.

Index

ADAMS, A L 103
ALEXANDER
   D L 35,39
   Ella 35,39
   Euna May 34,35,39
ALLEN
   L C 4
   L D 225
ANATUBY, Latice............................ 249
ANDERSON
   Joseph... 275
   R B 148,149
   R B, MD 146
ANGELL, W H 42
ANOATUBBY
   Jane.........................121,125,250,252
   Lankford............245,246,247,248,249,
   250,251,252
   Latice....................................246,251
   Laticia...........................245,246,249
   Lena............243,245,246,247,248,249,
   250,251,252,253
   Leticia 251
APALA
   Laticia 248
   Lattice... 252
   Letica.. 247
   Leticia........................247,248,252,253
APALLA, Letica 246,247
APELA, Leticia................................ 253
APPLE & FRANKLIN..................116,130
APPLER, Latice 251
ARMSTRONG
   J D 320
   J N 33,39
   J R.................................322,323,324
   Myrtle V 33,34,39
   William Henry........................33,34,39
ARNOLD, W H........................50,51,52
ARNOTE, W A 258
ARPELA, Letice.............................. 250
BACON, Chas E.........................242,243
BAIRD, W E 123,124,146,147,148
BAKER
   Danie 228
   Susan 228,229,230,231
BALL

E J........................19,20,21,69,215,235
   Myrtle V 34,39
BARD, Reford.................................... 74
BARKER, Eula................................. 192
BARTLEY
   J P..135,137
   J P, MD....................................135,137
BATES
   Emma 206,208,209,211
   M Pearl 206
   M Pearle 204,205,206,207,208,
   209,210,211
   May.. 207
   Orman Leycester 203,205,206,207,
   208,209,210,211
   Thomas Errol.............203,204,206,210
   W A 209
   William A..........204,205,206,207,208,
   209,210,211
BAXTER, J H.................................... 123
BEACH
   W W 312
   William Walter........................311,312
BEALL, Wm O 129,130,131
BEAM
   Andrew 244,245
   Simie... 253
   Sina... 244
   Sinie..248,249
   Sinnie.....................................245,246,248
BEAMS, Sinie 247
BEELER
   C A 35,39
   C A, MD 35
BELL, Robert S 99,100,170
BELT
   D J 172
   Jessie.. 247
   M D 120,172,173,247,248,250
   M D, MD....................................... 172
BENTON, E W................................... 18
BERKETT
   Eddie... 8
   George.. 8
   Jennie... 8
BERRY
   T M......................................281,282,283

Index

Thos M 280
Thos M, MD 280,284
BIRDWELL
   Annie 58,59,60
   Georgia Jackson 58,59,60
   H S 58,59,60
BIXBY, Tams 16,26,37,97,119,124, 165,170,177,184,285,294,296
BLEAKMORE, W P 159
BLEVINS
   Josephene 110
   Josephine 108,109
   Lemuel F 109,110
   Willie F 109,110
BOBO, Lacey P 14,15
BOND, E H 287,288,289
BOTSFORD, Charles L 183
BOYD, Shimer P 85
BOYED, Shimer P 85
BRADLEY
   Colbert 325
   Dora 320,321,322,323,324,325
   Edna 319,320,321,322,323,324,325
   Edwin 85,86
   Edwin Harris 84,85,86,87,88,89
   Edwin R 87,88,89
   Edwin Ruthren 86
   Elizabeth 85
   Frank C 320,321
   Frank Colbert 320,322,323,324,325
   A J 271
   Nettie 86,87,88,89
   William 85
   Winter P 322,324
BRADY, W T 258
BRECKINRIDGE, C R 294,296
BROWALL
   H 25
   H, MD 24,25
BROWN
   Amelia 99,100,101,102
   Benson 1
   Chiggling 256,257
   Clarice Frances 102,103,104,105
   Cleo 1
   Eben Foster 102,103,104,105
   Ellen 114,115,116,117,118,119, 120,121,125,126,127,128,129,132
   H H 101
   J B 104
   J W 205
   Jno H 97,98
   Joe 114,115,116,117,118,119,120, 121,122,123,124,125,126,127,128,129,132
   John 102
   John Douglas 101,102
   John Douglass 97,99,100,101
   John H 99,100,101,102
   Joseph 132
   Josephine 113,114,115,116,117,118, 119,121,125,126,127,128,129,130,131,132
   L F 205
   Linda 256,257
   Lula 255,256,257
   Maud E 104,105
   Maude E 102,103,104
   Odis 115
   Odis L 113,114,115,116,117,118, 119,120,125,126,127,128,129,130,131,132
   Odus L 127,128
   Viola May 1,2
BUCHANAN, Eliza 67,72
BUCHANNAN, Eliza 67
BUCKMASTER
   J I 37,39
   J I, MD 37
BURCH
   A J 3
   A J, MD 3
BURDESHAW, W H 196,197,198,199, 200,201,202,203
BURGESS, J C 221
BURKETT
   Cecil Rayford 304,305,306,307,308
   George 2,4,7,304,305,306,307,308,309
   Mary B 304,305,306,307,308
   Maud 2
BURRIS
   J H 244,245
   Marion J 161
BUSBY, Oral C 258

Index

BUSH, J B 27
BYRD
  B F 196,197,198
  Benj F 195,196
  Benjamin F 198
  Daisy Monette 195,196,197,198
  G F 161
  Mamie 196,197
  Mamie E 195,196,198
  N 24
CAIN, P L 193
CALLAWAY
  J R 59
  James R 60
  James R, MD 59
CAMPBELL
  C M 28,37,38,67,68,97,98,165,
  166,170,171,177,178,285,286,321
  Edith L 72,73
  Edith Louise 74
  Fannie 72,73
  Francis C 74
  M 220
  Montford T 72,73,74
CANTRELL, W T 321
CARAWAY
  E J 151,152
  Ida Ray 151,152
  Mary 151,152
CARLISLE, J H 77,78
CARPENTER, Jim 202,203
CARR & ROBERTS 230
CARRELL
  I N 86,88,89
  Isaac N 88
  J C 87
CARSON
  W W 317
  W W, MD 317
CARTER
  Colbert 265,266
  Dorset 153,154
  Dorsett 154
  Katie P 266
  Minnie 265,266
  Retia P 265,266
CASEY

  John Wesley 217,218,219
  John Westley 215,216,217
  Lula May 216,217,218,219
  Newt H 216,217,218,219
  Newton L 218
CASS, D H 164
CHAPMAN, A A 313,314,316
CHEADLE, Lucy 168
CHILDRESS, Dr J M 92
CHILDS, J S 153,154
CHITWOOD
  David P 2,3
  Joseph Hoyt 2,3
  Mary F 2,3
  Mary T 11
CLARK
  Amelia 43,44
  J H 283
  Melia 42
CLOPTON
  Blanch 7
  Blanche 3,4,5,6,7,8,9
  R M 9
  Rolla M 4,6,7,8,9
  Rolla Montgomery 5,6
  Susan 4,5,7
  Susie 5,6,8
COCHRAN, R M 73
COFFEY, Nina E 220
COHEE, Mandy 201
COLBART
  Iva Louis 287
  Lillie 287
  Thos R 287
COLBERT
  Alberta 175,176,179
  Bruce 50,51,52,53
  D C 50,52,53,54
  Daniel 251
  Daugherty C 51,52
  Dougherty C 53
  Ira Lois 289
  Iva Lois 284,287,288
  Iva Los 290
  Lillie 286,287,288,289
  Netter 50
  Nettie 51,52,53

Nettie Row 50
Nettie Rowe 50,51
Ode 285,289,290
Peggy 168,169
Pegy 168
Sam Louis 175,176,179,180
Sam T 179
Sam Tilden 180
Sam Tildon 175,176,179
Samuel T 177,178,180
Thomas R 287,288,289,290
Thomas R (Ode) 289
COLBY
   J H 182,183
   J H, MD 182
COLEMAN, P S 142,143
COLLINS
   Annie 79,80,81,82
   Ben F 79,80,81,82
   Dan 292
   Danni 290,291
   Dannie 291,292
   Garland W 290
   Garland Wardlow 290,291,292
   Lousie Maud 79,80,81,82
   Nancie 290,291
   Nancy 291,292
COOK, F C 300
CORNELLS, E F 309
COX
   B F 164,167
   Bertha 165,166
   Robert Calhoun 105
COYL
   Cecil Earl 40
   Jim 37
COYLE
   Cecil Earl 36,37,39
   Cicil Earl 39
   James T 40
   James Thomas 36,37,39
   Jim 38
   Ola Pearl 36,37,39
CRANFILL
   A G 315,316
   A G, MD 315
CRAVENS

C T 267,268
   Mary 267,269
   Willie 267,268
CRAWFORD, Jno P 162,163
CULBERT
   Iva Lois 286
   Thomas R 286
CULBERTSON, C E 111,112,113
DABNEY
   J A 298
   J A, MD 298
DAVENPORT, C J 59
DAVIDSON
   Charles A 220
   Chas A 221
DAVIS
   E E 189
   Ella 128
   Ellen 123,124,127
DAWSON
   E L 73,74
   E L, MD 73
DEATON, H L 135
DICK
   Josephine 40,41,42,43,44,46
   Josie 40,41
   Lee Roy 40,41
   Leroy 40,41,42,43,44,45,46
   Taylor 40,41,42,43,44,45,46
DICKSON
   Thomas B 223
   Thos B 223
DIFENDAFER, Chas T 226
DIXON, Thomas B 222
DOBSON, John H 168
DOSS, W P 24
DOUGLASS, Nancy L 228
DOWNING
   Mattie 263,264
   Mose 263,264
   Roy Thomas 263,264
DUDLEY, R P 201
EASLEY
   Etta 323,325
   J H 323,325
EBISCH, C F 239,240
EDDLEMAN

Index

Dale 23,24,25
Martha Frances Mead 23,24,25
Mrs J P 25
O T 23,24,25,26,27
R L 26
ENGLISH, Z H 50,53
ESKEW, Chas H 103
EWING, C H 43
EZZARD, John T 104,222,223
FANNIN, E J 26,27
FAULK, A A 90
FAUST, W D 26
FIELD
   Dr K W 75
   K W, MD 75
FIELDS
   J W 96
   J W, MD 96
FLETCHER
   Burney Johnson 132,133,134
   J H 134
   John Henry 132,133,134
   Sallie V 132,133,134
FLOWERS, J R 171
FOLSUM, Charley 162,163
FOSTER, W E 76
FOWLER, O R 152
FOYIL, W A 188,189,191
FRANKLIN
   E O 311
   E Q 93
   Mr 115,117,118
   Wirt 114,144
FROST, S W 280,281,282
FRYAR, Maggie 28
FRYE
   Bertha 163,164,167
   Florence Maryett 167
   Florence Marzett 163,164
   S J 165,166
   Samuel 167
   Samuel J 163,164,167
FULTON, J S 297
GARDNER
   J T 47,48
   W T 159
   W T, MD 159

GARSIDE, Fannie 296,297,298
GARSIDES
   Alex 295,296
   Ben 295,296
   Fannie 293,294,295,296
   Jim 295,296
   Joe, Jr 295,296
   Joseph 295
   Mattie 295,296
   Nellie 295,296
GERARD, G R 160
GILKERSON, C S 309
GLAZE, M F 107,108
GOBEN
   H G 264
   H G, MD 264
GODFREY
   Addie 190
   Addie Mary 188,189,190,191
   Annie 188,189,190,191
   Bessie Annie 188,189,191
   Dot 207
   Ed 188,189,190,191
   Mary Pearle 209
GOFORTH
   Clifton Leeper 141
   Cordelia 105,106
   Irene Stella 105,106
   Jos H 105
   Joseph H 106
   Mary H 106
GOINS
   Charles C 183,184
   Charles Calvin 180,181,182,183,184
   Charles R 184
   Charles Reuben 180,182,183,184
   Charley Calvin 181
   Charley Reuben 182
   Josephine 184
   Josephine Lucy 180,181,183,184
   Melinda Alzina 185,186,187
   S 183
   Sallie 183,184
   Sally 180,181,182,183,184
   Susan 181,183,186,187,216,217,
218,219
   W L 183

Index

GREEN
  G W 204
  G W, MD 204
GREENE
  G W 207,210
  G W, MD 207
GREENWOOD
  Alice 312,313,314,315,316
  Sim 314,315
  Simeon 313
  Simon 316
GREGORY, L E 256,257
GRIGGS, Victor 228
GRIMES, C L 213
GRISHAM
  G L 229,230
  M C 229,230
HAM, P P 300
HANNA, D H 206
HANNIGAN, J H 280
HARDEN
  Andrew J 199,200
  Elizabeth 199
  A J 199
  Viola Iona 198,199
HARDICKE, Dave 254
HARDIN
  Andrew 200
  Elizabeth 200
  Viola Iona 200
HARDWICKE
  Brit 254,255
  Dave 254,255
  Minnie 254,255
HARDY
  Walter 232,233
  Walter, MD 232,234
HARKINS
  Charley 167,168
  Charlie 169
  Lucy May 167,168,169
  Lula 167,168,169
  Mary 168
HARLAND, Elijah 278
HARNED, Myrtie E 305,306,307
HARP
  J M 204

Lillie 204
HARRIS
  Battiest 224,225
  Isaac 224,225
  Isac 225
  Lila 224,225
  Sarah 225
HARRISON
  A P 18
  W F 161,260
  W H 18
HARTIN, B V 77,78
HARTLEY, J H 305
HASSELL
  Bernice 214,215
  W T 214,215
  Willie 214,215
HAWKINS
  Millie 160,161,162,163
  Nelson 160,161,162,163
  Nicy 160,161,162,163
HAYES
  Charley 295
  Daniel 295
  Edward 295
  Maggie 295
  Minnie 295
HAYNES
  W F 213,214
  W F, MD 213
  W T 212
HEARRELL, Ada 239,240
HEDRICK, Caroline............................ 1
HERRING
  Hugh 195
  Mary 194,195
  W F 195
HILL, Sherwood W 319
HODGES, J P 202,203
HOLSOM, Noel J 18
HOMER
  S J 106
  Sol 106
HOOK, H P 68
HOUSTON, R K 309
HUDGEONS
  Josie 259

Index

Josie Leader 260,261,262,263
A R 259,260,261,262,263
Roy 259,260,261,262,263
S 261,263
HUGHES
   A B 239,240
   Mamie 239,240
   Thomas Jefferson 239,240
HUTCHINS
   Ira William 137,138
   J R 138
   Lizzie 137,138
   Mrs C V 138
   William Andrew 137,138
HYDE, R Scott 12
I.MATUBBY
   Hannah 270
   Susan 270,273
IMATUBBY, Hannah 272,273
IMMOHOTICHEY
   Jesse 47,48,49
   Jonas 47,48,49
   Lena 47,48,49
   Lena Underwood 48
   Mrs Jesse 48
IMOTICHEY, Lena 49
JACKSON
   Dr S W 111
   S W 113
   S W, MD 111
JAMES
   Anna 312
   Annie 310,311,312
   Eliza 68,69,70,71
   Emerson 310,311,312
   Lavader Jewel 309,310,311,312
   Lela 66,68,69,70,71,72
   Levada Jewel 310
   Minnie 69
   Turner 67,68,69,70,71,72
JANY, A L 168
JEFFERSON
   Mrs 118
   Susan Brown 117
JOHNSON, O L 16,226,227
JOHNSTON
   D P 120,128,130

D R 121,122,127,244,245,246,254, 255,256,257
JONES
   E A 99,100,101
   E A, MD 99,100
   Ellen 270,271,272,273
   Frank W 289,290
   Rena 269,270,271,272,273
   Wesley 270,271,272,273
JORDAN
   Agnes Mon Tressa 222
   Agnes Mon Trussa Jordan 222
   Agnes Monnie Tressa 223
   Agnes Montressa 219
   Agness Monnie Tressa 222
   George 221
   George W 219,222,223
   William T 219,222
   William Thomas 222,223,224
KEEL, Colbert 47,48
KEENER, J S 199,200
KEMP
   Anne 281
   Annie 279,280,281,282,283,284
   Frank 279,280,281,282,283,284
   Mary Alice 279,280,281,283,284
   Mary Allice 280,281,282
KENNEDY, D S 297,298,299
KERN, W S 317,318,319
KIBBEY, F P 102
KING
   Angela Gertrude 231,233,234
   B T 50,53
   Callie Boyd 232,233
   Christine Patricia 231,232,234
   Felix 234
   Felix J 232,233
KINNER, Lillie 276,277
KIRBY, C A 152
KIZER, F M 207
KUNTZ, J H 103
LANDRUM
   Agnes Montressa 219,220,223
   Monnie 221,223
LANE, Frances R 116,118
LANNOM
   Cordelia 107,108

Index

Leona James 107,108
William R 107,108
LAWRENCE, Honorable William R.... 62
LEADER, Josie 259,260,262
LEGATE, Amandy 103
LEGGETT, J A 120,125
LEONARD, Boone 12
LEWALLEN
   W P 61
   W P, MD 61
LEWIS
   C H 225
   Polly 256,257
LINEBAUGH, D N 297
LISTAN, H G 150
LIVELY
   C O 192,193
   C O, MD 193
LOGAN, Dr C E 258,259
LOOMIS
   B H 216,217
   O H 181,182,183,185,186,187, 216,217
LOONEY
   B R 53
   B R, MD 52
   J T 235,236
   J T, MD 235
LOVE
   Annie 58,59
   Bernice Lee 240,241,242,243
   George Edward Richmond 227,228, 229,230,231
   Mart 241,242,243
   Minnie 241,242,243
   Nona 227,228,229,230,231
   Sam 229
   Sam N 227,228,229,230,231
LOVETTE, Joe 319
LUCAS, W M 194,195
LUNTZ, Henry 79,80,81
LUTTRELL, C T 204,205,208
LUTTRESS
   C T 206
   Fannie 206
LYLES, Era 266
LYNG, Mary 308,309

MABLEY
   Benjamin E 140
   Tennie 140
MANDRELL, S W 120
MANSFIELD, MCMURRAY &
   CORNISH 131
MARR, Fred T 28
MARSH, Affie E 12,23
MARTIN
   W H 42
   Wm L 42
MASHBURN
   J H 241,242,291
   Laura A 241,242,291
MASON, Sarah Jane 14
MAYES
   T G 302
   Thomas Gardner 302
MAYS
   Birdy 299,300,301
   T G 300,301
   Thomas Gardner 299,300
   Thomas Gardner, Jr 301
MAYTUBBY, Peter, Jr 106
MCARTHUR
   C L 214
   Claire L 212
MCBRIDE, Howard 43
MCCARLEY
   W H 65
   W H, MD 65,66,292
MCCOY
   Bethena 226,227
   Levi 226,227
   N H 177
   Wesley 226,227
MCDANIEL, R E 189
MCDANIELS, A S 77,78
MCDAVITT, J C 311,312
MCDONALD
   Albert 272
   Albert S 272,273
   A B 271
MCGILL
   Eliza 194,195
   Frances Mary 195
   Frances May 194

Index

Mach 194
  Noah 194,195
  Rosa 194
MCKEEL
  Cora C 317,318,319
  J F 319
  John F 317,318,319
  Robert Blake 317,318,319
MCKINLEY, J J 3,11
MCKINNEY
  Cecial Berthal 295,296
  Harris 294,295,296
  A L 87,88
  Laura Etta 294,295,296
  Martha 295
  Maude Lee 295,296
  Oyd 294,295,296
  Polly 293,295,296
MCKINNIE, Polly 295,296
MCMILLAN, R 228
MCMORRIES, Lee W 189,191
MEAD
  F E 94
  Martha F 26,27
  Martha Frances 25
  S M 63,94,241,242,267,268,291,310
MEANS, J T 98
MEEKS, Ardil C 107,108
MELLISH, G W 135,136
MELTON, Ado 84
MERCHANT
  Flora 171
  Florence 170,171,175
  Frances 169
  T M 169
MERITT, J S 140
MERRIMAN, Crecie 254,255
MILLER
  H C 85,86
  Helen C 28,85,309
  Volina 309
MOBLEY
  Benjamin E 139,140
  Grady Elazor 139,140
  Tennie 139,140
MONROE, Josephine 41,42,43,44
MOORE

H M 225
J E 3,11
J N 38
Nancy 313,314,315,316
MOORMAN, K 87
MORRISON
  E W 303,304
  E W, MD 303
  H E 61
MUNROE, Josephine 41
MURPHY, Mary L 75,83
MURRAY
  Henton 64,65
  Henton Lenard 64,65
  Hinton 66
  Laura 21
  M C 63,64
  Mattie 63,64,65,66
  Maye 63,64
MURRY
  Henton 63
  Henton Lenard 62,63
  Mattie 63
NED, Watson 116
NEEDLES, T B 173,225,294,296
NICHOLS
  Hannah 257,258,259
  Louis 257,258,259
  Ora 257,258,259
NISLER, W T 29
NOEUTUBBY
  Lankford 244
  Laticia 244
  Lena 243,244
NORMAN
  C J 319
  J F 4,5,6
NOTLEY, W Y 76
O'BRYAN, J B 49
O'DONBY, W J 270,271
OKUYMBBY, Sylvie 122
PACKARD, Emma C 109
PARKER, W E 256,257
PARKS, Robert Calhoun 104
PATE, J R 120
PATER, Harvey 47
PATTERSON

Index

Edwin Johnson..........................212,213
Edwin Johnston 211,212,214
James E.......................211,212,213,214
Mollie J.......................211,212,213,214
PEARSON, J A W.......................107,108
PERKINS, Virgil A.............................. 61
PERRY, Ola Edith.............................. 139
PETER
    Harvey.. 48
    Jane..48,49
PETERS
    W L..83,84
    W L, MD... 83
PHELPS
    G M... 5
    Jas J... 5
PHILLIPS
    Mary Joyce...................................74,75
    Mrs W T... 75
    Nettie A.. 75
    William Thomas.............................. 75
PLUNKETT
    Benj J, MD..................................... 176
    Benjamin J..................................... 179
    Dr B J... 176
POE, Annie... 108
POLK
    F 3
    T 10
POLLOCK
    Georgia...............................111,112,113
    Georgie.....................................111,112
    Janice.................................110,112,113
    Junie..................................110,111,113
    Lee.....................................111,112,113
    Mrs A D...............................112,113
PORTER, Elsie............................202,203
POUND
    Mattie..10,11
    Tom...10,11
    Walker Theo.................................10,11
PRENTICE, J R..........................289,290
PRIDDY
    Cecil Lewis...................................... 62
    Marguerite.................................60,61,62
    Melvin.......................................60,61,62
    Siddie..60,61

PUGH, M R............. 185,186,187,216,217
RAY
    Bernard E....................................19,20
    Henry L......................................19,20
    Mollie....................................19,20,215
    Thelma.. 19
REAM
    Alinton Guy.............................236,238
    Allinton Guy.....................236,237,238
    Boudinot................................235,236
    Mattie.....................................235,236
    Ona O'Neal.........................236,237,238
    Ona Oneal...................................... 237
    R L.. 238
    Robert Lee.........................236,237,238
    Vinnie..................................234,235,236
REASOR, J M................................... 272
RENEGAR
    J F..90,91
    J F, MD..90,91
REXROAT, U T....................232,233,234
RICHARD, W................................... 237
RIDER
    Geo E................................155,156,157
    George E..................................157,158
    Maud E.. 104
    Thomas.. 103
RILEY, Chillion.................................. 105
RINGLE, J F.. 132
ROBINSON, Frank L...................109,110
ROLLOW
    J K.. 29
    T P.. 29
ROWE
    Letitia.. 51
    Robert C.. 50
ROWLEY, H B..........................189,190
SANDS, Pearl.............................37,38,40
SAUNDERS, Sarah Jane.......313,314,316
SCHIELE, Victoria......................196,197
SCHULE, Victoria............................. 198
SCOTT, John ?................................... 103
SELF
    Fannie.......................293,296,297,298
    James..293,299
    James W............................296,297,298
    Joseph W..................293,294,298,299

Index

Sarah Arinda 293,294,296,297,299
SETTLE
  W E 110
  W E, MD 109
SEXTON, T J 18
SHANNON
  Laura G 82,83,84
  Mrs William T 83
  W T 82
  William T 82,83,84
  Winnie Elizabeth 82,83,84
SHARP, J F 183
SHEPARD, Effie 10
SHIPPEY
  Dr E E 13
  E E 16,23
  E E, MD 13,16
SITTEL
  Edward 142,143,144,145
  Geneva 141,142,143,144,145
  Malvina 143,144
  Mary 142,143,144,145
SKEEN
  Cicero A 55,56
  Emily Francis 57
  M P .. 19,20,21,56,57,58,70,71,237,238
  Matilda 55,56
SLATER, G B 87
SLOVER, G W 133,134
SMITH
  E K 64,65,66,92,292
  Helen A 85
  Joseph P 217,218
  Tena 29,30
  W W 258
SNELL, Daniel 6,7
SPARKS, Mattie 261,263
SPEAKE, J W 321
SPENCER, Geo R 140
STATLER, Price 261
STATONS
  H A 302,303,304
  Marina B 302,303,304
  Sam Potts 302,303,304
STEEL, Amelia 99,100
STEELE
  Amelia 99

Amelia M 97,98,101
STEIN
  A J 10,11
  A K 3
STEPHENSON
  Annie 95,96
  Philip 95,96
  Phillip 96
  Victoria 95,96
  Victory 95
STEWART
  Charley Elmer 28,29,30,31
  Charlie Elmer 31
  John 28,29,30,31,32
  John B 28
  Maggie 30
  Maggie Fryar 28,29,30,31
STICK
  Alice 275
  Minnie 274
  Thomas 277
STOUT
  Jeff 200,201,202,203
  Mica 200,202,203
  Mickie 200,201
  Tennie 200,201,202,203
STUBBLEFIELD
  C 286
  Lillie 285,290
SURRELL
  Emily Frances Skeen 55,56
  Emily Francis 56,57,58
  Emily Francis Skeen 55
  J O 57,58
  John O 55,56,57
  Matilda Pocahontas 55,56,57,58
SUTHERLAND
  L B 22
  L B, MD 22
TAYLOR
  Frank R 91
  Frank Ralston 89,90
  Frank Roston 90
  J I 150,151
  J I, MD 150
  Mary Ann 89,90,91
  Stephen Lee 89,90,91

THAXTON
- Earnest Lenord 267
- Earnest Leonard 266,268,269
- Lida 269
- Rosa E 268,269
- Rose E 267
- Tullas 267,268,269

THOM
- Salanie 161,163
- Salena 162

THOMAS
- Charles Cruce 158,159
- Charles W 159
- Chas W 158
- Minnie G 158,159

THOMPSON
- Bell 227
- Belle 227
- Della May 160
- Virginia May 160
- W H 160
- William H 160

TIERNE, J F 76

TINSLEY
- Edith Audrey 192,193
- Eula 192,193
- V T 192
- Vester F 193
- Vester T 192,193

TISDEL, C J 62

TORBETT, S M 24

TROUT
- Ada 153
- Buck 153
- Roland 153

TROUTE
- Ada 153,154
- Ada Phillips 153,154
- Buck 153,154
- Roland 152,153,154

TRUAX
- Dr Geo H 260
- Geo H 262
- Geo H, MD 260

TRUE
- J L 187
- John L 185,186,187
- Lena May 185,186,187
- Lottie Belle 185,186,187
- Melinda Alzina 185,186,187

TUCKER, S P 22
TURNER, Robt F 61

TUSSY
- Henry B 149,150,151
- Lilla 150,151
- Lillie 149,150,151
- Lottie Kate 149,150,151

UNDERWOOD, Lena 48,49

VANDIVER
- James B 276,277,278
- O J 269

VAUGHN, John 176

VENABLE
- Dollie 92,93,94
- Dovie 93,94
- Robert L 92,93,94
- Ruth 92,93,94

VINYARD, J R 315
WAD, Huston 171

WALDON
- Hosea 76,77,78
- James H 7,9
- Roy Oscar 76,77
- Sophie 77,78
- Susie 76,77,78
- Turner Clyde 76,77,78

WALKER, Chas P ... 192,265,266,268,269
WALLACE, J W 201

WALTON
- Kutman 274,275,276,277,278
- Minnie 274,275,276
- Simon 274,275,276

WALTREP
- P M 81,82
- P M, MD 80,81
- Powhatan M 79

WARD
- Florence 175
- Frances 169,172,173,174,175
- Houston 169,171,172,173,174,175
- Huston 170
- Morine 169,172,173,174,175

WATERS, N R 178
WATKINS

Index

Emma A 154,155,156,157,158
George W 154,155,156,157,158
Rosalee Levina ... 154,155,156,157,158
WEAKLEY, A B 136
WEBSTER, J M 133
WELCH
   Affie E 11,12,13,15,16,17,23
   C A 18
   Clayton 14,16
   J S 155,156,157,158
   J S, MD 155,156
   Nellie 17,18
   Nellie A 14,16,17
   Paul B 15,16,17,23
   Paul Branum 11,12,13
   R C 18
   Robert C 11,12,13,14,15,16,17,23
   W T 33,39
   W T, MD 34
WEST
   John 271,273
   A T 40,41,43,264
WHARTON
   Dr J T 287
   J F 289
   J T 287,288
   J T, MD 288
WHITE
   Dora 320,321
   E 322
   Mattie E 320
   Myran 116
   Myron 118
WILKINSON, J B 136,137
WILLIAMS
   J E 1,2,301,306,309,321
   John L 166
WILLIAMSON
   Edward 21,22
   Laura 21,22
   Shirley 21,22
WILLIS
   Holmes 146,147,148,149
   Juanita 145,146,147,148,149
   Viola 146,147,148,149
WILLSON
   Anna Aleen 135
John D 135
Lillie Louella 136
Lillie Luella 135
WILSON
   Anna Aleen 134,135,136,137
   John D 135,136,137
   Lillie Louella 136,137
   Lillie Luella 135
WITT, Alberta 177,178,180
WOLF, Johnnie 247
WOLFE, Delpha 251
WOMACK, Oda 305
WOOD
   J E 33,34,35,36,37,39
   John C 13,15
WORSHAM
   Jewel 140
   Lucrecia 140
WORTON, J H 286
WRIGHT, T L 173
YEISER
   C C 241,243
   C C, MD 241,243